A HEADLEY COMPENDIUM

including

'HEADLEY 1066–1966'
by Canon Tudor Jones

and items from

Headley Miscellany, Vols 1 to 6

∾ ∾ ∾

compiled by

John Owen Smith

A Headley Compendium

Published 2011

Typeset and published by John Owen Smith
19 Kay Crescent, Headley Down, Hampshire GU35 8AH

Tel: 01428 712892 – Fax: 08700 516554
wordsmith@johnowensmith.co.uk
www.johnowensmith.co.uk

ISBN 978-1-873855-62-1

Printed and bound in Great Britain by CPI Antony Rowe, Chippenham and Eastbourne

Contents

Continued.../

Contents (continued)

Introduction

It is not easy to record the history of a parish in a consistent manner, let alone to give an understandable picture of its progress through the centuries. Some information is no longer available, some is inconsistent, some is incomprehensible to the modern eye and mind, and always there is the feeling that such facts as we have are a mere snapshot, and a fairly random one at that, of fragments of the full picture.

So we must take our hats off to Canon Tudor Jones who, at the end of his 30-year incumbency as rector of Headley, sat down to write *Headley 1066–1966*, which is still the nearest we have to a complete history of our parish.

The 'some other lover of Headley' who he hoped would 'one day make good' his document has not arrived, or at least has not yet dared to embark on such an exhaustive task. However, the arrival of computers and the world-wide web, which 'TJ' could never have envisaged, has given us the means to bring the particulars and anecdotes of the parish to an ever wider audience in new ways—and while these may not always have the benefit of the same studied learning and deliberation which Tudor Jones brought to his work, they do offer a vast storehouse of facts, figures and images to which he had no ready access.

They include tales and photographs sent to us from the four corners of the world by descendants of Headley people who have discovered their roots here using the 'new technology.' Also we have information transcribed from public records now available to be retrieved by all at the mere 'click of a mouse.'

In this book you will find the contents of Canon Tudor Jones' book faithfully reproduced, with just the occasional footnote or editorial comment added by me where it seemed appropriate.

Following on, I have added as a second section all the articles previously published in the six volumes of *Headley Miscellany* which were produced annually by The Headley Society from 1999–2005. It now replaces these six booklets—not only a more convenient way of buying the set, but also slightly cheaper.

I hope you enjoy your excursion into Headley's history.

John Owen Smith
December 2010

Acknowledgements

My thanks to the family of Canon Tudor Jones for permission to republish his work. Also to Betty White whose idea it was to create the *Headley Miscellany* series as a means of disseminating the historical information we had collected in Headley. This work now continues to reach a world-wide audience via the village website.

When the names are listed of those who have loved and actively recorded Headley history, along with Wallis Hay Laverty and James Spencer Tudor Jones will be included Joyce Mary Eileen Stevens (née Suter). Born in the village, she founded The Headley Society and was active in promoting the value of history—she has been an inspiration to those of us who continue to record and retell the stories of the parish, and has been greatly missed since her death in 2007.

Another who has been a fount of knowledge, especially in matters to do with farming, was David Hadfield. Many is the meeting we have held in his farmhouse listening to his fascinating tales. Sadly he, too, has passed away now and another gap is left in our knowledge.

The original cover of Canon Tudor Jones' book *(opposite)* was designed by Hester Whittle. For the cover of this compendium, I am grateful to Wendy Bennett for permission to use one of her colourful watercolours of the village.

Finally, my thanks of course to all those who have contributed the articles which we are now republishing. I think you will find their stories both interesting and informative.

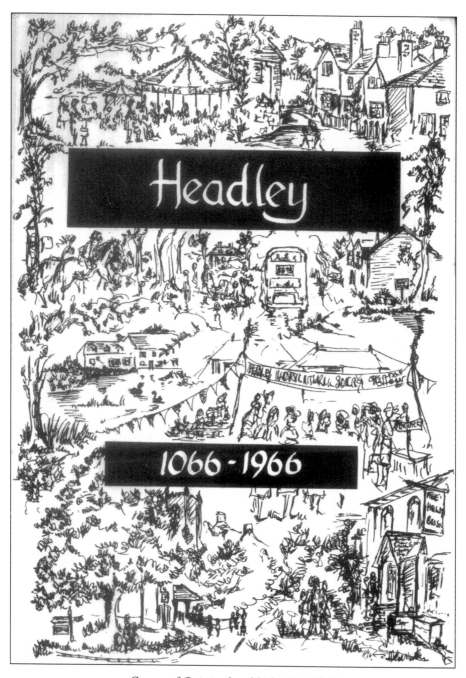

Cover of Original published in 1966
Artwork by Hester Whittle

HEADLEY

The Story of a Hampshire Parish
1066–1966

J.S. Tudor Jones
(Rector of Headley 1934–1965)

The Roman poet, Horace, wrote:

Ille terrarum mihi praeter omnes Angulus ridet:

which may be translated:

It is that corner of the world above all others which
has a smile for me.

Canon James Spencer Tudor Jones, Rector of Headley 1934–1965

Foreword

Round about the years 1952–56 it was my pleasure and privilege to give a lift to Church each Sunday morning to Walter Piggott, a small farmer from Lindford. Hardly a week passed but he told me some interesting facts about the Headley he had known as a boy. Many times have I reproached myself because I did not record these reminiscences, but the idea was then born in me to write something of the old days. When, on retirement, I was able to get down to research I found many sources of help. I must acknowledge with great gratitude the kindness of the Provost and Fellows of the Queen's College, Oxford, who gave me permission to study all their papers concerning the parish. I am also much indebted to Mrs Cottrill, the Hampshire County Archivist, for making available the Blunt papers and other ancient documents now safely housed at Winchester; to the Rev Dr Scott of Frensham for the loan of books and many other kindnesses; to Hester Whittle for the delightful cover, sketches and map which she has so skilfully drawn; to Joyce Stevens, who has written the chapters on the School and the workhouse riot, and, with my wife, has helped me by transcribing miscellaneous information; to my successor, the Rev David Bentley, for permission to inspect the Headley registers, and above all, to the notebooks left by Mr Laverty and his parish magazines.

There is a family legend to the effect that when they were away at school and subsequently in different parts of the Commonwealth, the letters I used to send to our three daughters were in such terrible handwriting that (after a quick glance to see that all was apparently well at home) they were put on one side to read at a more convenient season! That story makes me all the more grateful to Miss Garlick for her speedy and accurate typing of the manuscript of this book.

Much more could have been written had costs of production allowed: although the printers, Messrs. Unwin Brothers Limited of Old Woking, have been most reasonable. I hope that in the future, some other lover of Headley will one day make good what has had, perforce, to be omitted, and correct any mistakes which may, inadvertently, have been made.

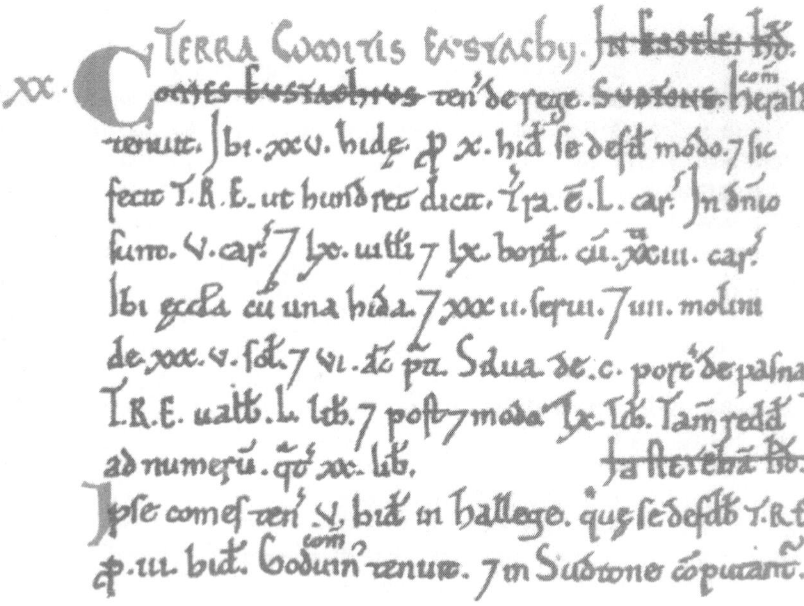

TERRA COMITIS EVSTACHIJ. In Castelei hd.
.XX. Comes Eustachius ten' de rege. Sudtone. Heraldus com
tenuit. Ibi .xxv. hidæ. p x. hid se defd modo. 7 sic
fecit T.R.E. ut hundret dicit. Tra. ē. L. car. In dnio
sunt. V. car. 7 lx. uitti 7 lx. bord. cu. xxiii. car.
Ibi eccla cu una hida. 7 xxxii. serui. 7 iii. molini
de .xxx. v. sol. 7 vi. ac pti. Silua de .c. porc de pasnag.
T.R.E. uatb. L. lib. 7 post 7 modo. lx. lib. Tam redd
ad numeru. qd xx. lib. In Afletebrige hd.
Ipse comes ten. V. hid in Hallega. que se defdb T.R.E.
p .iii. hid. Goduin com tenuit. 7 in Sudtone coputant.

The reference to Headley in the Domesday Book

An Outline of Nine Centuries

"If all the parsons had, for the last thirty years, employed their leisure time in writing the histories of their various parishes ... neither their situation nor that of their flocks would, perhaps, have been the worse for it at this day." Cobbett, from whose *Rural Rides* this quotation comes, was no lover of parsons. The parson who has ventured to write this book has "for the last thirty years" lived in a parish he came to love and, as evidence of this, has ventured in his retirement to record some of the old happenings for which, in his case, he had no 'leisure time' in his active ministry. It was my good fortune to follow a rector who, perhaps in less hurried days, made copious notes of the past life of Headley, and while I am beholden to many sources, old and new, it is to the Reverend WH Laverty that I owe the greatest debt.

Headley is a parish with a long history but, as in the case of very many isolated settlements of Saxon and later times, very little is known of its earliest days. The first known reference is in the famous Domesday Book, which William the Conqueror, who came to England exactly 900 years ago, caused to be compiled.[†] Says Sir Winston Churchill, "The history of many an English village begins with an entry in Domesday Book."

A reproduction of the paragraph in Domesday relating to Headley (where it is called Hallege) is shown opposite. The translation is as follows "Earl Eustace holds five hides in Hallege which were assessed in the time of King Edward as three hides. They were held by Earl Godwin, and are reckoned as part of Sutton" (Sutton refers to Bishop's Sutton, in which Manor Headley was then situate).

Earl (or Count) Eustace III of Boulogne, had a son, Count Eustace IV. He married Mary of Scotland, and their daughter Matilda married King Stephen, and so the Manor became Crown property in 1136. Subsequently the King exchanged this Manor with his brother, Henry de Blois, Bishop of Winchester, for Merton Manor, and the Priors of Merton became the first known patrons of the living.

It is interesting to note that, contrary to earlier belief, there is no reference to a mill in Domesday, though Mr Laverty appeared to believe such was the case. Undoubtedly there were mills in Headley, and indeed a perambulation of the parish taken in the reign of Edward VI mentions five, "one built on Frensham Pond, another lying between the highway called 'Grevat Lane' on the west and a river bank and a meadow called 'Kyttsmede' on the east, a fulling-mill or watercourse held by Thomas Fygg (members of the Figg family lived during my time at Fullers Vale), a mill held by Richard Gyll, and a messuage and fulling-mill abutting on Lacyes Marsh".

The word 'hide' mentioned in Domesday, according to the experts, does

---

[†] Written in 1966

not mean an area of land but an assessment of value: how much, in fact, it was worth to William!

The extent to which William had his new country tabulated is seen from the following extract from the Anglo-Saxon Chronicle: "Then he sent all over England into every shire to ascertain how many hundreds of 'hides' of land there were in each shire, and how much land and livestock the King himself owned in the country, and what annual dues were lawfully his from each shire. He also had it recorded how much land his archbishops had, and his Diocesan bishops, his abbots, and his earls, and—though I may be going into too great detail—what or how each man who was a landowner here in England had in land or in livestock, and how much money it was worth. So very thoroughly did he have the enquiry carried out that there was not a single hide, not even—it is shameful to record it, but it did not seem shameful to him to do—not even one ox, nor one cow, nor one pig which escaped notice in his survey."

The curtain now closes on the parish for more than 100 years and it is not till 1314 that the name of the first recorded Rector appears. He was GEOFFREY DE HOVILE, and he was succeeded in that year by WALTER DE BROLNESBOURNE. Presumably Geoffrey was a Prior of Merton: at any rate his successor was presented to the living by the Priory, who remained patrons till the Dissolution of the Monasteries in 1538.

Walter de Brolnesbourne was succeeded by ROBERT (surname unknown), for it is recorded that in 1368 JOHN PODISDONE was instituted priest of the Church of Hethleghe in succession to Robert on the presentation of the Prior and canons of Merton. In 1377 THOMAS DRAPERE, a sub-dean and penitentiary of Exeter Cathedral exchanged livings with John Podisdone and in 1380 THOMAS AUMENET rector of Beaumond exchanged with Drapere.

It may be convenient at this stage to enumerate a list of Rectors, with notes on some of them in future pages.

circa 1414 SIR JOHN MASSEY.

1443 JAMES BLAKEDON. Of the Order of Friars Preachers, "sub-penitentiary of the English nation in the Roman court: on his petition showing that by Apostolic Dispensation he is beneficed a parson of the Church of Headley in the Diocese of Winton, and that the Pope provided him to the Cathedral Church of Achonry in Ireland of which Bishopric a great part is of no value because it is inhabited by rebels; and that he may occupy the premises any papal grace, statute etc. notwithstanding" (Patent Rolls 21 Henry VI). This seems to mean that Blakedon enjoyed the emoluments of Headley though living in Rome.

ROBERT THORNETONE.

1460 JOHN HAMOND.

1472 ROBERT GEST.

1474 WILLIAM COLE.

1479 JOHN MACY.

1494 JOHN FYSHE.

1524 JOHN UNTHANKE. Probably the last pre-Reformation Rector.

On the Dissolution of the Monasteries in 1538 the patronage passed into the hands of the King who granted it to Sir John Gate in 1551. Gate however does not seem to have made any appointments and in 1558 Queen Mary restored the patronage to Winchester.
　　Subsequently the advowson again passed to the Crown and Queen Elizabeth appointed:

In 1575 THOMAS DRAKE who is described as 'Minister'

In 1586 WILLIAM DONNELL (?Daniell) was 'Parson'.

There is a note that King Charles I presented in 1631 AVERIE THOMPSON to the living but that Cromwell's ministers dispossessed him in 1644. However, at the Restoration he was reinstated, but soon afterwards Charles II presented six livings, of which Headley was one, to the Queen's College, Oxford, "in consideration of their help to him in his troubles" by a gift of all their plate. Records show that Averie Thompson was (re) appointed by the Provost and Scholars in 1660.
　　Like all his successors at Hedleigh, up to and including Mr Laverty, Thompson was a Fellow of the College.

1670 (Dec. 4) JOHN BEEBY. He was a Londoner, irregularly elected a Fellow in 1654 during the Commonwealth. He died 'of a malignant fever' and was buried in Queen's College Chapel. Previously Vicar of Culham, Oxon.

1673 (Feb. 7) WILLIAM SYMPSON. He married Mary Bayley at Headley in 1675 and she died in 1686. There is a stone let into the wall over the Rectory stable door marked 'S. 1680 W. M.' which may stand for Sympson 1680 William Mary. William Sympson was buried in 1695 "in Woolen only" *[see **The Registers** later]*.

1695 (Aug. 17) WILLIAM ROOK B.D. "A Fellow of Queen's College with a mathematical reputation." He was, like many other Queensmen, including the compiler of this book, a Cumbrian, having been born at Workington.

1717 (July 3) ROBERT RAILTON. He died the following year, his widow surviving him by 14 years. He gave £300 for the marble work at the east end of the Queen's College Chapel. He was a native of Carlisle, and previously Vicar of Marston, Oxon.

1718 (Dec. 24) GEORGE HOLME. Dr Holme appears to have been inducted in the same month as that in which Robert Railton died. He built and endowed the original Holme School, which is still called after him, though, alas a suggestion by the Parish Council in 1966 to call the houses opposite the school 'Holme Way' was rejected by the District Council. Perhaps under the inspiration of his predecessor, Dr Holme gave the marble pavement in the Queen's College Chapel.

The following is an extract from the Salisbury Journal of Monday, July 15th, 1765.
"Salisbury, July 15. On the 3rd inst. died at Headley, near Petersfield, Hants, in the 90th year of his age, the REV. GEORGE HOLME, D.D., rector of that parish, which he enjoyed 47 years. He was an affectionate husband, a faithful friend, and a humane master. His many benevolent acts will not soon be forgot by his parishioners, of which his endowing a charity school is a proof."
The last entry in the registers made by Dr Holme is that of the baptism on June 15th 1765, of George, the son of James and Anne White; when Dr Holme's writing is perfectly firm and good. A further extensive note on Dr Holme will be found in the Chapter headed 'The Holme School'.[†]

1765 (Oct. 19) WILLIAM SEWELL. The monument to him in the Church describes him as 'a man of extensive learning and undoubted charity.' In contrast to some of his predecessors and certainly his immediate successor, Wm. Sewell for 35 years "spent the whole of this time in the bosom of his parishioners". Various incidents relating to his incumbency will be found on later pages [see **An Odd Fellow**].

1801 (Jan) HENRY SMITH D.D. Dr Smith was for the greater part of his incumbency non-resident, and held the curacy of Bromley in Kent. Cases of non-residence, like this, made the Queen's College resolve in 1809 that no Fellow be appointed to a College living without giving "a positive and solemn assurance of his resolution to reside constantly upon it" except in peculiar circumstances as eg. ill health (this happened in the case of Robert Dickinson). This action of Henry Smith's led to an extraordinary assize case

---

[†] And in the *Headley Miscellany* article on p.91 written by Joyce Stevens

at Taunton which excited great curiosity at the time, and the details of which are reproduced in full later *[see **A Strange Case**]*. He was also from the north having been born at St Bees.

Smith was described as a square, very burly man of great physical strength. He and his Clerk, it is said, could consume more alcohol without showing any effect than any two men in the parish. He kept a pack of harriers and was famed as a rider to hounds. Stricter views of clerical decorum came in about that time, and a hint from the Bishop caused him to give up sport and sober down.

1818 (Oct 2) ROBERT DICKINSON. He too was a great deal non-resident, but suffered from ill-health, though he was described as "a jolly big old farmer". Though he lived till 1847 his name appears for the last time in the registers in 1834. There is an entry in the Baptism Register of 1813–1852 to this effect: 'On Ascension Day, May 12 1836, the Porch of the Church was injured, the spire and interior of the Tower destroyed by fire. Divine Providence was pleased to arrest the further progress of the flames. Praise ye the Lord.'

1848 (April) JOSEPH BALLANTINE DYKES. He too was a Cumbrian from near Cockermouth, and a chair made for him by the village carpenter there was given by his daughter to the Church and is now the Rector's chair in the Vestry. Mr Dykes largely altered the Church after the fire of 1836, which had damaged part of the building. He built a new Porch, rebuilt the walls, and raised the floor nearly 3 feet (as can be seen in the Tower) and added the Chancel and a Vestry. Previously there was a gallery which would hold 100 persons, the music being provided by bassoon, clarinet and bass viol, and a story is told that no one was allowed to sing except those invited into the gallery. One Peter Alder used to sit in the middle, and he had the longest nose ever seen, so long that it used noticeably to wag. There was a 'Three Decker' in the Church and two aisles.

It is uncertain if and when the Church was out of use between the fire and the restoration, but the records show that George Wm. Hampton was married in the Barn in May 1858 and that Minnie Langrish was christened there in January 1859.

1872 (July) WALLIS HAY LAVERTY *[see later chapter **1872–1928**]*

1929 (Sept.) MICHAEL RIDLEY. In his short ministry he reorganised the Church finances, made the parish conscious of its place in the family of the diocese, and the Churchwardens and Church Council of their responsibilities in the government of the affairs of the church. Above all, he held in Lent one year a highly successful School of Prayer to which lay folk 'hungry for spiritual teaching' came in large numbers. He left after 4¼ years to become Vicar of S. Gabriel's, Warwick Square, and later Rector of Finchley and

Deputy Priest-in-Ordinary to the King. In the fullness of his powers he died on Michaelmas Day 1953 at the age of 53.

1934 (June) JAMES SPENCER TUDOR JONES. Yet another Cumbrian!

1966 (April) DAVID EDWARD BENTLEY. He was appointed by the Queen's College but was the first Rector since 1660 who was not a member of the College. He is a B.A. of the University of Leeds.

To which we may now add:—

- 1974 (Nov) DEREK LEONARD HAMILTON HEAD

- 1984 WILLIAM MICHAEL POWELL

- 1990 (Nov) RICHARD (DICK) WILLIAM WOODGER

- 1999 (March) MICHAEL SEMPLE – until Oct 2010

The Church

Much of the history of any community is centred round the Church, and Headley's Church is no exception. For more than 800 years—in one form or another—it has stood as a witness to the Christian way of life. Eustace of Boulogne and his household were French speaking. The Headley people were then Saxons. The services of the Church were in Latin. But from those days through all the changes the centuries have brought, the Faith taught in the church has provided the answer to the vital questions that successive generations have asked, and it has survived because in every age men have found that it supplied their needs. When we come through the door we are following the footsteps of the men of Headley who passed through during the Wars of the Roses, maybe to receive the blessing of the priest of those days and then to cut their bows from the yews planted in the Churchyard. When we kneel at the altar, our lips are touching the same chalice from which for 400 years (it was made in 1567) the men and women of Headley have received the Holy Communion of the Body and Blood of Christ. What stories this building could tell if it could speak—from the days of our Saxon forefathers who had to surrender to the Normans, to the men of yesterday who died rather than surrender in the last Great War, and whose names are inscribed in the beautifully illuminated Book near the west wall.

Many structural changes have, of course, taken place since the first days. In William Sewell's time the Church had a spire. In 1903 the following note appeared in the Parish Magazine written by a certain Archdeacon Norris:

"If I had not seen the sketch of your church as it was in 1842, I could not have divined the original plan of the building. Its present arrangement is altogether modern; no ancient church ever had a Western Tower occupying half the width of the Nave. Western Towers were almost always so placed as to form abutments to the walls, or to the arcades of the Nave. Your tower fulfils neither purpose: its south wall is in line with the axis of the wide modern Nave; its north wall is some 18 inches further north than the north wall of the Nave. Thus I was forced to the conclusion that the disproportionately wide Nave of 1859 occupied the area which originally had been occupied by a Nave and a side Aisle. But whether the Aisle had been on the north or the south side I could not have determined without the aid of your sketch.

Your sketch shows that in 1842 the slopes of the roof were not symmetrical, the southern slopes being shorter than the northern—the northern having been lengthened to cover a side aisle. This north-side aisle seems to have been separated from the Nave by an Arcade. For you will observe that after the removal of the Chancel two buttresses were erected against the Nave's eastern gable; the southern buttress of smaller projection sufficed as abutment to the south wall of the Nave; the other buttress is of much greater dimensions, and is placed just where an Arcade between Nave and north Aisle would need abutment to counteract its Eastward thrust. Those who thus repaired the church would never have placed so large a buttress in this position, unless there had been standing an Arcade behind it, requiring something to lean against at this eastern end, as it leaned against the Tower at its western end. I take it, the demolition of the old Chancel (whose width is exactly shown by these two buttresses) had so weakened the Arcade that it would have become ruinous but for this buttress.

The Church in 1842

The Northern wall of the new Nave of 1859 seems to have been built a little to the South of the line on which the wall of the north side originally stood. The ancient arch of the Tower—of no great height, but high enough to show that the side Aisle must have had an independent roof of its own, not a "lean-to"—is internally the only indisputable relic of the ancient structure. The restorers spared the ancient Tower, which was built, I take it, in Richard II's reign. The pinnacles and parapet are of later date. There is one problem left which I cannot solve—how to account for the apparently ancient beams which now extend over the whole width of the modern Nave. That they are ancient appears from their being shaped with an adze, not with a saw. If they existed in the ancient church, they must have spanned the whole width of Nave and Aisle, resting upon the Arcade in some way (as at Grasmere Church, in Westmoreland). But this is so unlikely that I prefer to suppose that they were brought from some neighbouring barn, or other ancient building."

The following note was written in 1935 by P. M. Johnston, F.S.A.

"There has been a Church on the present site since the 12th century at least—possibly succeeding to a Saxon Church of timber. Of this 12th century building only one feature remains—a plain Late Norman doorway, now built into the Vestry, which was probably the Priest's doorway in the N. wall of the Chancel, removed to its present position when the Vestry and Organ Chamber were built. With the exception of the picturesque 14th century Tower at the N.W. of the Nave, the walls of the Church were entirely re-built, with some modifications in the plan, in 1859, at a time when scant respect was shown for ancient things, and when our fathers were only too ready to exchange old lamps for new. It is pleasing, therefore, to record that in this case so many original features were preserved from the ancient fabric and re-built in the re-construction. First and foremost among these is the magnificent roof of wide span and massive timbers, which sits so grandly upon the Nave walls. It dates from the last quarter of the 14th century, and its great width (about 26ft.) is quite exceptional in a Parish Church. Its tie-beams, king-posts and wall-plates are all heavily moulded, and the braced collar and rafter construction is very massive. On one king-post near the west end is carved the head of a man—possibly meant for the master-carpenter, who took an affectionate pride in his work.

The Chancel roof is modern and poor: the Chancel arch appears to date from 1859, but possibly some of the stones may be old ones re-worked. In the north-east window of the Chancel, however, almost completely hidden, is a magnificent panel of painted glass, of brilliant colouring, dating from about 1260. It represents the martyrdom of a Saint and is a very valuable relic of medieval art, of the same period and bearing marked resemblance to the world-famous glass in Chartres Cathedral.

There are several large 17th and 18th century monumental tablets on the walls deserving notice, but otherwise all the fittings and furnishings of the Church are modern, except, perhaps, the Font, of 15th century type, octagonal, with quatrefoil panels on the bowl. This, if old, has been re-worked.

Of the other ancient features incorporated in the re-built walls there are: a short 13th century lancet in the south wall of the Chancel; a good two-light window of about 1380 in the south wall of the Nave; and a fine three-light window, with somewhat elaborate super-tracery, in the west wall, of the same date, which, from the evidence of a water-colour drawing preserved in the Vestry, would appear to have been removed in 1859 from its original position as the east window of the Chancel.

The south doorway, like these windows, is of *clunch*, or Surrey 'Fire-stone'—not very suitable for external use, owing to its soft texture. It has a flat four-centred head and is of about 1500. The oak door was presented by a Miss Ballantine Dykes in memory of her sister.

The Tower of Headley Church is a beautiful little feature. Excepting the parapet, with its battlements and pinnacles, which replaces the spire, burnt in

1836, the tower is of about 1380. It has no buttresses, but the walls are solidly constructed of hard sandstone rubble, partly plaster-coated *[it was re-plastered in 1996—Ed]*, with quoinings and string-course of sandstone ashlar, and charming tracery windows of two-lights in the white clunch, dug from under the chalk in the neighbouring hills. There are four of these pretty windows in the top or bell-stage, a single-light trefoiled opening in the middle storey; and another two-light window like those above, but with the addition of a hood-moulding in the west wall of the ground storey. Finally, there is an excellent 14th century arch leading from the Tower to the Nave."
[This is a shortened and amended version of his original report, which may be read on the village website—Ed]

The Communion vessels are among the oldest in the land. The official description of the chalice is as follows: The bowl is plain, slightly tapered, and has a round stem and small banded knop. There are vertical bands with stamped moulding above and below the stem, and the foot is domed. The paten cover is domed with small foot. The height of the chalice is 7¼ inches and the weight is 8 oz 15 dwt. The diameter of the cover is 4³/₈ inches and the weight 3 oz 3 dwt. Marks: London Assay for 1567 (small block letter K with dot below it) and RD linked letters for Robert Danbe.

The Flagon was given by Dr Holme in 1734. The body is tankard-shaped, engraved with the sacred monogram within rays, and has a splayed foot. It has an S-handle, and a domed cover with thumb-piece. The height is 13½ ins and the weight 50 oz 12 dwt. Marks: London Assay for 1734, and EV with crescent above and amulet below for Edward Vincent. Inscription: *S. Stae Trinitatis Honori, et in usum Ecclesiae de Hedley. Com. Southton. D.D.D. Georgius Holme, S.T.P. ejusdem Ecclesiae Rector A.D. 1734.*

There are also two pewter Alms Plates, one of which has apparently been a paten, inscribed 'Hedly'.

The fire of 1836

Mr Henry Knight told Mr Laverty that he was on the roof assisting to extinguish the flames tho' his friends tried to persuade him to come down. By-and-bye the shingle of the spire had all burnt away leaving only a solitary upright iron rod on which the vane was. So in order to prevent this from falling on the roof, the people below fired bullets! at the vane, but with no effect, for by and bye it fell into the old gallery and of course set it on fire. The fire broke out in a shed which was then close by the Church (the churchyard not being so big as now) owing to some straw catching alight from matches with which some children were playing. A drawing of the Church as it was according to the best of Mr Knight's recollection *[see opposite]* is to be found in Macmillan's edition of White's Selborne (1875), illustrated by Mr Laverty's father (Professor De la Motte).

The Church before 1836

Memorials on the walls of the church

(1)   Here lies William Huggins Esq. first a scholar of Charterhouse, then a Fellow of Magdalen College, Oxford. His genius was so happy, quick and versatile that he easily acquired whatever befits a scholar and a gentleman. He was versed in well-nigh every branch of literature and made a special study of Italian poetry.   He enriched his native language by a faithful translation of the great Poet Dante and the inspired songs of Aristo.   In private life he was courteous, polite and witty; in public serious, of proved integrity and most patriotic.   Though fit to move in a Court, he lived modestly in the country far from the Court. [This refers to the fact that in his early years he held a Court appointment.] His life was one of leisure, but his leisure was never without occupation. By his administration of the laws, by composing the differences of neighbours, by helping all according to his means, he gained respect as a citizen and a magistrate. He died on July the 3rd AD1761, aged 65.   [William Huggins lived at Heath House "later Headley Park".]

(2)   Sacred to the memory of Catharine, the deeply regretted wife of George Holme, D.D., Rector of this Church, the fifth daughter of John Leigh, Esq., of North Court in the Isle of Wight. She was a truly remarkable woman, adorned with intellectual gifts as well as physical beauty, in whom the fire of continual devotion to God, ready charity towards her neighbour, and wifely love for her husband burnt unceasingly. She gave a hundred pounds to increase the value of this Benefice, also eighty pounds to build Hedley School; also, when dying, she left twenty pounds to the poor, whom she had always assisted in her lifetime.   After enduring for more than 10 years with wonderful patience the torture of a painful disease, she fell asleep peacefully in the Lord on June the 3rd, AD1760, aged 80.

Her husband, deeply mourning, set up this monument, that the memory of her many and great virtues might not quickly perish, and that some record might survive of his own love for his excellent wife.[†]

(3)   To the memory of the Reverend William Sewell, Clerk, A.M. Rector of this Parish and Fellow of Queen's College, Oxford. A man of extensive learning and unbounded charity. He was presented to the Rectory of Headley in the year 1765 and continued to hold it till the time of his death in the year 1800, a period of 35 years, the whole of which time he spent in the bosom of his parishioners, discharging the religious and moral duties of his profession with unceasing diligence and most exemplary piety. He died on the 18th day of October 1800 in the 80th year of his age. [So much for the official eulogy, but his grandson presents a slightly different picture—see p.35]

[†] A new memorial to her husband, Dr George Holme, has now been placed next to hers, dedicated on 29th October 2000

Other mural tablets commemorate Dame Anna Maria Gatehouse, the daughter and heiress of William Huggins; the Rev John Parson, a curate of Mr Dickinson's, 1822–29; Mrs Henrietta Dickinson, wife of the above; Mr Parish, the wife of Admiral Parish; Dr Bailey; Brigadier General E Stokes-Roberts; Mr and Mrs Smithes of Eveley; Mr WT Phillips of Hilland and his son John, the latter a Lt Colonel in the R.A. who died of wounds in North Africa 1943; The Rev WH Laverty; Mr GA McAndrew of Headley Park, a Churchwarden for many years; and Mr William Gamblen, who was Postmaster for more than 60 years, Parish Clerk for 45 years, and Chorister for 75 years.

A tablet in memory of the men who died in the War of 1914–1918 is placed on the south wall to the left of the door and a memorial book wherein is inscribed the names and brief particulars of the 48 men of the parish who fell in the War of 1939–1945 is to be found in an oaken case placed against the west wall. The page commemorating each man is displayed twice a year.

The book is exquisitely produced, the main calligrapher being the late Graily Hewitt of Liss, a prominent member of the Society of Scribes and Illuminators. *[Ida Henstock of Petersfield the illuminator – Joyce Stevens]*

On the title page are recorded the words of Robert Brooke:

> *These laid the world away: poured out the red*
> *Sweet wine of youth: gave up the years to be*
> *Of work and joy, and that unhoped serene,*
> *That men call age.*

The case of Hampshire oak was made by H Barnsley of Froxfield. Mr Barnsley was at that time commissioned by the Government of Southern Rhodesia to make caskets for presentation to King George VI, and, for the Canadian Government, special chairs for Westminster Abbey.

The Churchyard

The original Churchyard was a small area of ground immediately round the Church and it is there that the earliest graves are situate. Mr Dykes added half an acre to the West in 1868, and in 1909 Mr Laverty added a further acre to the West of the Rectory garden. The third addition, between Mr Laverty's part and the Council houses, was brought into use in 1965 and this should be sufficient for the needs of the parish for a considerable time, particularly since in these days there are so many cremations. To provide for the reverent interment of the ashes of those cremated, a plot of ground, surrounded by a hedge and planted with rose bushes, has been set apart on the south side of Mr Dykes' addition.

In his earlier years Mr Laverty deciphered all the headstones in the Churchyard. Some of the more ancient are very beautifully carved and others unusual in design or inscription. One near the Vestry door shows an early portrayal of the manner in which the resurrection was pictured, a coffin with a pushed back lid carved on it; another has an inscription thus:

> *Lo! here we lie*
> *All covered with cold clay*

Not very appropriate in a light and sandy soil; another in memory of a boy of ten years who lived at Stream and whose parents went afterwards to America:

> *The cup of life just with his lips he pressed,*
> *He found it bitter and declined the rest.*

And, finally, *'Her death was occasioned by the bite of a mad dog'.*

An unusual and most interesting stone coffin lid, on which the outline of a sword (denoting a priest) is faintly traced, can be seen leaning against the wall to the right of the door leading into the Rectory garden.

The sundial near the main door was made by Rilbright of London in 1784, when John and William Lee were Churchwardens. It was still used by the Clerk to tell the time in 1875, the clock not being given till 1900.

The 1914–1919 War Memorial commemorating the 96 Headley men who fell in that war was unveiled on July 4th 1920 by Major General WD Brownlow, C.B. It stands between the east end of the Church and the road. *[The 48 names from the World War 2 Roll of Honour were added to the Memorial in 1995 – Ed].*

Some people apparently asked for a Tablet to be placed inside the Church and this was unveiled in September 1920 by Mr WT Phillips, JP of Hilland.

A very handsome seat given by Sir Harry Brittain in memory of his wife Alida and designed by Mr John Reid is situate on the west side of the porch. Lady Brittain's memorial stone is by the same eminent Scottish sculptor.

The Lych Gate in the making

The Lych Gate was erected to commemorate the Queen's Coronation and was dedicated in May 1954. The work was designed and carried out entirely by Headley men, among whom were Messrs RL Robinson, EE Nash, KJ O'Brien, J Wakeford and H Fyfield, the overall supervision being in the hands of Mr CK Johnson-Burt, the designer of the Mulberry Harbour in 1944. Inscribed on the arch above the Gate on entering are the words 'Enter into his gates with thanksgiving,' while on leaving the Churchyard the words 'Go forth into the world in peace' catch the eye. A photograph of the opening of the Gate appeared in 'The Times'.

The Registers

The Headley Registers are among the oldest in the land. Fearon and Williams in their *Hampshire Registers* quote Headley's earliest entry first of the illustrations they give, from "delightful little paper books". In 1538 Thomas Cromwell issued his famous Injunctions of which the twelfth reads: Item, that you and every parson, vicar or curate within the Diocese, shall for every Church keep one book or register, wherein ye shall write the day and year of every wedding, christening and burying made in your parish for your time, and so every man succeeding you likewise, and also there insert every person's name that shall be so wedded, christened or buried.

In those days it would take some time before these Injunctions were circulated and observed, especially in such a backwater as Headley, so it is interesting to note that the first entries, below, are at such an early date.

A°. D^i. 1540. De Baptizatis. The xixth daye off Marche was chrystened Agnes Phylpe the daughter off John and Johane Phylpe.

A°. D^i. 1539. De Maritatis. The 1st daye off July was marryed Robert Hardyng and Kateryn Woolffe.

A°. D^i. 1539. De Sepultis. The xxvith daye off Marche was burryed Wyllyam Rawlyne off the age of iiii years; the ffathers name Rychard Rawlyne, the mothers Johane Rawlyne.

A brother of the late Lady O'Brien conferred a great boon on the parish by transcribing all the entries up to the year 1927, and, in addition, the Registers are indexed (the Marriages for 420 years, the Baptisms and Burials for 270 years).

The following places are mentioned in the early registers, the figures showing the earliest date at which each is found: Almshouse 1612; Alton 1614; Erverd (now Arford) 1620 and Erford 1623; Barvarde 1562 and Barford Mill 1614; Bevells 1603; Binsted 1618; Brydge 1568 and Bridge 1591; Bordon Lodge in the Forest 1567; Broxed 1585; Chirte 1613; Evelye 1576 and Eveley 1593; Farnahm 1572 and ffarnam 1574; ffrensam 1551 and Frensham 1579; Grashott 1564 and Grayshott 1584; Hasellmere 1597; Hatch 1594; Heath House 1555; Hedley Hill 1587; Hedley Wood 1599; Herne 1582 and Hearne 1618; Hilland 1596; Huntingford Bridge 1562; Lindford 1632; Linsted 1576;The Lodge 1591; Mathewes 1606; Moorhouse 1563; Sanders

Green 1567; Seamans (now Simmondstones) 1584 and Symons Green 1564; Slaford Bridge 1563 and Slaforth Bridge 1568; Stanford 1583; Streame 1619; Tratsworth 1627; Trotsford 1563 and Trotsforthe 1566; Wyshanger 1563.

Some of the more interesting entries in the Registers are as follows:

1570 'Bachelor of the age of 60'.

1572 'Robartt Lockyng committyng hymself to an unskylfull surgion was cutt at Farnahm and died and was ther buried'.

1573 'His mother comyng into this Parish by chance to se her mother and so was delyvered'.

1581 Rychard Fygg 'of the age of 95 yeares as he told me'.

1584 In the early registers the same name is often spelt differently in the same paragraph e.g. Nov. 1. Elizabeth Hardinge daughter of Thomas Hardynge. [During the centuries the name Headley has been spelt thus: Hallege (11th century); Hertelegh (13th), Hedle and Hetlegh (14th), Hedley (15th), Hethle and Hethelie (16th), Hedleigh (17th) Heathley (18th).]

1597 'Elizabeth Mylls a mayde.' 'John Morer a lame mann.'

1602 The name of the eldest child of William Coxe (Rector) put into the Baptism register with a flourish, but not so the second!

1609 May and June, 3 Northalls and 3 Hills buried within 4 weeks.

1618 'A poore travayling woman buried.'

1628 Baptised 'Elizabeth Geokene the minister's daughter of this Parish' (? Elizabeth Geokene Coxe).

1644 'Agnes, daughter of John and Mary Holloway was (by reason of waters overflowing) baptised at Kingsley.'

1654 The only marriage entered between 1654 and 1658 was performed by a J.P. (Edward Heighes Esq.). Thirteen 'Bands' were, however, published during that period.

In 1666 the Act for burying in woollen was passed. The penalties, not being at first sufficient, a new Act was passed in 1678. The purpose of the Act was to encourage the woollen trade, and to lessen the importation of linen. The penalty for non-observance was £5; a register had to be kept; there was an exception in the case of one dying of plague; and the Act was to be publicly read in churches for seven years on the Sunday after Aug. 2nd.

1690 'May 15th. Thomas the sonn of John Marland was interred. Affidavit was made before Mr Joseph Bush, Curate of Bramshott by John Marland that the said Thomas was buried in woollen only according to the Act. Attested under the hands and seals of Widow Jenks and Sarah Prior'.

Beginning with May 1690 a proper Register was kept of Burials and Affidavits as above. This ceases in 1792. But "Aff" is put to all the Burials from 27 June 1801 to the end of 1812.

1695 'Mr Wm. Sympson Rector of Hedley was interred the 11th of August. Affidavit was made before Mr Ed. Jenkins Vicar of Farnham by Joan Baker that the said Mr Sympson was buried in woolen only, witnesses Tho. Rowland, Hugh Evans'. And at the end of the year 'This is a true and full Register of all Burials in ye Parish of Hedley since the last Easter Sessions, April 13th 96. Wm. Rooke, Rector. April the 18th 1696, seene and allowed by us T. Jervoise, Cha. Cole'.

1700 June 15. Joan the wife of John Bristow, yeoman, was buried. In the affidavit register: 'Joan the wife of John Bristow was buried in linnen, the money forfeited according to the law in that behalf given to the informer, and the rest distributed to the poore'. [There is a note that in 1803 the widow of the late Rector was buried in linen.]

1700/01/03. Elizabeth, Rebecca, Sarah, daughters of Rector (Rooke) baptized.

1710 Aug 15. James Forde, Vicar of Farnham was married to Elizabeth Muggleston, also of Farnham.

1727 Joshua Hunt, adult aged 65 years, baptised.

1734 Benjamin Langwith, Dr in Divinity, Rector of Petworth, was married to Sarah Gregory of Dorking.

1739 March 2nd. 'A male infant dropt at the House near Frensham Great Pond on ye 10th of January last in the evening, was baptised by the name of William Pond.' Mr Laverty sagely remarks that Pond's descendants would never know how they came by their name!

1747 "Thomas Gatehouse, Jun. of Wallop, Esqre and Ann Maria Huggins eldest daughter of Wm. Huggins Esqre were married by Licence." This Thos. Gatehouse, afterwards Sir Thomas, used to drive from Nether Wallop in a four-in-hand, and a wooden bridge which stood over the water dividing Headley and Kingsley parishes was called 'Sir Thomas Gatehouse's Wooden Bridge'. It was afterwards in the middle of Bordon Camp. Mr Huggins, the wife's father, offered the use of his house in Headley Park to Dr. Smollett, on his 'enlargement from the King's Bench' but the doctor would not leave London. Sir T. Gatehouse is said to be the original of Sir T. Bulford in *'Humphrey Clinker'*.

Sir Thomas' daughter was married to Mr Daniel Knight of Eveley. This hasty widower 'married Miss Gatehouse some six weeks after the death of his first wife; and it is said that his son cried all through the wedding service.'

And as a tail-piece,

1874 Baptised Henriette Amelia Louise Flora Therese Seymour Saunders of Hilland. A formidable name indeed, but nothing approaching that of a Merseyside football fan who in 1966 had his child christened with all the eleven surnames of the successful Liverpool team!

The following entry in the Registers relates to the spire which was burnt in the fire of 1836: 'Memorandum 1803: That the Church Spire was new shingled this year and the present Weather-Cock or Vane (more properly called) was placed upon it the 13th December. The Vane is made of Copper with Iron Braces, weights 25 lbs and is in length 5ft 3ins. It was made at Bromley in Kent, and was the gift of the present Rector, Henry Smith; it cost six guineas without the carriage. Witness, John Fox, Curate.'

A Bishop Enquires

At various dates from 1559 (and probably before) the Bishops of Winchester (and Headley was then in that Diocese) issued what were known as Visitations—a series of questions concerning the affairs of the parishers. They are interesting as showing the kind of thing that most concerned the Church authorities at particular periods. The following are typical examples:

1559 It is ordered that all clergy are to see that all shrines, images and candlesticks are to be removed. The Wardens are asked if their clergy extolled pilgrimages and relics.

Do you know who in their houses keep undefaced images, pictures or other monuments of superstition, and adore them?

Have you taken down all glass with images on it and defaced all pictures or images on the walls?

1590 TO THE CLERGY. You are questioned as to any who have intruded themselves who have not been lawfully called, or if a deacon has usurped the Office of Minister? Whether lay persons have read openly in Divine Service or solemnised Matrimony, or ministered any Sacrament? If any say or sing in private Conventicle, Mass, or any service contrary to the laws of this realm? Do they baptise in basons or in Fonts? Do they minister the Holy Communion in wafer bread or common bread, in profane cuppes, dishes, bowls, or in a decent Communion Cup kept for the same purpose only, or whether the communicant stands, sits or kneels? Whether at Perambulation they say any other rite or ceremony than to say or sing in English the Psalm with the Litany and one Homily?

TO THE LAITIE. Whether all images, shrines and other monuments of idolatry and superstition be put out of your parishes? Whether the roode lofts be pulled down and a partition made between Chancel and Church?

As time goes on these questions become less searching. The next Visitation of which extracts are quoted is that of 1691.

Is your Parish Church in repair? Doth the minister endeavour to reclaim all Popish Resusants (sic) if any such be visiting your parish? Doth he baptise without Godfather or Godmother? Does he celebrate the Lord's Supper often, so that every one of the parishioners may receive three times a year at least, Easter being one? Doth he marry in private houses or hath he married at other hours than 8 to 12? Doth your minister and parishioners observe the yearly Perambulation in Rogation Week for preserving the bounds of the parish? Doth every parishioner kneel at prayer and Sacrament and stand once the Creed and Gospel are read?

From 'Visitation' of 1714:

TO CHURCHWARDENS AND SIDESMEN

Is there a large Bible of last translation? Have you a Register Book and a bier and herse cloth for burials? Is your churchyard fenced? Is your minister ordained according to the laws of the Church of England and legally inducted? Is he resident or how long has he been absent without urgent necessity? Does he instruct the youths and endeavour to reform profane people? Does he neglect to visit the sick or baptise a sick or dying child?

And that of 1801:

Does your Minister, if residing, read once a month in your Church the Common Prayer and himself in person? Doth he four times a year read the Act of Parliament against profane cursing or swearing? Are there any parishioners who are late or who are noisy in your Churchyard during Divine Service? Is your Parish Clerk and Sexton 20 at least, and honest? Are his wages duly paid him and when a person is dying, doth he, upon notice given him thereof, toll a bell that the neighbours may be warned therebye to meditate on their own death and commend the soul of the dying person to the Grace and Mercy of God? Do your Churchwardens know who comes late to church or depart before the whole is ended?

Headley During The Commonwealth

The first Rector appointed by Queens College Oxford was Averie Thompson in 1632. When Cromwell ousted Charles I from the throne, most of the loyal clergy, including the Rector, were dispossessed of their livings in the year 1644. Instead of regular clergy, itinerant preachers were employed who rode about the country to teach the people the new and fanatical religion. Nothing is known as to what happened to Averie Thompson until he was restored to his living in 1660, but Dr Scott records that John Longworth, vicar of the neighbouring parish of Selborne, after he was dispossessed "retired to a little tenement about one hundred and fifty yards from the church, where he earned a small pittance by the practise of physic... On the Sunday after his [Longworth's] deprivation, his puritanical successor began his sermon from Psalm 20.8 'They are brought down and fallen; but we are risen and stand upright'."

In 1652 the following document was issued:—

"To the Honble the Comttee of Parliamt concerning plundered ministers.

The humble petition of the provost and schollars of Queen's College in the University of Oxford.

Sheweth,

that whereas your petitioners are the undoubted patrons of the Rectoryes of Heidley and Carisbrooke and of the Vicaridge of Godshill in the County of Southampton and of the Vicaridge of Holy-Roods in the Towne of Southampton, which sayd Rectoryes and Vicarsidges for the severall delinquencyes of the respective Incumbents, have been for diversye years siquestrated and to continue during which time severall provisions of ministers have bene made for the severall parishes, who by reason of their frequent removealls have not taken just care for the payment of the tenths yeerly due to the Comonwealth, nor for the necessary reparation of the Houses belonging to their respective Churches, by means whereof the right of yr petitioners is

33

prejudiced, and those who shall hereafter be presented by them like to be much damnifyed, in being compelled to pay the Tenth, and other incumbent charges in arrier, and being left without remedy for the dilapidations that have accrued during the sequestrations for prevention and remedy whereof.

Yr. petitioners humbly pray

That it would please this Honble Comttee to graunt that when and as often as any minister enjoying the sequestration of any Benefice of the patronage of your petitioners shall be removed by death, cession or otherwise, the care of providing for those Churches may be permitted to your petitioners and their successors, they not dominating any person to any place but such of their Society as for their guifts and abilityes for the worke of the ministery, and their affections to the present Governmt that be approved by the Honble Comttee."

An Odd Fellow

A certain amount of information, amusing and otherwise, is available concerning William Sewell (Rector 1765–1800).

The first extract is from a letter to a friend by the Rev R Radcliffe, a Fellow of Queen's.

"Our very best living was vacant in summer by the death of the immortal Holmes (sic), and has fallen to the share of the very oddest Fellow belonging to us. You will know that I mean Dr Sewell."

From the Queen's College Register: "Oct. 14.1765. Agreed at a meeting of the Fellows, the Provost being absent [he had had a stroke in the spring of the year], that William Sewell, MA, be presented to the Rectory of Headleigh, alias Heathleigh, vacant by the death of Dr. Holme."

The following is written by his grandson, another William Sewell, a Fellow of Exeter College, Oxford, and the founder of Radley and St Columba's College, Dublin, in Volume I of his 'Reminiscences'.

"He was a Fellow of Queen's College, Oxford, a man of learning, great in Hebrew and mathematics, very small indeed, I suspect, in knowledge of the world. I often heard him spoken of by my father and mother and aunts. He seems to have lived on at Queen's College, as men did in those days, waiting for a good College living until they were wholly unfit for it. He took the College living of Headley in Hampshire, somewhere under Hindhead between Petersfield and Farnham, and married, as I have said, Miss Clarke of the Isle of Wight, of whom I only know that she died a martyr to rheumatic gout. And great-aunt Hanbury has often told me that she had to watch by her mother at night without sleeping, so long that at last she herself lost the power of sleep and was obliged to have her eyelids closed by others, by force. She seems to have borne her sufferings with saintly patience, and after the death of my grandfather lived and died at Farnham in Surrey. My grandfather himself must, by all accounts, have been a representative man. He might have sat for a picture of his class—the old College Fellow transplanted into a large wild living. And how totally unlike the same class in the present day! The details I have heard drop from my father led me to think of my grandfather as a grave, quaint old man with a wig; immersed in his Hebrew and mathematics, and allowing the world around him to go on as it liked. There was a time when he kept a carriage, probably soon after his marriage, and I have heard of his going out to dinner in it. But the horses, which in the morning had been engaged with the plough, were sadly disinclined to drag the heavy unwieldy vehicle through the ruts and mire of the North Hants lanes, and they came to a standstill. The coachman's whip was useless, till my grandfather got out of the carriage, took his penknife and applied it in such a determined way to the animals' flanks, that they started off with my

35

grandmother, leaving himself behind in the mud.

My grandfather was a County magistrate, but he allowed my aunts to relieve him in the duty of signing papers and other official acts of the hand, when he was himself immersed in his Hebrew. "Sir," said my aunt one Sunday to him, "the bells are going for church; had you not better get ready?" "Wait a minute, Fanny, wait a minute." Fanny waited a minute. Five minutes passed and my aunt renewed her warning. "Wait a minute, Fanny, wait; do not interrupt me again." He was warned and again refused to move. "But, Sir, the people are all in church." "Let them wait, Fanny, let them wait." And they did wait, till their patience was exhausted—and when at last he went, he met them at the door coming out.

One bitter cold December Sunday the singers were indulging in a very long anthem. My grandfather was in the pulpit, impatient to commence his sermon, and still more impatient of the cold. He looked to the gallery, but in vain; made signs, but no symptom of cessation. Then he caught the eye of the clerk, but the clerk persisted in a bass solo in which he was deeply interested. At last my grandfather waved his handkerchief to the performers—but still no stop. So he got down out of the pulpit, went up into the gallery, took the clerk by the shoulders and shook him well. "Won't you stop?" he said. "Won't you stop?"

I have often heard my father describe the burying the dead at night when the smallpox was raging. Only my father to hold the lantern over the grave, and the wind howling in the leafless trees.

The living was a good one, but I suspect there was no worldly wisdom to manage finances and that at one time they fell into disorder, and my father postponed his own marriage to enable him to assist his family. This consisted of three daughters, Fanny, Lydia and Elizabeth, and at least another son, Barnabas, besides my father Thomas. I am not sure that there was not a third son.[†] But Barnabas died, I believe, in India, and I have no trace of anyone else.'

*****

Headley is the next parish to Selborne and when Wm. Sewell became Rector of Headley, Gilbert White had for some years been Curate of Selborne. The two men were friends, and one letter from Sewell to White has been preserved, and is printed below. It is taken from 'Life and Letters of G. White' Holt-White, ii, 12–14.

Headley, Aug. 7. 1777
Revd. Sir,
Out of a large pot of Medals (about 3 years since) which were found in Wulmere pond, I collected a regular series from Claudius Drusus to

---

[†] The parish Register shows he had 7 children baptised: Elizabeth, Lydia, William, Frances, Thomas, Barnabas and John, who died aged 1.

Commodus included; that is, Medals of all the Roman Emperors from AD 43 to AD 194. Vespasian, a General under Claudius Drusus, about AD 47, marched down with a Roman Army this way, from the parts where London now is, towards Porchester, S. Hampton and the Isle of Wight. It is beautiful on Headley Heath and Common to observe the Entrenchments of the Romans and Britains over against each other; the first advancing, the other retreating. The Romans crossed Headly River at Stanford, and advanced to the place which now is Wulmere pond; and there fixed an abiding Station or City, which remained for near 150 years; when they seem to have been expelled thence by the Britains, or perhaps by an earthquake or some other cause. Great treasures even now lye buried in that pond....

The greatest curiosity thereabouts is, as I said, the advancement of the Roman Army to the S.W. over Hindhead, and over Headly upper Heath and Common.

I am, Sir, most respectfully,
Your obedient servant
Wm. Sewell

Memorandum

At the last Interview with Mr Lee of Headley Wood and Mr Knight, two of the principal Farmers, they proposed to take the Tithes at my Valuation, if an Allowance of Thirty Pounds is made to them, for the Trouble of Collecting and the Risk of Losing something by bad Tenants. My Opinion is that, though the Valuation is a very fair one and moderate for each Tenant, to take his own Tithes, yet it would be worthwhile for Mr Sewell to allow them 20£, rather than to have the trouble and losses which perhaps will be unavoidable in Collecting from such a Number of Tenants, whose Property lies at a considerable Distance from the Parsonage House and Barns, and several of these Tenants in narrow circumstances, or, indeed, if better Terms cannot be made with Messrs Lee & Knight, it would be prudent to close with them; because, from the great distance, that many of the lands lie from the Parsonage, and the Trouble the Tenants would give to any Stranger, that takes the Tithes, in Kind, from the Losses he would sustain, and the additional Expenses he would beat (?) in collecting, probably near double the Sum, which Messrs Lee & Knight demand, must be allowed out of the Valuation to a Tenant, who takes the Tithes in Kind, in order to enable him to pay his Rent. Mr Baker, another of the principal Tenants, when I last saw him, offered 35£ per Annum from the Glebe, which was valued at £ 37. 16. 0.

Signed B. Pryce
A true Copy, Wm. Sewell.

Headley, June 6, 1774 – The Agreement with John Caiger

We whose Names are hereunto subscribed, in Public Vestry summoned for the Purpose, Do hereby consent and agree to Release, transfer and Make over to Mr John Caiger of the parish of Headley, Inn-holder, In consideration of the sum of One hundred and thirty pounds payable to the Church-Wardens, Overseers and principal inhabitants of the said Parish on Michs day next 1774. All that cottage and parcel of Land, part of the Land called Vintners, situate and lying at Hedley-hill in the West-part of the Way there, between the land of Martha Dunce on the South, Pit Lane on the North and with the West end abutteth upon the Land of the Parsonage. And the said John Caiger doth for himself hereby Agree to purchase the above premises of the sd Parish and to pay One hundred and thirty pounds for the same on Michael-mas day next as aforesaid, for the use of the said Church-Wardens, Overseers and principal Inhabitants of the said Parish of Headley for the time being and their successors, On their making over and conveying to him the said John Caiger the premises aforesaid free from all Incumbrances whatever, the said John Caiger paying for the said conveyances and all other charges attending the same. In witness whereof we the said Rector, Church-Wardens, Overseers and principal Inhabitants of the sd Parish of Headley in the County of Southampton aforesaid Do hereunto set our hands in confirmation of the above Agreement this 6th day of June 1774.

Wm. Sewell Rector.   John Caiger
John Clear, W. Brider: Church-Wardens
Thos. Hunt, Wm. Channell: Over-Seers

There followed 20 names, and underneath this—

June 6th 1774. I hereby acknowledge to have received of and from the said Purchaser John Caiger the sum of Half a guinea, In Earnest and in part of the within sum of One hundred and thirty pounds. I say Received for the use of the said Parish Officers etc. etc. by me. Thos. Gatehouse.

Note on the above. Ancient maps make it clear that Vintners was on the site of what is now Wakeford's butcher's shop. It was in fact the *Holly Bush* before the public house was moved to the other side of the road and the post where the sign of the *Holly Bush* used to hang can still be seen. "Hedley-hill" was the name then given to Headley High Street, "Martha Dunce's" was Mrs Heelis' house called Duncesfield and "Pit Lane" is now Mill Lane.

This was the house where Cobbett had his refreshment *[see articles on Cobbett in Headley, pp.56 and 190]*.

Valuation of the Parsonage of Headley, in the County of Hants, taken, August, 1783

PARSONAGE HOUSE AND HOMESTEAD

A very good House, pleasantly situated on a dry healthy soil, consisting of two Parlours, and Hall, a Kitchen and Pantry, on the Ground-Floor; four Bed-Chambers, six Garrets, four Under-Ground Cellars, with a Brewhouse, Milkhouse and other convenient Offices; also of two spatious Barns, a Stable, Cowpens, Granary, Waggon-House, Fuel-House, Ash-House etc. The Gardens, Yard and Rickyard amount to about   1¾ Acres

A Plot of arable, joining the Rickyard, about	¾
The Herbage of the Church-Yard	½
Total	3 Acres

The above House and land is worth about 15£ per Annum. The Plot, the Herbage of the Church-Yard and that of the Rickyards should be reserved to the House, together with proper Stable-Room, the use of the Farm-Yard for Pigs, the exclusive use of it for Poultry, and the Run of a Cow there.

Tenant should covenant to thatch the Buildings, allow straw for litter, and also to carry Mr Sewell's Fuel from the Heath.

The Holme School[†]

Today we take the presence of schools so much for granted, that we can easily forget that there was a time when education was neither compulsory nor free. What happened to the children of our village in those days?

Apparently there were several little dame-schools scattered about the parish where reading and writing were taught, but these catered for very few children, and those only the fortunate few whose parents could afford to pay a few pence a week for their schooling.

William Voller, who was 73 in October 1772, remembered being taught to read by Widow Steele, who kept a little school at Whitelady's House at the Park Gate. At the opposite end of the parish in the early eighteen hundreds there was a small day-school kept by a man who lived in a cottage at Hollywater, and John Pink, born in 1803, used to tell how the boys took their place in class according to the way they said their multiplication table. About this time, too, there was a school at what we now know as the Wheatsheaf, run by a Mr Kersley of Headley Wood; another run by Caleb Parnham, first at Heath House and afterwards on the Green, and a third at Standford kept by Mrs Piggott. I believe she lived at Reynolds, opposite Standford Corn Mill, and her pupils were taught French; that is to say, they could count up to twenty, and chant the days of the week, and the months of the year! At the end of term it is said she treated the children to a piece of cake and a sip of wine.

Later in the century there was a school for little children at Moore House, on the road to Frensham, one at Standford built by the father of Mr George Warren for the 'Bible Christians', and another built and supported by Mr HH Allen of Eveley (now Standford Grange) in connection with the Plymouth Brethren's Iron Room.

All these schools have long since disappeared, but one has survived and flourished for more than two hundred years, the one founded in 1755 by Dr George Holme, Rector of Headley from 1718 to 1765.[‡] This generous and far-seeing man obtained half an acre of 'the Lord's Waste' from the Bishop of Winchester (Lord of the Manor of Bishop's Sutton) on which to build a school, and a house for the Master, and endowed it with the revenues from fifteen acres of land at Linstead, two acres at Thurstoes (Whitmore Vale) and property at Ashe in Surrey.

The first trustees of the Charity were:—
   the Rev Joseph Browne, DD, Rector of Bramshott,
   the Rev Duncombe Bristowe, DD, Vicar of Selborne,
   the Rev Edmund Yalden, Vicar of Newton Valance,

[†] This chapter written by Joyce Stevens in 1966
[‡] See more about Dr Holme on p.91

the Rev Richard Yalden, Rector of Greatham,
the Rev Richard Willis, Rector of Hartley Maudit,
Richard Turner of Headley (Yeoman),
William Collins of Headley (Yeoman),
and the Foundation Deed stated that "Dr Holme (for the common good of the said Parish of Headley and for furthering and promoting the useful education of young persons of both sexes of the said Parish of Headley, more particularly of such children as are or shall be born of poor and indigent parents) has for some time past instituted and set up a charity school in the said Parish for teaching and instructing 12 poor children of either sex of the said Parish (or in case of a deficiency of such children therein, of poor children of the Parishes of Bramshott and Kingsley in the said County) in such principles of learning and knowledge as are most proper for such young persons, that is to say, the boys in Reading, Writing and Common Arithmetic, and the girls in Reading and Writing and Arithmetic and in Sewing and Knitting."

Any number of children could attend the school, but only 12 could benefit from the Charity; the rest had to pay. There is no record of the amount they paid in those early days, but James Barnett, when an old man, said that the fees were sixpence a week in 1830, but reading and sewing were extras, and cost twopence more. In 1874 the very young Mr Laverty seems to have found that the financial arrangements for the school were all rather vague, and needed to be put on a sound business footing, and so he and the other Trustees drew up a new scale of fees, as follows:—

	Labourers	Journeymen	Tradesmen and Small Farmers	Farmers
One child	2d.	3d.	4d.	9d.
Two children	3d.	4d.	6d.	1s. 6d.
Three or more	4d.	5d.	8d.	2s. 0d.

– an interesting commentary on the life of our village then, both socially and economically.

Dr Holme's school was at first called Headley Charity School, and consisted of the house for the Master and one room (now used as a Staff Room) known as The Gallery, because the fixed benches were arranged on a series of steps as in a theatre. This gallery remained until about 1930, and many middle-aged Headley people still vividly remember their introduction to the world of learning in this room.

Just over one hundred years after its founding Mr Ballantine Dykes drew up a new scheme for the administration of the school. Dr Holme had envisaged the Trustees as serving for life and when their number was reduced to three by death—no provision was made for resignation or removal—those three should immediately elect five new trustees to make up the original number of eight; the Rector 'for the time being' automatically being one of the eight. Mr Dykes' revised scheme of 1859 named the Rector, the Churchwardens, the surviving trustees and not more than five subscribers of

£1 each as being responsible for the running of the school. The children were to pay, with the exception of 12 poor children, who would be educated free as a reward for good conduct or proficiency of work. The Conscience Clause was to apply; that is to say, the children need not attend church nor receive Catechism instruction; and the school was to be open for Inspection.

In 1871 Mr Dykes enlarged the building by the addition of the room which now forms the northern half of the large room divided by a partition. (Scholars of the early part of this century remember that in their day a dusty, moth-eaten, red baize curtain was the only division between the two rooms. It was, of course, anything but sound-proof, and those who sat near it could communicate with the neighbouring class through the holes!) This addition was paid for partly by a building grant of £71-5-0 from the Treasury, and partly by a voluntary 6d rate from parishioners. By accepting a Government grant the school became a Public Elementary School under the meaning of the Education Act of 1870, and was called officially the Headley National School. The voluntary rate brought other consequences. Since they had helped to pay for enlarging the school, parishioners quite naturally assumed that they should take some part in its management, and almost the first task that faced the new Rector, then only 25 years old, was to point out to them at a Vestry Meeting that they could claim no jurisdiction over the National School, which remained as before in the hands of the Rector and Trustees. Instead of forming "a Council and Committee for the Management of the schools" the Vestry was induced to limit itself to the appointment of a "Council for the management of the education of the poor children of the parish", and the first members were The Rector, the Churchwardens, Mr Allen, Mr Dixie, Mr I'Anson, Mr Gay, Mr Langrish, Mr Lickfold, Mr Parker, Mr Petar, Mr Phillips, Mr Price, Mr Warren and Mr Woods.

Mr Laverty certainly had some difficult problems to face during his first years as Rector. There were now four different groups of people concerned with the School:

(1)   The original Trustees administering the Holme Charity.
(2)   The Rector.
(3)   The trustees (ie. subscribers) of Mr Dykes' 1859 scheme.
(4)   The Education Council of the Parish formed to raise funds.

Who, therefore, was responsible for engaging and paying the Master?

There was also a further complication in that there existed a separate Infants' School, in the house at the other end of the Green now part of Square House, founded and built in 1824 by a Mr Wheeler in opposition to Dr Holme's School. He was a curate here who, when he left the village, joined the Roman Catholic Church, and when Mr Laverty arrived in 1872 the Infants' School seemed to be no man's property, since Mr Wheeler's family never claimed it, and Mr Dykes had apparently taken it over and run it with the National School. Eventually, after a great deal of correspondence and legal advice, the Infants' School was sold in 1878 and the money used further to enlarge the National School by the addition of three more classrooms. The sale of the little school also helped the Education Council in another way, for with all the children being taught under one roof, they need only employ one fully Certificated Teacher instead of two, and so saved themselves £30 a year.

Finance must have been a worry to the Council, for their Income and Expenditure were very difficult to predict. There was a guaranteed £13 or £14 a year from the original endowment, but the rest of the income was made up of voluntary contributions, the voluntary rate, the 'school pence' paid by the parents of the scholars, and a Grant from the Government, which depended upon the result of the Annual Examination by H.M.I. and the attendance. In 1873–4 for instance, the estimated grant of £40 proved too optimistic as "there were more failures than we expected", and the actual grant was £30. 16. 0. For the following year the Council attempted to budget as follows:—

Estimated Expenditure		**Estimated Income**	
Mr Fillmore (Headmaster)	100. 0. 0.	Balance	13. 0. 0.
Miss Harrap	50. 0. 0.	Endowment	13. 0. 0.
The Infants' Mistress		Grant (say)	40. 0. 0.
(This was before the		Pence (say)	20. 0. 0.
Infants' School was sold)		6d. rate	103.10. 0.
Burraston	14.10. 0.		
Assistant Teachers	15. 0. 0.		
Expenses	10. 0. 0.		
	189.10. 0.		**189.10. 0.**

The failures of the previous year were explained by the fact that only two girls were sent in for the examination, whereas there ought to have been thirty, as there were boys. The trouble was that the girls were kept at home to mind the babies, and so Mr Laverty brought forward to the Education Council a scheme for taking care, during school hours, of children under three years old. "And this new Babies' Department could be worked with one woman if we employ the girls who will then be set free to come to school. We shall get their service for nothing; for their grant will amount to 18/-, which we do not now get; as for paying the woman we should charge the babies ½d or 1d a day. The advantages to parents are:—

1.   Better for babies.

2.   Those who have an elder girl will have no expense, for she will receive more than they pay for babies."

This plan was approved by the Council, but whether it ever came to fruition I have not been able to discover!

What bad old days those were in some ways, and yet what an inspiring example of public service was set for us by those men of Headley, who spent their time and energy in ensuring education for the children of our village long before it was provided by the Government.

They spent their own money too. Many of the old accounts show that after paying the Master and his assistants, and buying equipment, cleaning materials, coal and bavins—a lovely old Headley word—there was a deficit at the end of the year which was paid out of their own pockets by Mr Dykes and Mr Laverty.

Apparently some rate-payers objected to the 'voluntary' rate, which helped to swell the funds, but Mr Laverty pointed out that if a School Board were to be formed, a compulsory rate would have to be imposed and it would be much higher than the 4d or 6d they were already paying.

In spite of all these difficulties money was found for prizes for the children who did well at the annual Inspection, and there is an illuminating list for July 1873:—

Hori Chandler Std. VI (The Monitor)	s. d.
Smith's and Major's Geography	8
Grammar	8
History of England	8
Jones' Standard Arithmetic	6
John Heywood's 3d Atlas	3
	2. 9.
George Hack Std. II	
Jones' Standard Arithmetic Part 1	2½
Reader for Standard III	10
John Heywood's 3d Atlas	3
	1. 3½
Sarah Burrows (Infant)	
Picture Book	6
Ball	3
	9

Little Sarah at least was still allowed to enjoy some relaxation!

Her Majesty's Inspector for that year reported favourably on the work and said that the discipline was good, but that the scanty attendance of girls in all the classes was to be regretted.

In those days it was common practice to make public the Inspector's Report after his annual visit, and several of these reports are printed in the early Parish Magazines, but for records of the first of the dozen or so men who have been Headmasters during these 200 years, we have to rely largely on oral tradition.

The Parish Clerk in 1752 was Nathaniel Bayley. He had been a schoolmaster, and when Dr Holme built and endowed the school he appointed Nathaniel the master, and he and his son and grandson were clerks and schoolmasters of Headley until 1861. Bayley the third, although apparently retired, was in actual possession of the school buildings when Mr Dykes became Rector in 1848, and it was only with great difficulty that the buildings were recovered, and then only by allowing Bayley to retain them for his life. When he had signed the deed, he threw down the pen, burst into tears and said, "I've signed away my birthright."

'Old Nat', as the first schoolmaster was called, had two daughters, Sarah and Anne; three sons, William, Nathaniel and John; and two half-starved lurchers, who went with him everywhere. When he rang the bells for weddings he used to ring once towards the Robin Hood, once towards the Holly Bush, and once towards Frensham Road. Then when he got his fee he used to say to his wife, "Come along, Hannah, we'll all go and have some'ut to drink". He was very fond of beer.

John Matthews (1790–1875), the last Pound-keeper who lived at 'the old shop at Hilland', remembered being at school for two or three years under Nathaniel. The father used to teach at one end of the room and the son at the other. It was the best school for miles around, he said, and children used to come from all parts.

William Bayley, who succeeded his father in 1798, was reputed to have a very violent temper, and was described as not fit to be a schoolmaster. He had a long black ruler, as heavy as iron, for ruling paper for writing—there were no printed copy-books then—and with this he would hit the boys. Denyer, a boy from Liphook, used to plague him, and he tried to hit him with the ruler, and missed when the boy ran away and dodged, but cut a piece of another boy's ear right out. Mr Henry Knight, the carpenter and builder of Arford, told this story to Mr Laverty, and old Mr Eli Shrubb remembered William Bayley walking up the road to Church hitching up his breeches, one hand in front and the other behind. He was bitten by a mad dog in 1807 and as a result, it was said, at certain times of the year he could not bend!

Mrs George Cole (Fanny Fullick) said the first shilling she ever earned was given to her by Mrs Bayley, the schoolmistress, for knitting. As she had always heard you should put money in the bank, she put it in the bank in Curtis Lane, and never saw it again.

William Bayley died in 1819 and was succeeded by his son William, who was followed by Furness, his son-in-law. From 1861 to 1867 the Headmaster was Mr Pollard, whose 12 year old daughter played the harmonium in church.

When Mr Laverty arrived the Headmaster was Mr Fillmore, a young man of thirty. He had been trained at Highbury and his salary was £95 a year. For this, in addition to his normal duties, he had to train a pupil-teacher, conduct evening-classes and play the harmonium in church. He was a very tidy man, and could sing a comic song rather well. In those days there were regular concerts in the school-room, the profits from which seem often to have been used to defray the expenses of the Parish Magazine. After one of these concerts, at which 220 people were present, the following paragraph appeared in the Hampshire Post for December 17th 1880:—

"Our correspondent thought the two pieces rendered by Mr Fillmore were in rather bad taste, and not in unison with the rest of the programme". The programme was made up of readings, songs, recitations, and whistling, and Mr Fillmore sang The Little Brown Jug, and the Brewer's Only Daughter.

Mr Laverty thought the article was written in spite, and the following month the paper made amends: "The Rev WH Laverty, in favouring us with the above programme, desires us to state that, in calling upon Mr Fillmore, the Chairman, Mr Edmund Woodthorpe of Grayshott, said that though as a rule he declined to take notice of anonymous correspondents yet he felt he might break through the rule on the present occasion. To the Hampshire Post last month there had been sent a notice of Mr Fillmore's songs which was incorrect. There was nothing objectionable whatever, except indeed to one who altogether objected to comic songs; but he grieved to say that there were people who did object to all fun and jollity. The Chairman's words were interrupted more than once by loud cheering from all parts of the room."

Mr Edwards followed Mr Fillmore, and then in 1890 came Mr CH Beck, a man still remembered with respect and affection by many Headley people. He "reigned" for thirty-three years, and with the Rector and the Clerk (Mr William Gamblen) worked hard for the good of the village. Indeed he was the ideal village schoolmaster, who entered wholeheartedly into every aspect of its life. He set a very high standard of work and H.M.I's reports were always good, resulting in the highest possible Grants. He ran evening classes in English, Art, Science, and Handwork, organised entertainments, and ran a club for the lads of the village. For many years he was on the Committee of the Horticultural Society which he and Mr Laverty founded, and he proved to be a very good Organist and Choirmaster. In the first year of his appointment he robed the choir, appealing to 'the gentry' for money, and a local paper reported that "a full choral service is now taken in place of the somewhat dull monotone." There is a record of the choir treat for August 1890. They went to Bentley to catch the 7.30am train for Southampton and then on to Cowes for lunch. From there they went by train to Ryde where they spent the afternoon, returning home via Portsmouth and Liphook and reaching Headley at 10.30pm. Some day!

One of the most interesting features of Mr Beck's time at the school was the annual Bird and Tree Competition. This was run by the Royal Society for the Protection of Birds and was organised on a county basis all over England. A team of children selected one bird and one tree each, and observed them in detail throughout the year, drawing sketches and writing essays. From 1911 to 1925 the judges' comments are full of praise for the work of the Headley children. "The Headley papers are like the eager, intimate talk of boys and girls telling of what has genuinely interested them; so natural and spontaneous. They are written with a real feeling for nature which tells that something in the heart as well as in the head has been awakened to a true outlook on wild life."

"Drawings are most exceptionally clever and artistic, firmness of touch and delicacy of colouring being very noteworthy."

"All the papers begin with appropriate lines of poetry wonderfully well selected. If all those of past years have been preserved the school must now have a considerable anthology."

In 1918... "It is interesting to learn that the Headley school-children gathered herbs and flowers for making ointments and medicines for the soldiers and sailors," and in 1922 Florence Courtnage, who studied the beech tree, noted the use of its nuts in medicine, and as a coffee substitute. She also wrote, "On Beech Hill Common are a number of beech trees planted by Bird and Tree boys and girls now so well grown that birds can nest in them."

In 1924 Edgar King (Mrs Wakeford's nephew) watched some blackbird nestlings all day, having his meals brought out to him, and found that the male and female visited the nest 168 times. The judges remarked, "It is hard to deny the shield to a School which can furnish a boy like that."

Year after year the children won medals and certificates for excellent work and were frequently placed second in the whole county, until at last in 1919 a team consisting of Grace Budd (now Mrs Worman), Stanley Dicker, Lizzie Heather, William James, Beryl Kemp, Annie Kenward, Felicia LeFeuvre, Ivy Parfect, and Maggie Watts, won the County Shield.

It would be interesting to know how many of the prize-winners of those days still cherish their medals and certificates. Among them were Edward Warner (the present Verger) and his brother Eric, Leonard Carter, Gladys Hounsome, George Blanchard, Elsie Wood, Ellen and William Heather, Henry Passingham, Dorothy Eddey, Arthur Dopson and Florence Maidwell.

Mr Beck retired in 1926, aged 66, but this gentle and unassuming man had worn himself out in the service of the people of Headley. He lived for only three years more, dying three months after Mr Laverty, who had written in the Parish Magazine about him, "We have worked together excellently well for over 30 years." It was certainly the end of an era when these two outstanding men had gone.

From 1923 to 1926 Mr FC Beadle was Headmaster. He came from Bristol and had had experience chiefly in Grammar Schools. His time here was spent chiefly in experimenting with the Dalton plan, a system of independent study, and he soon went out to South Africa as Principal of a College.

The last of the old-fashioned village school-masters was Mr VA Amos. He was a very talented but unpredictable man, an excellent teacher and very artistic and capable with his hands. Everything that he did, he did well, taking up fresh interests with burning enthusiasm until he tired of them, and turned to something else. At different times he ran the Sunday Schools and the Scouts; took up book-binding and weaving; built lily-pools at his own house, the Rectory and the School; produced plays and pageants; and illuminated two beautiful lists for the church, of past Rectors, and of benefactors. He became a licensed Lay Reader in 1927 and travelled all over the Deanery preaching and conducting services, yet when he died in 1949 he was an avowed agnostic, leaving directions that no religious service was to be held at his burial.

He was the last Headmaster to take an active part in village life, and actually to live in the village. The School is now controlled by the Government, being taken out of the hands of the Church when the County demanded that an impossibly large sum of money must be spent on building and modernisation.

But still, carrying on the tradition of more than 200 years, the present Headmaster, Mr Lea, and his staff devote their lives to the service of our children as their predecessors, named and unnamed, have done throughout the generations. And still there are children in The Holme School whose ancestors were taught there when it was opened in 1755.

The Fauntleroys

Among Miss Blunt's papers there is the following "Anecdote". Fauntleroy—alias 'Enfant le Roy' whose Ancestor (by the by) was a Natural son of one of our Kings, who Begot him upon a Miller's daughter of Crondal when Hunting in the adjoining Forest called Alice Holt, and gave him the Headley, alias Hethely Estate, situate at the very Edge of the Forest (many hundred years ago) then called Heath House. *Extracted from an ancient manuscript, 31 December 1770.*

In some notes by Mr Laverty he states that by the end of the 17th century the original family of Fauntleroy had disappeared. But there was living at Curtis Farm 150 years ago Fauntleroy the banker who was hanged for forgery. He forged, not for himself but for his bank; and his case finally put an end to hanging for forgery. He was "a tall man and used to wear white trousers, white waistcoat and black coat." Two Headley farmers went up to his execution.

In this connection the following story was told to a friend of mine by a present-day parishioner (Mrs W) as follows: Long, long ago in a cottage on Weaver's Down there lived a man and a woman named Gosden and Gauntlett, who had twelve children. The parents were unmarried and the children seem to have been known by either surname indiscriminately. One of the daughters was the victim of the King, and her son became known as Fauntleroy. The parents made her leave home, but provided her with a cottage in Shamble Fields. When the son grew up he stole some bonds, or deeds of property, and to escape from the law, hid them in Curtis Farm, which was unoccupied at the time. He did not live there, but only used it as a refuge. The Mrs W's Mother told her this story, and it has always been handed down in her family, because Gosden and Gauntlett eventually married and had a thirteenth child who was Mrs W's mother's ancestor. This child, being born in wedlock, inherited her parent's cottage, and Mrs W was born there. She remembers that when she was a child, Curtis Farm was for sale, and her father seriously thought of buying it.

The Fauntleroy's Title to the 12th part of the Headley Estate

In the 3rd year of Kg Edward 6th 1558. Sir Ro Pexall of Beaurepair, Knight was seized in See of the Manor of Broxhead.

On whose death One 12th part of the said Mannor descended to Elizabeth Jobson, wife of John Jobson of Hatfield-Peverel in Essex Esquire, son and heir apparent of Sir Francis Jobson Knight—And by the said Elizabeth and John Jobson were Lawfully conveyed to Sir John Savage of Beaurepaire Knight—

And by him to Edward Savage, one of his Natural Sons—

And by the said Edward Savage unto Richd Burrell

And by the said Richard Burrell since conveyed to Thomas Tayler and his Heirs for ever.

And by the said Thomas Tayler and Richard Burrell by Indenture bearing date 15th May 2 King Charles 1626. Conveyed to John Fauntleroy of Headley in the county of Southampton Gentleman, as per description over-leaf. John Shrub the said informant further tells ye, that in his memory, one John Morer kept Mr Fauntleroy's Flock of Sheep upon Broxhead Common, which strayed into the Forest-Liberty upon which Adams had nearly lost his Place on this Acct. and the other Keepers, with the Hayward drove them to the Forest-Pound at Holy-Water—Where they confined them so long, that the sheep were much impoverished. And upon complaint made by Mr Fauntleroy, Orders were immediately issued, That as many sheep as had apparently suffered from such confinement, should be made good, by an equal number of Deer, out of Woolmer Forest, which at that time (abt Anno 1713) was fully stocked.

John Shrub.

The Deer were not all distroyed till the year 1742, when the Kings Hounds came down on purpose. — John Cleare, 28th Feb. 1773

The Keepers, once claimed the Liberty of Woolmer Forest, to extend as far down as Mr Lee's, Hedge Corner, leading to Lyndford Bridge. But Mr Vickary, the then Lord of the Manor of Broxhead, soon convinced them to the contrary, and obliged them ever afterwards to keep within their own Forest-Bounds, so anciently established and so notoriously well-known.

John Shrub aged 76
27th Feby. 1773

In the Fauntleroy's title to the Headley Estate there is this note: "The Common of Broxhead extends itself from the corner of Old Lands along the Moore southwards, and so along a ditch leading up beyond Bordon Lodge so far or thereabouts as many ancient people have reported, as the lord can lay his line iii times and throw his horn; and so from thence down the Ditch Eastwards, down to the river which is called by the name of Lynford River." The late Sir Charles Owen (quoted by Major AG Wade in his book on Alice Holt Forest) gave as his opinion that 'line' was the actual measuring rope used in those days, while 'throwing' his horn probably meant sounding his horn, a note of proprietorship of the area in question. The eastern boundaries of Alice Holt Forest were then probably the streams to the south, west and north of Broxhead, crossed at various points by Washford, Lindford and Huntingford bridges.

A Strange Case

Extract from the Taunton Courier, August 4th 1814:— "The assizes for the County commenced at the Castle on Tuesday, the 19th. The Right Hon. Sir V Gibbs presided at the Nisi Prius Bar.

Holme, Clerk, v. Smith, D. D. The defendant is a Doctor of Divinity and Rector of Headley. The plaintiff is a clergyman, and resided at the parsonage house at Headley. The action was brought by the plaintiff to recover a penalty for non-residence, under the 43rd Geo iii, c. 84, and 53rd Geo iii, c. 149. The first act enacts that the Rector shall reside on his Rectory, and the latter provides that if he cannot or do not reside there he shall keep a licensed curate to perform the duties of his Church. It appeared, that though Dr Smith kept no resident licensed curate as he ought to do under the latter Act, yet the plaintiff himself had actually resided there and did the duties which he now came into Court to complain were neglected, and the Rector, though he had not so licenced the plaintiff as his curate, had actually nominated him as such to the bishop, but such nomination appeared to have been informal. Much animadversion was made by the defendant's counsel on the plaintiffs conduct in bringing the action, and the learned judge, Sir Vicary Gibbs, made some observations of the same nature thereon; but observed that, however improper or unbecoming a Christian, a gentleman, and a neighbour, towards the defendant, yet the action must be treated in the same manner as others of the same kind, inasmuch as the plaintiff had a right to bring such action, the defendant not having complied with the before-mentioned statutes. The annual value of the living, and the rector's absence from it being proved, the jury, under the direction of his lordship, gave a verdict for one-third of that value after deducting out-goings, agreeable to the provisions of the act."

Dr Smith was Rector from 1800 to 1818. Mr James Holme (presumably no relation of Dr Holme, an earlier rector) signs as curate from June 1813 to Dec 1814.

A Miscellany

Mr Dykes was once served a bad trick by old Mrs B of Lindford. She sent to him to say that her husband was ill of the small-pox. Mr Dykes got in a great fright; told her to keep at home, and he would sent her all she wanted; so down went Port Wine and all good things; and Mrs B even went so far as to say that if he shut off supplies she would come up to the Rectory. The whole thing is now believed to have been a hoax.

Mr Dykes was once asked to have evening instead of afternoon service in the winter. The Clerk (Mr Speakman) was told to ask him, and the answer as reported by Mr Speakman was a refusal 'as it would make the village IMMORTAL.'

Mr Dykes died on the evening before Good Friday. Mr Lickfold was carting coal for him at the time, and Shiba Fullick was one of the carters. A little intoxicated, Shiba was making a good row on Friday morning as they were finishing the carting. "Don't make so much noise," said Flackney the Butler, "the governor's gone." "Where's he gone to this wet morning?" said Shiba.

During the great drought of 1864 an extensive fire took place in Woolmer Forest, which was only extinguished by the exertions of more than 1,000 persons employed incessantly for three days and nights digging trenches. The fire began near Trottsford and destroyed the wood which extended from Headley to Petersfield.

Canon Capes of Bramshott writes in 1901, "Some residents can still remember and can name the man who, tiring of his wife's company, took her with the halter round her neck, which was thought enough to make the contract legal, and sold her at Headley Fair."

"1791 Affidavits of all burials in wollen, of all persons, buried in the parish of Headley, Hants, from Easter 1783 to Easter 1791, being eight years: and the whole number buried there as aforesaid, in that period of eight years, that is, 14 per annum at an average. And the whole number of inhabitants of the said parish being about 800; therefore, if 800 be divided by 14, it will appear that a 56th or a 57th part dyed yearly."

A copy of an agreement between Mr Rooke, Rector of Hedley, and Mr Richard Knight for a seat in the chancell. — Nov. 11. 1707
Whereas Mr William Rooke Rector of Hedley hath given to Mr Richard Knight to erect a seat in ye chancell. These are to certify that neither I the said Richard Knight nor any claiming from me shall have any right by this

grant any longer than during the pleasure of him ye said William Rooke, or his successor for the time being for ever.

In witness thereof I have sett my hand ye day and yeare about written
Richard Knight
Witnesses hereunto: John Caiger, William Franklin

Breefs were authorisations for the collecting for some particular charitable object. There were very few prior to the Restoration in 1660, but in 1583 the registers record "The second day of March was Thomas Brownyng, collector for the hospytall of Hyghgatt at Hedley. The same day was William More, Collector of Hammersmyth Hospytall there also." These appear to be collections from house to house.

Later instances are as follows:
- Hedleigh Church 1696. May 24. Collected for the breef for St. Olave, Southwark 0. 5s. 2d.
- Southton Heathly a rate made for ye poore of the parish April 30 Anno domini 1705. This amounted to £24. 1. 6. from 96 persons, the Rector (Rooke) heading the list with £2. The total was a considerable sum for those days.

In one of his notebooks Mr Laverty writes thus—May M came 15. 2. 84 to ask for some mutton for Mrs Wm. S. "She had a bad cold, but was not in bed; hadn't seen the doctor." Gave her 1/- worth. Asked Wm. S; he "never sent". Went to Mrs M's; found her at dinner. "Mutton was for her," she said. "May made a mistake!!" I pulled the door to pretty roughly and came away...

Wm. M (a brother of May's) died in Farnham Asylum at 11 years of age. Bewitched by an old woman (when a baby) to whom they had refused something; which said old woman asked after him the day he died, and herself fell down dead the same day on her way home.

From the Hindhead Herald 1921.

In a lately issued 'Mathematical Gazette' there is an interesting reminiscence of the Rector of Headley. It is an account of the Mathematical Association of which the Rector was, and still is, a member. The writer speaks of half a century ago, when the Association had just been formed, and says, "Resolutions were passed approving certain details or principles to be adopted in any syllabus. The matter which gave most chance of a fight was a list of proposals drawn up by the Rev WH Laverty. The most important of them was as follows: That the separation which has hitherto been maintained between the methods of algebra and geometry is artificial. That it is useless to draw a distinction between commensurable and incommensurable quantities, seeing that by the use of infinitesimals, incommensurables may be brought under the same methods of proof as commensurables"!!

Lent weddings. It is recorded that Mr Laverty, having been asked if any weddings were coming off soon, replied in the following verse used long ago at Oxford:

> Marriages throughout Lent's season,
> Few are in the papers found;
> Births and deaths, as if no reason
> Could stop either, still abound.
> As the rushing of the waters
> That were long by mill-dam pent.
> Lo! The sons of men and daughters
> Getting married after Lent.

There is a Board in the Vestry which reads: The Incorporated Society for Building etc. Churches granted £140, AD 1858, towards rebuilding this Church, by which additional accommodation has been obtained for 63 persons. The entire area will accommodate 379 at the least. The sittings are all free and subject to annual assignment by the Churchwardens, suitable provision being made for the poorer inhabitants.

"379 at least." It is difficult to believe that this figure is anything but an exaggeration on the part of the Society.

From the Parish Magazine

March 1909 In case of Fire in any part of the parish where there is a supply of water, a telegram or mounted messenger may be sent to the Bordon Camp Fire Brigade, which will be pleased to attend.

March 1923 The Post Office announced that the official name of the Telephone Call Office which has been established on 'Stone Hill' will be 'Headley Down'.

December 1925 From Mr McAndrew of Headley Park we have had a wonderful gift of a Village Hall, primarily for the use of the Women's Institute, but also for general purposes, and to him and Mrs Perry and others who have provided the furnishing etc, we owe a deep debt of gratitude.

One of the first uses to which the Hall was put was for the Bazaar organised by Major Hooper to help pay the great sum required for 'Dilapidations' (at the Rectory) both now and annually. I need hardly say that my family and I are most thankful for the splendid result.

Paper lent to Mr Laverty by Mr Geo. Warren.

I hereby certify that I have received into the Registry of the Lord Bishop of Winchester a Certificate that a Room on the premises of William Warren, paper maker at Bramshot in the County of Hants and Diocese of Winchester is set apart, by a Congregation of His Majesty's Protestant Subjects Dissenting from the Church of England, as and for a Place of Public Worship and

Service of Almighty God. Dated at Winchester, the 26th Day of November 1830.[†] C. Wooldridge, Deputy Registrar.

A letter received by Mr Laverty in 1910.
"Sir,
I have been asked by Mrs C.F. to tell you that she for-bids the bands of her son Harry for he his under age. And her son Harry also asked me to tell you that he wishes to withdraw his bands."

Feb. 1923. The London papers had an account in December of the clever way PC Bundy (still living with his daughter in the Liphook Road) saved the life of a kitten on Beech Hill. The following is from the official organ of the Swiss Union for the protection of animals; La vie d'un petit minet, tombé dans un puits profond, fut sauvée d'une manière remarquable. Après avoir essayé deux fois de rattraper le petit chat dans un seau; un 'policeman' attacha une corde à la chatte mère, et la fit descendre dans le puits; la dessus elle saisit le petit par le cou et le tint jusqu' à ce que tous les deux fussent mis en sûreté. (par le cou = by the neck!)

[†] The same week that the Riot happened – see p.57.

Cobbett's visits to Headley

November 24, 1822

'Upon leaving Greatham we came out upon Woolmer Forest.... I asked a man the way to Thursley. "You must go to Liphook, sir," said he. "But," I said, "I will not go to Liphook." These people seem to be posted at all these stages to turn me aside from my purpose, and to make me go over that Hindhead, which I had resolved to avoid. I went on a little further, and asked another man the way to Headley, which lies on the western foot of Hindhead, whence I knew there must be a road to Thursley without going over that miserable hill. The man told me that I must go through the forest. I asked him whether it was a good road: "It is a sound road," said he, laying a weighty emphasis upon the word 'sound.' "Do people go it?" said I. "Ye–es," said he. "Oh then," I said to my man, "as it is a sound road keep you close to my heel, and do not attempt to go aside, not even for a foot." Indeed, it was a sound road. The rain of the night had made the fresh horse tracks visible. And we got to Headley in a short time, over a sand road, which seemed so delightful after the flints and stone and dirt and sloughs that we had passed over and through since the morning....

'... We got to Headley, the sign of the Holly Bush, just at dusk, and just as it began to rain. I had neither eaten nor drunk since eight o'clock in the morning; and as it was a nice little public-house, I at first intended to stay all night, an intention which I afterwards very indiscreetly gave up. I had laid my plan, which included the getting to Thursley that night. When, therefore, I had got some cold bacon and bread, and some milk, I began to feel ashamed of stopping short of my plan.'

Cobbett bargained with a man for three shillings to guide him so as to avoid Hindhead, but the guide lost his way and they eventually arrived 'on the turnpike some hundred yards on the Liphook side of the buildings called the Hut.... It is odd how differently one is affected by the same sight, under different circumstances. At the 'Holly Bush' at Headley there was a room full of Fellows in white smock frocks, drinking and smoking and talking, and I, who was then dry and warm, moralised within myself on their folly in spending their time in such a way. But when I got down from Hindhead to the public-house at Road Lane, with my skin soaking and my teeth chattering, I thought just such another group, whom I saw through the window sitting round a good fire with pipes in their mouths, the wisest assembly I had ever set eyes on.'

The following August Cobbett was more fortunate, and he speaks in glowing terms of the road from Headley through Churt to Thursley: 'a prettier ride I never had in the course of my life'.

See more about Cobbett's visit to Headley on p.190

Troubled Times[†]

"If the rising of 1830 had succeeded, and won back for the labourer his lost livelihood, the day when the Headley workhouse was thrown down would be remembered by the poor as the day of the taking of the Bastille. But this rebellion failed, and the men who led that last struggle for the labourer passed into the forgetfulness of death and exile."

J L and Barbara Hammond, "The Village Labourer 1760–1832"

It is an astonishing fact that, while he chronicled every available item of Headley's history right back to Domesday book, and no detail was too small to escape his notice, Mr Laverty scarcely mentions the riot at the Workhouse. Yet surely this was the most momentous event of all, reflecting the dreadful conditions under which the majority of village people were forced to exist, and resulting in the most tragic consequences for many unfortunate Headley families.

Considering that he came here only forty years after the event I find this omission almost inexplicable, for there must have been many still alive who could have given him vivid eye-witness accounts of what actually happened. Of course, as a clergyman receiving generous tithes, he represented part of a system that the farm labourers were fighting, and perhaps there was still too much bitterness aroused by the savage punishments for them to talk freely to him.

To understand what led to the uprising it is necessary to go back hundreds of years, long before the Norman Conquest in fact. England looked very different then. The country was not divided by hedges and fences into a patch-work of comparatively small fields. Most of the land was forest, such as Alice Holt is now, and villages grew up in the clearings. The church, with a cluster of cottages around it, stood in the centre of what was virtually one huge open field, and everyone in the village, including the Lord of the Manor, shared in the farming of the land. The "field" was divided into strips, each an acre or half-an-acre in size, and one man's holding might be scattered in many different places, but at least it was fair, for in this way everyone shared good and poor land. Also, every year, the strips were re-allocated.

In this part of England the two-field system of farming was followed; that is to say, all the available land was divided into two great fields, one of which was used for growing grain, while the other lay fallow, and in the following year the position was reversed. The meadows by the river were enclosed by hurdles for hay, but when the hay was cut, every man could run a cow, some pigs or geese on this land. The fallow field also was used in this way, as also was the "waste" or common. In addition to his strips in the open field the

---

[†] This chapter written by Joyce Stevens

Lord also had his own demesne land round the Manor house, and he usually owned the Mill. The villagers worked the Lord's land for him for a proportion of the year, and their corn was ground in his mill. Naturally he exacted a share of their flour as payment.

In Headley one can imagine that the great fields stretched from the Church out to Headley Park, down to Lindford Bridge, and right across the present Playing Fields to Standford, bounded by the river in all directions. The School Green was part of the Lord's Waste and Broxhead to the west and Headley Down to the east are remains of the extensive commons.

In these days each village was self-supporting, cut off from the next by thick forests and rough tracks, almost impassable in the winter months. The people of the village, rich and poor alike, were dependent upon each other, co-operating in working the land, and yet each possessed a sturdy independence.

This system of farming lasted an incredibly long time, continuing in parts of the country until the late eighteenth century, but then the second Enclosure movement really got into its stride. A more economical and scientific system of farming was needed to feed the ever-growing population, and artificial grasses, root crops and new methods of growing grain could be used by go-ahead farmers, who had been held back by the old system. Scattered strips with their baulks and headlands were wasteful of land, and gradually even large areas of the commons, waste and forests were enclosed and made productive by the wealthy landlord class. The Napoleonic Wars too made it essential for England to produce more food, which had been raised to almost famine prices.

Enclosures were a necessary step but they led to great hardships among the poor, and created a new class in England – the landless labourer. The money he received as compensation for loss of commoner's rights was not enough to set him up as a small farmer, nor even to pay for fencing the plot of land that might have been allotted to him. Money was not as useful to him as land rights and it was soon dissipated in the ale-house or elsewhere. Prices were soaring, and wages were low – lower in Hampshire than anywhere else in the southern counties; often not more than seven shillings a week. The Speenhamland system of helping the poor, based upon the changing price of a loaf of bread, offered him charity instead of raising his wages.

The Combination Act prevented him from forming a Trades Union with his fellows. The Act of Settlement [of 1662] prevented him from moving to another parish in an industrial town in search of work. The Game Laws threatened him with imprisonment, whipping or transportation if he went poaching to find food for his family, and he also ran the risk of being maimed for life in a man-trap. New methods of farming, especially the new threshing machines, led to unemployment. The former sturdy independent rural labourer was becoming a pauper, dependent upon charity.

To try to deal with the situation, groups of Parishes combined to form Unions to provide a house where infirm, aged paupers, and orphan or illegitimate children could be sheltered. The also guaranteed to find work for the labourers by sending them the rounds of the rate payers of the parish, who each had to promise to employ the men for a certain number of days, according to the rateable value of their property. The Parishes of Headley, Bramshott and Kingsley combined in this way, and in 1795 they built a House of Industry, as it was first rather grandly called. This was the house along the Liphook Road which we now know as Headley Grange.

There is no need to go into detail about the dreaded Workhouse system; Charles Dickens and the poet Crabbe have described that eloquently enough. The important point is that in 1830 when all over the southern counties the desperate labourers revolted against the conditions described in the previous paragraphs – breaking up threshing machines, and setting fire to ricks and barns – in this district it was the hated Workhouses that they attacked.

The scene is vividly described in J L and B Hammond's book, *The Village Labourer*:

"The mob first went to Mr Cobbold, Vicar of Selborne, and demanded that he should reduce his tithes, telling him with some bluntness, 'we must have a touch of your tithes: we think £300 a year quite enough for you... £4 a week is quite enough.' Mr Cobbold was thoroughly alarmed, and consented to sign a paper promising to reduce his tithes which amounted to something over £600, by half that sum. The mob were accompanied by a good many farmers who had agreed to raise wages if the labourers would undertake to obtain a reduction of tithes, and these farmers signed the paper also. After Mr Cobbold's surrender the mob went on to the workhouse at Headley, which served the parishes of Bramshott, Headley and Kingsley. Their leader was a certain Robert Holdaway, a wheelwright, who had been for a short time a publican. He was a widower, with eight small children, described by the witnesses at his trial as a man of excellent character, quiet, industrious, and inoffensive. The master of the workhouse greeted Holdaway with 'What, Holdy, are you here?' 'Yes, but I mean you no harm nor your wife nor your goods: so get them out as soon as you can, for the house must come down.' The master warned him that there were old people and sick children in the house. Holdaway promised that they should be protected, asked where they were, and said the window would be marked. What followed is described in the evidence given by the master of the workhouse: 'There was not a room left entire, except that in which the sick children were. These were removed into the yard on two beds, and covered over, and kept from harm all the time. This was done by the mob. They were left there because there was no room for them in the sick ward. The sick ward was full of infirm old paupers. It was not touched, but of all the rest of the place not a room was left entire.' The farmers looked on whilst the destruction proceeded and one at least of the labourers in the mob declared afterwards that his master had forced him to join."

The Rev WW Capes, a former Rector of Bramshott, tells how Mr Curtis, who lived at The Reedens (now Wodehouse) met the mob on their way and they spoke to him with glee of what was done.

"Oh! Mr Curtis, it is a pity you were not at Headley when we broke into the Workhouse. You would have laughed if you had seen the tiles fly. Tell the people at Alton to look out as we are intending to attack the Workhouse and Breweries."

Mr Curtis, the owner of the shop then called Church Gate Stores, was Parish Constable at the time.[†]

The riots spread right across Hampshire throughout November 1830, but with the aid of troops the labourers were subdued and the first Special Commission was opened at Winchester on December 18th. There were more than 300 prisoners, for the most part charged with breaking machines, and demanding money with threats, and after being tried in batches, 6 were sentenced to death, 95 to transportation for life, 36 to transportation for various periods, 65 to imprisonment with hard labour and 67 were acquitted.

These severe sentences, when not a single life had been taken by the rioters and not a single person wounded, produced an outburst of public opinion, and all classes except the magistrates, joined in petitions to the Government for mercy. The *Times* Correspondent at Winchester wrote 'The scenes of distress in and about the jail are most terrible. The number of men who are to be torn from their homes and connexions is so great that there is scarcely a hamlet in the county into which anguish and tribulation have not entered. Wives, sisters, mothers, children, beset the gates daily, and the governor of the jail informs me that the scenes he is obliged to witness at the time of locking up the prison are truly heartbreaking.'

One of the men condemned to death was Robert Holdaway, the leader of the attack on the Workhouse at Headley, but as a result of the public outcry his life was spared, together with three others of the six originally to be executed. However, the Government compelled all the prisoners who had been condemned by the Commission to witness the hanging of the two whom public opinion had been powerless to save. "'At this moment I cast my eyes down into the felons' yard, and saw many of the convicts weeping bitterly, some burying their faces in their smock frocks, others wringing their hands convulsively, and others leaning for support against the wall of the yard and unable to cast their eyes upwards.' This was the last vision of English justice that each labourer carried to his distant and dreaded servitude, a scene that would never fade from his mind." (*The Village Labourer*)

And we must remember that these men in the felons' yard were not criminals; they were the ordinary, decent men of our Hampshire villages; the carpenters, joiners, smiths and bricklayers, shoemakers, shepherds and small-holders who had thrown in their lot with the poor, who regularly took in Cobbett's Register and who, therefore, had become dangerous "politicians".

Of Robert Holdaway we hear no more; and what of his eight, small, motherless children? Did they spend the rest of their lives in the gaunt

---

[†] This is incorrect – it was another Mr Curtis who they met at East Worldham

barracks of the Workhouse or were they fortunate enough to be cared for by relatives or friends?[†]

Transportation, even if only for seven years, was equal to sentence of death, for passages home were not part of the bargain, and no man was likely to be able to come by enough money ever to return to England at the end of his sentence. When the families of the Headley men stood outside Winchester prison they knew that they saw each other for the last time; this was Goodbye, for ever.

After the shock of the sudden uprisings and their terrible consequences, some attempts were made to improve the conditions of the poor, and it was at this time that land was set aside in each parish for allotments. Headley Workhouse was sold in 1870, and became a private house, but for many years after that "The Union" at Alton remained a fate to be dreaded by people becoming too old or infirm to earn a living.

How incredible this all seems to us now, living in a Welfare State, with National Insurance, medical services, child allowances, free milk in schools – and continual demands for higher pay! All the Hampshire labourers of 1830 asked was 2/- a day, and they worked from daylight till dark, six days a week.

Ninety years later, after the first World War, a Memorial was erected outside the Church. Subsequently, news arrived of the death in a Prisoner of War Camp of one more man, whose name had been omitted from the original List. He was William Holdaway, of Beech Hill.

See more about the Workhouse Riot on p.123

[†] At least some of these questions have now been answered in *One Monday in November* by John Owen Smith

Queen Victoria's Jubilee in Headley

From the local paper of July 1887:—

On Sunday a very full and earnest congregation assembled at the parish church to hear Madame Patey's 'Oh! rest in the Lord' from Mendelssohn's Elijah. The singing of the National Anthem brought to an appropriate conclusion a hearty service in thanksgiving to God for the Queen's prosperous reign. The National Anthem was sung and the appropriate prayers and thanksgivings used in the afternoon at Greyshott and in the evening at Headley.

On Tuesday the residents of Headley celebrated Her Majesty's Jubilee by holding a very successful festival in the Rectory grounds. On the same occasion the Foresters, Court Forget-me-Not, held their fifth anniversary at the same place. It can thus be easily understood by those who know the energy and zeal that the Headley people always display when they put their hands to any undertaking of this character that the festivities of Tuesday gave satisfaction to all. Indeed, it was such a day of merrymaking and general rejoicing as has rarely if ever taken place in this parish before. The village was tastefully decorated with flags, banners, and evergreens, and loyal mottoes were displayed in prominent positions. Venetian poles were placed on each side of the thoroughfare in High Street, from which were suspended festoons of flags of every colour and nationality. Bunting was also displayed from the Church tower, and the Rectory windows. Mr W Rogers' place of business, which faces down the street, attracted general admiration for its artistic decoration of flags, evergreens, and a conspicuous portrait of the Queen over the main entrance. The Holly Bush Inn, a short distance away, was also decorated with foliage, and both made up a very pretty rural scene.

The day's proceedings commenced about 11am when the Foresters—adults and juveniles—assembled at the Court House previous to a general parade of the parish. Some were on horseback, in the costume of Robin Hood and his trusty followers. A procession having been formed, headed by the excellent band of the Alton Volunteers corps, visits were paid to The Oaks, the residence of Major General Parish, CB; The Firs, the seat of JG Patey, Esq; Mrs Vincent's residence where the processionists were provided with light refreshment; Harford House, the residence of Colonel Norman; Headley Grange, the residence of TS Hahn, Esq; and Crabtree House, the residence of S Bewsher, Esq.

1872–1928

And so we come to the times of Mr Laverty *[see photo on p.224]*. The Rev WH Laverty was, like many of his predecessors, a Fellow of the Queen's College, Oxford. He was one of the University's leading mathematicians, and a distinguished career in this branch of learning seemed assured to him. But—he fell in love, and as all Fellows at that period had to be bachelors (there being no married quarters in College), another position had to be found for him. Fortunately, the living of Headley was then of some value, and so in 1872 he became Rector and his almost historic incumbency did not end till he died in harness in 1928. Mr Laverty was, when appointed, aged 25 (five years younger than the present Rector, whom God preserve!) and the following story was told about him. When news arrived that a young man was coming as Rector, certain people expressed a fear that being young and coming from Oxford, he would be dreadfully 'high church'. This feeling was not diminished when on the Rector's arrival he cleaned up the Church and put a little colour on the walls, but Mr Bettesworth, the Churchwarden, said, "The world wags, and Mr Laverty's a young man, and you can't expect him to stand still like an old man as Mr Dykes."

In the three months' interregnum the following notice was given to the Churchwardens: "The Churchwardens have the care of the benefice during a vacancy. Having first taken out a sequestration from the spiritual court they are to manage all the profits and expenses for him that shall next succeed: plough and sow his glebe, take in the crop, collect tithes, thrash out and sell corn, repair houses and fences and the like. They should take care that during the vacancy the Church shall be duly served by a Curate approved by the Bishop, whom they are to pay out of the profits of the benefice. And if the successor thinks himself aggrieved by them he may appeal to the ecclesiastical judge".

The following letter was also sent to the Churchwardens: "Gentlemen, As Executor under the will of my Brother, your late Rector, I hereby give you formal notice that it is my desire that the money lent by my Brother for the purchase of land to enlarge the Churchyard be repaid to me at once.

Your obedient servant
............"

The "young man" got to work at once, but nothing he did could have alarmed his older parishioners. In November 1872 the 'Monthly Illustrated Journal' was begun, and this, under various names, has continued to be issued ever since. Headley was then truly a village community with a comparatively small population, and the Journal records very little but births, marriages and deaths, and the hymns to be sung each Sunday. Many ancestors of present-day residents appear in the lists from the registers as, eg. Shrubb, Burrows,

Fullick, Glaysher, Fyfield..

A significant change was announced to the effect that there would be a Celebration of the Holy Communion every fortnight, which was obviously an advance on the custom which had prevailed in previous years. A service each Sunday at 3pm was begun at Grayshott (which was then in the parish and called Greyshott!).

A Provident Club and a Shoe Club were formed and some of the rules of the latter state: "those children only are to be admitted who attend the Day School; the weekly subscription is one penny; interest will depend on the regular attendance of the children at school; and further interest will be given for regular attendance at the Sunday School."

On Christmas Day 1873 the old folks who came from a distance were treated to a Christmas Dinner at the Rectory; others, who could not come, received, some a present of food, and others a blanket. The money saved by means of the Provident and Shoe Clubs came acceptably to many; an average of 5/- was given as interest, those depositors who had children receiving some more, some less, according to the attendance of their children at the schools.

The Cricket Club was formed in 1872 and played its first match on May 12th, and the first perambulation of the bounds of the parish took place the same year, though there were records of similar perambulations in 1723 and 1772. Mr Laverty organised other 'beating the bounds' on several occasions till advancing years compelled him to give up that activity. It was revived again in 1936, and on one or two occasions since then it has been carried out.

The Wednesday Cricket Team before the First World War

Mr Laverty tells some interesting stories of those early years of which the following are examples. "At the autumn manoeuvres [of 1874?] Dan Collins the Blacksmith shoed a horse for Prince Arthur (Duke of Connaught) but would take no pay, so the Prince said he would send him a pipe. In the following year the Prince again went to Collins when he reminded him of his promise, and the Prince tied a knot in his pocket handkerchief so as to be sure to remember it." In the same year the said Dan Collins "having ridden to Selborne (he very seldom did ride) and according to his usual habit (as I am told) got tipsy, rode back and on White Hill soon after looking in at the 'Prince of Wales' was thrown. He was taken home in a cart and put to bed, his friends thinking he was merely tipsy. However next morning he was discovered putting his legs into his coat sleeves. A doctor was called for but he never rallied." [There was still a Collins at the Blacksmiths when I came.]

Early in 1857 Abraham Keeling murdered Esther Fullick, aged 11, who was nursemaid to Keeling's grandchild, and then committed suicide. He lived at the "small farm across the water at Headley Mill," presumably now Stream Farm. The intention had been to bury him at Wellfield Corner, but eventually he was buried in the Churchyard at night, near the wall opposite the Church porch, stones being flung on the coffin by the onlookers. (His may well have been the bones found by men working at the enlargement of the Buttery a year or so ago.)

It is manifestly impossible to enumerate all the changes that occurred during Mr Laverty's fifty-eight years 'reign'. ('Reign' is surely the right word to use, for undoubtedly he ruled the parish, and his authority increased as his years). A summary of the chief events was circulated on the occasion of his Jubilee as Rector and the more important are here reproduced.

1872 Churchyard planted with shrubs.
     Perambulations of parish boundaries began.
1873 Services commenced in Grayshott Schoolroom (and continued for 15
     years).
1874 East Window erected in memory of the Rev JB Dykes.
1878 Allotments started near the Grange.
     Main schoolroom enlarged.
1882 Reredos erected in memory of Mr JR Phillips.
1885 Pipe organ substituted for American organ.
     Flower Show first instituted and Rectory field arranged as Cricket
     Ground (the Club started in 1872).
1886 Penny Dinners introduced.
1887 Church redecorated and new heating apparatus installed.
     Pulpit erected in memory of Mrs JR Phillips and lectern presented by
     Mrs Laverty's four sisters, all married in the church.
1888 Further addition to the Holme School.
     Telegraph office opened.

1890 London children given holiday accommodation.
1891 Chestnut tree planted in High Street to mark site of stocks.
1892 Chancel screen erected in memory of General HW Parish.
1894 West window erected in memory of Admiral John Parish. First Parish Council elected (the Rector acting as Hon. Clerk till 1919).
1896 Further enlargement of the Holme School.
1900 Clock installed in memory of a son of Sir Robert and Lady Wright. Commencement of Bordon Camp. Tobacco, etc, sent to our soldiers in South Africa.
1901 Separation of Grayshott into independent parish.
Conversion of Beech Hill allotments into a Recreation Ground.
1905 Mothers' Union started by Mrs John Parish (who for some years had conducted Mothers' meetings).
1906 Headley Working Men's Institute founded.
1908 Vestry enlarged.
1909 An acre added to the Churchyard.
1912 Beech Hill Social Club and Bordon Working Men's Club founded.
1913 Deadwater Council School (now Mill Chase Primary School) built.
1914-19 Several lists printed of Soldiers and Sailors serving in the War, including those who were lost, to whom Memorials were erected in Church and Churchyard in 1920.
1920 Erection of Community Church at Stone Hill (now Headley Down).
1922 Oak Choir stalls erected in memory of the late Rector and Mrs Dykes, and their two sons.

Of all but a very few of the above Mr Laverty must have been the instigator, and no one will doubt that his influence in the parish was outstanding. Someone who came to Headley soon after his death sends a few notes about this exceptional man. "This brilliant young mathematical Fellow of Queen's wanted to get married when it was not permitted, and therefore decided to be ordained. He had no vocation in the ordinary sense, but he was intensely conscientious. The village could set their clocks by him, setting out to visit on his bicycle at 2pm, or maybe 2.30, and he visited every house in the parish twice a year. The visits were brief ones and he often left tracts about such things as sleeping with open windows etc. He could not face sick visits, and used to send the daughters to visit the sick with baskets of eggs and more tracts.

No Bishop was allowed in the church and no churchwarden in the vestry! The Rector pocketed the collections and paid all the bills, and such was the esteem in which he was held that no one had any doubt but that he was out of pocket.

A photograph in one of the parish registers shows him as a small man who normally wore a knickerbocker suit and a black or speckled straw hat, and, at any rate in his later years, a grey beard.

In eight volumes of notebook which Mr Laverty left containing short biographies of his parishioners, there are many instances of the practical help which he gave to those who had met with misfortune. For instance, a letter sent to likely subscribers says "George Holden, who carries the letters between Headley and Liphook, has the misfortune to lose his pony. As he is in somewhat delicate health he will not be able to carry out his duties unless he can drive. Contributions towards the purchase of a new pony may be given to the bearer." The result was £3. 13. 0.

"The trial of L. and W. B. on the charge of setting fire to a piece of common on the Grayshott road is to take place at the end of this month. The boys declare their innocence and many believe that a mistake has been made; and it is of the utmost importance that the evidence should be subject to searching cross-examination. For the Law-Expenses a sum of 10 guineas is required, and donations are asked towards this. Donors are understood as not in any way forejudging the case, but only as helping to secure a fair trial for the boys." £7 odd was apparently subscribed, but there is no mention of the result of the trial.

Here it may be appropriate to include this appreciation, which shows what members of another church thought of him.

To The Revd WH Laverty, Rector of Headley in the County of Hants. 1872–1922

Dear Sir,

In commemorating your Golden Wedding and Jubilee of Rectorship, we, the Trustees of the Stone Hill Community Church, take this opportunity of assuring you how greatly we appreciate the kindly interest, generous gifts and practical sympathy which you have given to us in the establishment of a non-sectarian Church in an outlying part of your Parish.

Some of us have for a great number of years resided in your Parish, and we recall the many improvements and benefits which you have secured for Headley during the 50 years of your Incumbency.

We recall particularly the acquisition of seven beautiful windows in memory of Mr Dykes the previous Rector, Miss Isabel I'Anson, Mr I'Anson, Admiral Parish, Mr Hubbuck and Mr CAW McAndrew. The erection of Reredos and Pulpit in memory of Mr and Mrs JR Phillips, and Clock in memory of the son of Sir Robert Wright. The installation of Pipe Organ in 1885, the enlargement of Vestry in 1908, and the Memorials to those fallen in the Great War in 1920. The formation of the first Parish Council in 1894, to which for 25 years you acted as Hon. Clerk. The establishment of a separate Church at Grayshott following much arduous but valuable work there, a School at Deadwater and the decoration of Headley Church, enlargement of Church Yard and of Headley School and other improvements too numerous to detail.

To this very incomplete list of your achievements must be added the personal endearment to the inhabitants of your Parish which your Ministry has secured to you.

We wish you, Sir, the ever present joy of knowing that your life work has been well done, and we trust you will be spared to us for a great number of years.

Yours very sincerely,

(Signed)   Mary Jane Curtis

Sophia Ogden

Fanny Venning

Victor M James

TA Hayward

Charles H. Venning

Arthur Bishop Wilson

Lawrence H James, Chaplain

Trustees of Stone Hill Community Church.

Dated this 12th day of June, 1922.

The wise old man was then aged 75, but his work was not yet quite done. Shortly after the above letter was sent to him he persuaded the 'Laurence H James', a Methodist who had been appointed Chaplain to the Community Church, to be ordained into the Church of England and become his curate, whereupon the whole of the worshippers of the Stone Hill Church became Anglicans also, and ever since the Rectors of Headley have been asked to conduct services in 'the little church', even though its Trust Deed still declares it to be undenominational.

In the Parish Magazine of July 1928 there is this note (the last of many such that had appeared over the years) 'The number of houses at my Spring Visitation was 855'.

He conducted the funeral of Robert Matthews on December 1st and in the following month there is recorded among the deaths,

Dec. 27. Wallis Hay Laverty, Headley Rectory, aged 81 years.

The Parish Council

The first Parish Council, elected at a Poll taken on December 17, 1894, consisted of Rev WH Laverty, Miss CB I'Anson (Grayshott), Messrs CH Beck (the schoolmaster), George Bone (Bird's Nest Farm), Oliver Chapman (Grayshott), Thos. Carter (Eveley Gardens), Chas. David (Headley Green), Thos. Falkner (Standford), Albert Harding (Lindford), RS Gardner (Hatch House Farm), George Warren (Standford), A. Ingham Whitaker (Grayshott Hall). At its first meeting summoned by Sir Robert Wright as Chairman of the first parish meeting, Sir Robert was elected Chairman of the Council, and the Rev WH Laverty was elected Clerk, a position he occupied till 1919.

Extracts from the Minutes show that the Council in 1895 "having examined the plans of the proposed new railway called the Portsmouth, Basingstoke and Godalming Railway, consider that such a railway would be of advantage to Headley parish, provided that there be a station within a mile of Headley Street." The proposal evidently found favour with the authorities for a later minute records that a letter had been received from the solicitor to the proposed Company "that to all intents and purposes it is settled that the station is to be at Curtis Farm House or near thereto."

In spite of the above assurance nothing more was heard of the railway and Headley is still without its station.

Among other matters discussed at meetings of the Council prior to 1918 were:—

1898 the fact of many accidents at Wellfield Corner and a petition to the District Council to build a bridge at Headley Mill (still being discussed!)

1903 the lighting of the village (not yet realised!)

1907 application to the County Council to form a separate civil parish of the Western districts of Headley. (This was done in 1929 when the parish of Whitehill was formed and the districts of Bordon and Lindford—but not Standford—incorporated into it.)

1908 It was suggested that chairs instead of forms should be provided for the Council meetings. Urgent need for a road across Broxhead from Lindford Bridge to the Camp.

1909 An objection to "Mr Bide's great heap of manure" on Broxhead Common.

1910 The old Commoners (on Broxhead) were stated to be "the owners of the old properties in Lindford and up to Headley Street, Headley Wood, Headley Park, Trottsford, etc. The rights are those of feed and turf cutting, sporting rights and some digging of gravel for private use."

1914 'The hill rising from Arford Pond' was called 'Parfect's Hollow'.

1917 The attention of the Council was called to the forming of a Rat and

Sparrow Club.

1918 It was noted that subscriptions to the Rat and Sparrow Club will not cover the payments for tails.

The Chairmen of the Parish Council in those days were Sir Robert Wright, Mr A. Ingham Whitaker, Mr WT Phillips and Col FF Perry.

The Last Thirty Years

This chapter is perhaps the most difficult of all to write. Not only does it deal with incidents in which I, perforce, have taken an active part, but it is not easy, so soon after the events, to judge which of them is worthy of inclusion.

At my induction, the address of the then Archdeacon of Surrey (Ven. L.E. Blackburne) was based on the words 'Bear ye one another's burdens,' and right well did successive Parochial Church Councils lead their fellow members of the laity in co-operation and mutual understanding of a Rector's task. The other notable feature of the day was, as the congregation left the Church, the sight of two very tall and somewhat gaunt figures, draped from head to foot in protective clothing, and causing some confusion on the road. It was the Misses Pack-Beresford taking a swarm in the Churchyard hedge!

These ladies, who, with their brothers, then lived at Brambletye, were known as the 'new people' though they had come many years before. The words are indicative of the fact that in those days life ran very slowly in what was still an isolated community, and possibly I saw more changes in thirty years than any of my predecessors. It was an elderly population then—hardly a child went to the Holme School from the direction of the Church or the Holly Bush. There was no such place as Church Fields or the Erie Estate, and hardly more than a dozen houses down the Liphook Road. Further afield, neither the houses on the cricket field at Lindford, nor those on the way to Headley Mill, nor the Alexandra Park Estate at Bordon had been built, and "commuters" and "commuting", whether applied to people or the act, were unknown.

In 1935 Mr GA McAndrew of Headley Park, with his brother and sister, gave a set of six bells for the church (their father having given the Village Hall in 1925) and the same year Sir Charles O'Brien, who had represented the King as Governor first of the Seychelles and later of Barbados, unveiled a commemorative plaque on the Village Green to mark that King's (George V) Jubilee. The three beech trees planted at the same time did not survive.

In 1936 I revived the idea of 'treading the bounds' of the parish in spite of the fact that at the preliminary survey of the ground, Jack Lickfold, Len Maynard and I were chased first by a bull and then by the irate owner (until he saw who we were) in a far corner of the parish. In the same year Mr VA Amos designed and executed the list of Rectors, which now hangs on the West wall of the Church.

In 1937 the Church was enriched by oak Altar rails given in memory of Mr and Mrs Squarey, and many members of the congregation at the same time completed the scheme for the interior by the gift of oak pews, costing at that time, £12 each.

From 1938 onwards the parish, with the rest of the nation, lived under the shadow of war and I see there is recorded in the Parish Magazine a word of thanks to the late Major Heaslop, Major (now Colonel) Dudgeon, Mrs Heelis, the late Lady O'Brien and the Air-raid Wardens for 'the quiet and efficient way in which they dealt with the various branches of work for which they were responsible.' A list of all those serving was placed on the Church door, and twice weekly prayers were offered for their safe return. All men known to have served were after the war given a Certificate of Honour, designed by Hugh (now the Rev) Thomson-Glover.

An association for boys and girls known as the Youth Fellowship was begun in 1941 and has continued ever since. At that time the idea of such a village club so interested the educational authorities at Winchester that an official was sent down post haste to see what it was all about, but, to put us in our place, the idea of something for youth was not really new. In an ancient document it is recorded that in 1649 Mr Nicholas Moore built a gallery in the Church "for the youths of the parish"!

In 1949 an unusual event occurred—a Church became too small for its worshippers. Headley Down Church was considerably enlarged and beautified. Many of those who habitually attended the services were responsible for the additions and improvements, but to Mr RL Robinson the chief credit was due. An expert carpenter, he designed and made the oak altar rail, lectern, clergy desk and seat. All are examples of wonderful workmanship, and it is pleasant to record that an oak reredos to his memory was made by the same Mr Barnsley who was responsible for the War Memorial case in the Parish Church.

In June 1951 a considerable number of parishioners (some 180 in all) performed the Pageant of Headley, written by Eveline Clarke to commemorate the Festival of Britain (see p.161). The story of the Pageant depicted, first, the Headley villagers repelling the Danish invaders of AD894, the granting of Headley Mill to a Norman Knight by William the Conqueror, the havoc wrought by the Black Death in the 14th century and the consequent labour troubles which arose at that time. It went on to give a representation of an envoy from Elizabeth to grant a Charter to hold a fair in 1601, the ejection of the then Rector by Cromwell's men because of his refusal to discontinue the use of the Prayer Book (1645) *[see p.160]* and a visit to the Lord of the Manor by William Cobbett (1800) and the beginnings of the education of the labouring man. A representation of Headley's part in the celebration of the Exhibition of 1851 led on to the last Episode—a vision of the future (2051) when all the inventions of science are devoted to the benefit, and not the destruction of mankind.

In 1953 Mrs Clarke's genius produced another Pageant "Salute to Elizabeth", portraying eight Queens of England's past history, all in honour of the Coronation of our present gracious Queen. Both Pageants were performed in the spacious gardens of Wodehouse, then the home of Mr and Mrs Reginald Thackeray, to whose generosity the parish owed so much, and not least the gift of the Thackeray Pavilion on the Playing Fields.

The Coronation Pageant of 1953

Mention of the Playing Fields would be incomplete without a reference to the oaken gate placed at the village end of the Fields in memory of John Heather, a Youth Fellowship boy, "who played the game to the end".

"The Church among the people" was the heading of an article quoted by the Farnham Herald in September 1952 describing the blessing of the houses on the Alexandra Park estate. In the same month a most generous offer of £300 was made to start a fund for the provision of some religious/social centre which was completed in 1955 at a cost of £1,700.

'Has Headley a history?' When the Pageant of 1951 was being planned, this question was asked more than once. It was then hoped that at some future date a history of the place, which many of us had come to love, would be produced, and what Eveline Clarke so imaginatively wrote has now been supplemented in more prosaic fashion. Here it is, then, with all its imperfections, offered to all who would read with the same affection as Horace showed towards his native place.

In the early spring morning in our Farnham garden we hear the birds singing, and the volume of their song seems greater than I have ever heard before. On the first page of the first bound volume (1874–1877) of the Headley Parish Magazine (joined then, as it is still, to a national Church publication), there is an exquisite little sketch of a village church, a bird singing on a gravestone, and an old man pausing to look at a milestone outside the churchyard gate. The following lines are printed as an inset into the sketch. They may well have been remembered by Wallis Hay Laverty as he drew near to the end of his long service to his God in Headley, and they certainly have their message to his very unworthy successor:

I hear it singing, singing sweetly,
   Sweetly in an undertone;
Singing as if God had taught it—
   It is better further on!

Night and day it sings the same song.,
   Sings it while I sit alone:
Sings it that the heart may hear it—
   It is better further on!
Sits upon the grave and sings it,
   Sings it when the heart would groan;
Sings it when the shadows darken—
   It is better further on

Further on? But how much further?
   Count the milestones one by one?
No! No counting, only trusting—
   It is better further on!

Appendices

(1) Headley's Water Mills

Mr FW Simmonds of Rowledge, who is an authority on the subject, has very kindly sent me the following notes.

Like most other localities favoured with streams, Headley parish had its water mills from the earliest days, probably from Saxon times. Through the centuries water was the only power other than human and animal muscle—except in those places where windmills were developed later.

The Romans may have introduced water mills to this country. The Saxons certainly had them, for no fewer than 7,500 were numbered in William the Conqueror's famous Domesday Book, of which 318 were in Hampshire. Unfortunately, there seems to be no record of those, if any, which were then in Headley, but Headley Mill, still working in 1966, is thought to be a successor to a mill there at the Normans' great census, and Lower Barford Mill is said to have been another.

Every Saxon manor had its mill, at which the inhabitants were bound to have their corn ground – with a toll for the lord of the manor. The water mills through the ages, right up the advent of steam, electricity and modern transport, were vital to the life of the community.

The southern branch of the Wey, which forms part of the Surrey–Sussex boundary nearer its source, had already powered several water mills before reaching Headley and it supplied at least six within the parish before going on to join the northern tributary at Tilford. There were 11 mills between Alton and Farnham, seven in Farnham and another three dozen before the waters of the various Wey tributaries reached the Thames at Weybridge.

These figures, probably surprising to many people, indicate the importance of water mills to the small population of the past.

Water power, however, was used for other purposes besides grinding corn for humans, animals and poultry. At least two mills in Headley manufactured paper of various classes, including paper for the Bank of England. One of these was Stanford, or Standford Upper Mill, which was operated for many years in conjunction with the larger paper mill, formerly an iron mill, in neighbouring Bramshott.

There was a paper mill at Bramshott in 1689 and paper making is mentioned at Standford in 1739. Early last century both belonged to William Warren, later William Warren and Sons, and finally Warren Brothers. The Portal family, originally from France, the earliest makers of banknote paper in England and still at Laverstoke, seem to have taken over these two mills and were here until about 1924.

Rags for paper making were brought by road from London, the carrier returning with hops and possibly other agricultural produce. Paper used to be

75

subject to excise tax, hence some of the records available, but the early history of water mills is difficult to ascertain.

Certainly one of three mills which was at Barford, on the little stream which forms the Hampshire–Surrey boundary for several miles until it trickles into Frensham Great Pond, also made paper for at least 100 years. It was mentioned as such in 1777 and in the late 1880s and was working at one time in conjunction with Spicers, who had a paper mill at Alton from 1840 until 1909.

Reference has already been made to the five mills mentioned in the reign of Edward II.

The 1859 edition of White's extensive History and Directory of Hampshire credits the parish with two paper mills and several corn mills. Names given include: Oliver George, corn miller; William Warren and Sons (George Roe and Andrew), paper makers, Standford Mills (also at Reynolds and Hatch Farms); John Lickfold, farmer and miller, Lower House Farm. Farming and milling often went together, of course, and many millers were also maltsters.

Here may be interpolated a paragraph from Shorters' *Paper Mills in Hampshire*, published in volume XVIII of the Hants Field Club's Proceedings.

"I am indebted to Mrs J.M.E Stevens for sending me a complete list of the paper-makers mentioned in the records of Headley Parish; some of the entries may be connected with Bramshott, Barford and Standford papermills, but others cannot be separately linked with any one of these. The first relevant entry, William Eade, paper maker (daughter buried in 1739) may be connected with Standford, as may other entries of paper makers in the 18th century: Richard Beck (daughter baptised 1761), Sarah Wills, a paper-maker's daughter from Whitchurch (buried 1762), John Gosling (examined 1763).

The Headley Parish Registers record the following paper-makers at Standford: 1813, Richard Smith; 1828 James Tilbury and Richard Curtis (1828–31); 1830 Robert Puttick; 1832–6 Thomas Tilbury; 1832 James Stubble; 1836–41 James West; 1849–57 George Elstone; 1859 Edwin Eggar; 1874 William Suter, senior, foreman in Messrs. Warren's Mill, Standford."

Messrs Warren Bros. owned the Mill for the remainder of the 19th century. In 1885 and 1890 the following products were advertised as made by this firm at Bramshott and Standford Mills: Cartridges, White and Coloured Royal Hands, Small Hands, Middles, Browns and Paper Bags. These were made on two machines 54 inches in width. Later Directories, up to 1920, state that Bank of England papers were made at Bramshott by Messrs Portal on a machine 72 inches in width. The mill last appears in the 1924 edition of these Directories. (See Directory of Paper Makers 1885 and 1890.)

Mr Simmonds' notes now continue.

When it was published in 1908 the Victoria County History said there were "now" six mills:

1. Headley Park, formerly corn, now electricity and pumping.
2. Headley, corn.
3. Lower Standford, formerly corn, now disused.
4. Upper Standford, electricity, formerly paper making.
5. Barford Upper Mill, corn.
6. Barford Lower Mill, disused, formerly flock, previously paper.

The first two were larger mills with four pairs of stones each. Upper Standford Mill, now a ruin, and more recently known as Eveley Mill, became a laundry for the Eveley estate. The corn mill was the middle of the three Barford mills; the upper one was the paper mill.

Today undoubtedly the most interesting mill in the parish is Headley Mill, picturesquely situated by its large pond alongside B3004, the Bordon–Liphook Road. It has a breast-shot wheel, new in 1927 and still working daily to drive modern animal and poultry food machinery. Above are four pairs of the old style mill stones, which are kept in working order and occasionally started up to demonstrate the ancient craft of milling.

Nearly 4 ft in diameter and 10 ins thick, each stone scales about 15 cwt. The upper stone has to be perfectly balanced and adjusted to run close above the nether stone and the works as a whole form one of the most complete and latest sets of stone grinding machinery as it was before this system finally succumbed to the more efficient steel rollers.

Headley Mill is owned by Messrs J. Ellis and Sons Ltd, who are still using stones for grinding wholemeal flour at their Neatham Mill. Mr John Ellis, whose father bought Headley Mill in 1914, is one of the churchwardens.

You remember the Biblical maiden behind the mill stone? She had to pound corn between a circular hand-stone and a larger flat stone. Headley's mill stones also have their "damsels", mechanical rocking devices to feed the corn to the stones. Some of the timber in the mill is believed to date from the 16th century.

Also by the same road, Standford Lower Mill, already mentioned, has been converted within the last two years into a delightful residence. It used to have two pairs of stones and I believe it was working much later than V.C.H. indicates. Nothing remained of the wooden water wheel, but Mr George Matthews has retained the big vertical shaft and its spur wheel in his drawing room and a mill stone in the bedroom above, which used to be the milling floor.

The larger upper pond at Barford must have powered a sizeable mill at one time and this was the paper mill. I can remember the desolate ruins there nearly 50 years ago, but no trace remains today except the dam and some modern cottages.

Barford Middle Mill ground corn and was working until after World War

I, probably until about 1930, when one of the Barford dams broke. Mr P Dighton restored the mill house before the last war and Mr B Fairclough and his sister now live there. The vertical shaft, or spindle, about 15ft by 15 inches, now forms the newel post of the staircase. The gardens, woods and mill pond, with delightful show of daffodils in the spring, are occasionally opened to the public.

Barford Lower Mill was formerly a flock mill, preparing rags for paper making (probably for the upper mill) and was a derelict, completely gutted ruin for many years. It was converted into a residence about a decade ago by the late Major JH Virgo and, has an attractive water garden.

This mill is on record as having had the largest water wheel in Surrey, but the buildings are in Hampshire and the wheel was in the stream which forms the boundary. It also had auxiliary steam power at one time. The house was built in 1738 and the mill worked until about 1890 or 1900, employing 50 people. It – like Barford Middle Mill and probably others – is reputed to have been used by smugglers to hide contraband spirit brought from the coast, in a secret chamber reached through the water wheel. Middle Mill had a hidden staircase.

Headley Parish registers have a number of entries around 150 years ago of Batchelors, of Barford, Barford Upper Mill and Plastow Farm, Barford. Would this family have been connected with Mary Batchelor, who married Thomas Simmonds, of Bourne Mill, Farnham, in 1797, and Amelia Batchelor, who married William Simmonds, of Froyle Mill and Willey Mill, Farnham, in 1801, in each case at Farnham Parish Church? Probably brothers marrying sisters.

See more about the watermills of Headley on p.113

(2) A reference to White's Directory of Hampshire in the year 1878 produces a list of people resident in Headley in that year.

A selection is as follows:–

Mrs Sarah Bennett, The Green.

Edmund Bettesworth, farmer and hop grower, Bayfields. (He was also a Churchwarden. Hops were then grown in the parish.)

James Campbell, Hilland House.

Richard Curtis, draper and general furnisher, Churchgate.

Thomas Faulkner, wheelwright, shopkeeper and postmaster, Standford.

Chas. Fillmore, National schoolmaster.

Hon. Fitzalan Foley, Broxhead. (Now the official residence of the O.C., Bordon.)

Theophilus Sigmond Hahn, Headley Grange.

Mrs Mary Joliffe, Headley Villa. (Where was this?)

Sir Henry Keating, PC, Headley Park.

Wm. Langrish, Curtis House.

John Lickfold, farmer and miller, Headley Mill.

Mrs Mary Ann Marden, victualler, White House (now Frensham Pond Hotel).

Mr Edward Petar, farmer and hop planter, Headley Wood.

William Speakman, postmaster and parish clerk, Arford.

James Upperton, vict. Holly Bush.

Leslie Walker, Alexandra Park (Timothy White, the founder of the well-known firm of the same name, also lived there.)

John Wood, MD, surgeon, Standford.

The Directory also states "the parish includes the small hamlets of Lindford, Standford, Hollywater, Deadwater, Bank of England, Wishanger, Herne, Barford, Whitmore and Greyshott." Where was 'Bank of England'? I have a recollection that, even in my time, there was a district or house at the far end of Chase Road which old folk called by that name. Can anyone help here, perhaps for later editions? And why 'Bank of England'?

(3) The Expense of a Common Kiln of Lime

		£ s. d.
For Digging One Load of chalk	— 2. —	
For Bottle and Bag—more Worth—	— 1. —	
	— 3. —	
* 7 times this Sum Repeated for 1 kiln		1. 1. —
To Carriage of 7 Loads of Chalk	3. 10. —	
To Cutting 5 Loads of Heath at 2/6	12. 6	
To the Keeper's Fee 1/- per Load	— 5. —	4. 7. 6
To the Limeburners	— 5. —	
To an Assistant	— 3. —	
For Victuals and Drink	— 4. —	— 12. —
	Total	£6. — 6

Note:

That one large Load of Chalk put into the Kiln, will produce, when burnt, 45 Basket-bushels, to a Load.

My Kiln, on the Common, will hold 10 or 11 Loads of Chalk which will be sufficient for Four Acres, i.e. about 12 Dungcarts full. It must be Observed, there is a full load difference in laying or placing in the Chalk, and the only way to Reconcile that Matter is, by a Cup of Ale now and then, to the Burner.

Inform. THO. BENNETT. JOHN OSBORNE. GEO. WHEELER.

* For Digging a Load of Chalk W.C. says, is 1/6 Only, and three-pence per Load, instead of Bread and Cheese, which is much the Cheapest Way.

—On the Other Hand—

You Commonly send 2 or 3 Quarts of Drink—2 pound of Bread, and one pound of Cheese.

From Sir T Gatehouse's notebook.

(4) A copy of a much dilapidated manuscript relating to Tithe about the time of Dr. Holme.

A Court of the Small tithe in the year 171?

? of cows as many as you milk you must pay a penny a Cow to the Minester; for tithe, Calves if you have seven, there is one due for tithe, and if seventeen there is two and if there is ten, the seventh Calf as you have is due for tithe. Let him be good or bad, and where is not seven Calves for each Calf you must pay a penny to the Minester and if you weane them you must pay a half penny a Calf for the sale(?) of them and if you kill then you must pay the right Shoulder, and you are to keep a Calf a month after his ? before he is tithable;

What dry sheep you sell at the spring of the year in the Wool you are to pay a penny a sheep some say it is Three half pence a sheep, and if their is seven Lambs there is one due for the tithe and if their is two? ? seventeen and on ? if their is ever so many the oner [owner] is to take up the first two Lambs and the Parson the next.... Then the oner takes nine and the Parson the next and so on if there be ever so many.

The tithen day for Lambs is St Mark's Day, and if their is not seven lambs you must pay a half penny a Lamb. Pigs if their is seven you are to pay one to the Parson, the oner is to take up two and the Parson the next, the Pigs are to be three weeks old before they are tithable.

Ester dues you are to pay a penny or five Eggs and a penny garn and a penny Smoke and two pence for Offering Money as many as are above sixteen years of Age.

Apples and pears when you do or have gathered them you are to send the Parson word to come and take his tithe which is the tenth.

Gee's the same as Lambs.

No Latters (?) Grasse paid for tithes in Headly.

Trench Ground four shillings an Acre for tithe.
John Clear, John Bristow

(5) In Headley Parish are 700 inhabitants, as computed accurately, in February 1771, and proved from the Proportions of the Christenings and Burials-being the Same with those of Stoke Damerel (in Devonshire) a most healthy Place, and from the number of People there; for in each Place the Births are to the Burials, as 1 to an Half;

The Births at Headley, at a medium for Six Years last are 26—and the Burials 13; and the Number living 700.

At Stoke, aforesaid, the Births 122, the Burials 62, and the number Living 3,361. Whence, at each Place, the Deaths yearly are nearly 1 in 54.

But, yearly—

> at Norwich, 1 in 30
> at Rome, 1 in 22
> at Berlin, 1 in 19
> at Madeira, 1 in 50
> at Breslaw, 1 in 28

In the whole Prufsion 1 in 40

In London, 1 in 18

This shows, that Headley and its Environs, is as healthy as any Place perhaps in the World, and the Inhabitants, if all Continued, or Remained, here would be doubled in 40 years; In the Healthy Parts of America they are doubled in 25 Years, more Children being born there because they Marry all their Servants and Negros.

April 10, 1773.

(6) The Sum Total of the Inventory of the household goods and furniture of the Rev Dr Holmes (sic) of the parish of Headley in the County of Southampton Deicesd; taken this 3 day Debr. 1765.

	£ s. d.
The parlor next the garden	8. 8. 0
The best parlour	11. 8. 0
The........	1. 19. 6
The scarlet Bed Chamber	24. 19. 0
The yellow Bed Chamber	10. 4. 6
The Grene Bed Chamber	14. 3. 6
The Plad Bed Chamber	6. 17. 0
The Kitchen	11. 7. 8
The Milk house	0. 12. 4
The Brew house	8. 10. 0
The Ale Setter	4. 12. 0
The Maid's Roome Garrat	10. 12. 3
Bottles	4. 0. 4
Inn Goods	117. 9. 1
Out Goods	10. 5. 3
Marble Chimney Pieces	2. 1. 0
Total Sum	129. 15. 4

(7) An agreement for the establishment of the Headley and Kingsley Association for the prosecution of Felons. Dated 12th March, 1806.

It was agreed that certain sums might be paid to an Informer upon the conviction of an offender, over and above any reward by Act of Parliament: For Burglary, Horse Stealing, Arson, etc, £40; Cattle Maiming £20; Stealing Poultry £15; Stealing Wood or Underwood or Gates £5; Breaking Hedges, Stealing Turnips, etc, £2.

Members paid Subscriptions from 10/– upwards, according to the size of their holdings.

There were 19 Members of the Association including

> Mr John Clear, of Kingsley.
> Mr Charles Collins, of Headley.
> Mr Daniel Knight, of Headley.
> Mr Richard Knight, of Headley.
> Mr W Langrish, of Headley.

Mr Daniel Knight was the Treasurer, and the Solicitors were Messrs C and H Trimmer, of Alton.

There was a Committee of nine, any five of whom were entitled to commence a Prosecution.

End of the Original Headley 1066–1966

Joyce Stevens, founder of The Headley Society

HEADLEY MISCELLANY

Volumes 1–6

Previously published in serial form between 1999 and 2005

Church Path, Headley, from an old postcard—but where is it?

Preface

In the press report of a Headley Parish Council meeting in February 1973, it is recorded that Mrs Joyce Stevens thought that the possibility was worth exploring of forming a local civic society, as these, existing independently of parish councils, had a useful function. It went on to say that she had often thought of starting such a society in Headley and she would 'like the council to think about this and discuss it at some future time.'

Twelve years later in 1985, with the duties of parish office behind her, she founded The Headley Society with the motto: 'Respects the Past, Cares about the Present, and Looks to the Future.'

Since then, the Society has been active in all these spheres, and is today a forum for discussion and action in the locality.

One question which we considered for some time was how best to make available to a wider audience the interesting and valuable historical information which exists within the parish.

Some of this information is in people's heads, some in their houses, some already published but now unavailable or forgotten, some yet to be discovered. Much of it, when received, is of significant interest—but often there is too small a quantity of material relating to any particular topic to warrant publication by itself.

To address this problem, it was decided to bring out a series of *Headley Miscellany*, each issue of which containing a number of items of historical value, and this we began to do in 1999.

❧❧❧

The contents of the first six editions of *Headley Miscellany* have been consolidated here into one convenient volume.

Note that the sequence of material has been rearranged from the original series in order to bring subject matter together. In particular the contents of Canon Tudor Jones' book *Headley 1066–1966* together form the first part of this publication.

John Owen Smith
Chairman, The Headley Society 2010

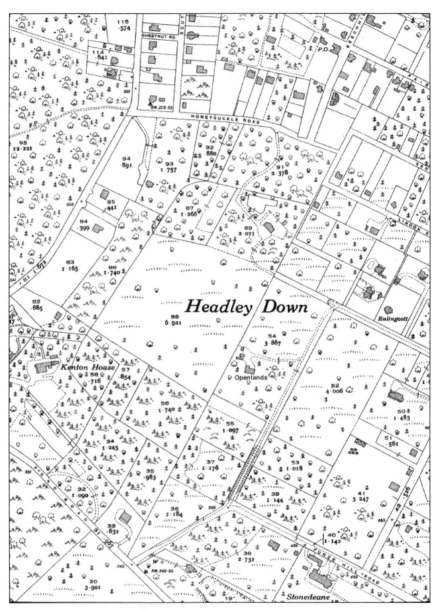

Part of Headley Down, including 'Openlands'— 1937

The Influence of Dr Wilks on Headley

Betty White—written in 1999

In 1923, at the age of 62, Dr Elizabeth Wilks and her husband, Mark, moved to Headley from London and set up home in Openlands, Furze Vale Road, Headley Down and became involved in Headley life. Mark Wilks was a teacher and Dr Elizabeth Wilks a past suffragette and campaigner for human rights. Although always dressed in black and rather formidable, she cared deeply for her fellow human beings.

When in 1932 a sewerage scheme for the district, with outfall near Huntingford Bridge, was suggested the Headley Rural Preservation Society, together with the rest of the Parish opposed the scheme.

Dr Wilks and a Mrs Parrott, concerned that a sewerage scheme was needed, visited every house in the Parish to ascertain if this was so. They discovered that very bad housing conditions with insufficient water supply abounded, but felt there was adequate sewerage. Dreadful overcrowding existed with families crowded into 2 rooms, parents and children sharing one bedroom. In one case eleven people, eight of working age, lived in a 2-roomed cottage. Dr Wilks and Mrs Parrot were joined by Miss Pack Beresford, a Parish and District Councillor, and they set out to ensure that every family in the Parish had decent housing.

The Parish Council, Rural District Council and even the Medical Officer for Health at that time, could not be persuaded to become involved. As the Rural Preservation Society also strongly objected to the building of suitable housing, the new Society—Headley Public Utility Society—was formed and registered in January 1933 under the Industrial and Provident Societies Act 1893, being one of the Friendly Societies, and the decision was made to build eight cottages for families in most urgent need.

These buildings were to be positioned near to the school, the village and the shops, and arranged circumferentially to the village, avoiding ribbon development. After much searching, 2 acres close to Curtis Lane was purchased for £200. The money required to build the houses was hard to come by with poor response from people in the Parish, therefore committee members raised £1,400 as loan stock and Dr Wilks and her husband lent the remaining £1,400 needed, on mortgage with 4% to be paid over 40 years.

The first eight cottages were built in 1933 and when £2,000 loan stock became available in 1936, the Wilks added a further £1,250 on mortgage, and cottages 9–16 were built. Care was taken to ensure that these buildings were well planned, with electric light and piped cold water and an outside bucket toilet, under cover, by the back door. A play area with swing and see-saw was provided and each cottage had sufficient garden for cultivation. The 2/6d weekly rent was collected by Mr & Mrs Parrott, who made sure that tenants kept the premises in good repair with well kept gardens free from litter, the latter being burnt by one of the cottage families.

Fond of children, sadly her own daughter had died at the age of 19 from peritonitis, Dr Wilks would hold summer picnics for the families and always gave a party at Christmas. She and her husband were a devoted couple and they lived in a simple wooden house, converted from a World War 1 hut, with few modern amenities.

Dr Wilks died in 1953 at 92 years of age, but her legacy remains. She stated in her will that her cottage—*Openlands*—should be used to house a needy person of the area and that this person should be found by word of mouth, never by advertising. A modest rent should be charged, the money going towards the upkeep and not for profit.

During her lifetime at *Openlands*, about 10 acres of land between the boundaries of Pond Road, Stonehill Road and Furze Vale Road, at one time known as Stonehill Park, had been purchased and this land remains today as wooded countryside for the use of Headley Down residents. The footpaths and the cottage are still maintained by Headley Public Utility Society although storms, especially the one in 1987, have caused severe damage and somewhat altered the layout. Fear of accidents not being insured has meant that the playground no longer functions, although the land is covered for normal usage.

The area was offered to the National Trust, but they declined—therefore the committee soldiers on administrating this land. As the brass plaque at the end of the Bridle Path in Furze Vale Road states:—

"OPENLANDS".
These woods are held in trust as a
Nature Reserve for your enjoyment.
Headley Public Utility Society Ltd.

The cottages at Openfields were taken over by the local council. Subsequently nine are now privately owned with the remaining seven belonging to the East Hampshire Housing Association.

These lines, penned by George Barrow and written by Elizabeth Wilks in an autograph book, give an insight into the woman who gave much to the village of Headley.

There's night and day, brothers,
both sweet things
Sun, moon and stars, brothers,
all sweet things:
There's likewise a wind on the heath,
Life is very sweet, brothers.
George Borrow

Elizabeth Wilks
born July 1861

90

Dr George Holme (1676–1765) Rector of Headley 1718–1765

Joyce Stevens—written in 1999

I was educated at two schools named after their founders: The Holme School, Headley, and Eggar's Grammar School, Alton. Of Dr Holme I knew nothing until many years had passed, but at Alton we remembered John Eggar at the annual Founder's Day Service in St Lawrence Church. It was a familiar local name, for the family came from Chawton and Bentley, and were farmers and land-owners. Another branch lived in Standford. The school was established by Act of Parliament in 1641, and this was the last public document signed by Charles I.

It was not until Canon Tudor Jones published his booklet on Headley in 1966 that I first learned anything about Dr Holme, and then strangely it was an announcement of his death in the Salisbury Journal of 15th July 1765. He had been Rector of Headley for 47 years and is described as "an affectionate husband, a faithful friend and a humane master. His many benevolent acts will not soon be forgot by his parishioners, of which his endowing a charity school is a proof." Exactly a month before his death at the age of 89 he baptised George White, and his writing in the Baptismal Register is firm and good.

Geo. Holme Rector

Members of The Headley Society had just completed a record of all the Monumental Inscriptions in the parish churchyard and were astonished to realise that no memorial to Dr Holme existed. There is a very elaborate marble tablet to his wife on the North wall of the nave, almost opposite the door. She died five years before her husband, and translated from the Latin it reads:—

Sacred to the memory of Catherine, the deeply regretted wife of George HOLME, D.D., Rector of this Church, the fifth daughter of John LEIGH, Esq., of North Court in the Isle of Wight. She was a truly remarkable woman, adorned with intellectual gifts as well as physical beauty, in whom the fire of continual devotion to God, ready charity towards her neighbour and wifely love for her husband burnt unceasingly. She gave a hundred pounds to increase the value of this Benefice, also eighty pounds to build

Headley School; also when dying, she left twenty pounds to the poor, whom she had always assisted in her lifetime. After enduring for more than ten years with wonderful patience the torture of a painful disease, she fell asleep peacefully in the Lord on June the 3rd, A.D. 1760, aged 80. Her husband, deeply mourning, set up this monument, that the memory of her many and great virtues might not quickly perish, and that some record might survive of his own love for his excellent wife.

With curiosity aroused, we began our researches. As the living has been in the gift of Queen's College, Oxford, for 340 years, that was the obvious place to start, and we are very much indebted to Mr John Kaye, Keeper of the Archives, for the wealth of information he provided.

It begins: "He was the son of Richard Holme, probably of Penrith, Cumberland...."

Penrith! Our previous Rector, Dick Woodger, had moved there last August, and his wife Janet is an experienced and enthusiastic genealogist. So now we had two sources of information: academic and genealogical.

From Queen's we know that he entered as "a poor child" (aged 18) in 1694. He moved up the foundation to become a taberdar (the name denoting a special gown worn by certain scholars on grants) in 1701, and Fellow in 1704. He took his BA in 1699, MA in 1702, and his BD and DD together in 1718 when he was presented to the Living of Headley aged 42.

Next comes an intriguing aside. "He served for some time as a chaplain at Algiers." How surprising! Chaplain to whom or what, and what did the post entail? Clearly another line of research was called for, because Algeria was a Moslem country inhabited by Arabs and Berbers, and the whole Mediterranean coastline was plagued by the fierce Barbary pirates led by the two Barbarossa brothers.

It seems a very adventurous move for a young man, straight from the sheltered life of Oxford. Did he want to see the world before settling down, or was he inspired by missionary zeal, or the chance to make some money? The journey itself would have been long and hazardous.

Back to Queen's College for enlightenment. Mr Kaye could tell me only that several Queen's fellows are recorded as having taken up this appointment with the Merchants of Algiers, a board of traders maintaining a 'factory' there. They had nothing to do with the college, nor a Bishop, nor any public body, but must have been Protestants.

So I turned again to Janet Woodger, who provided two addresses: the Most Revd Chais Abdel Malik (President Bishop of the Episcopal Church Jerusalem and the Middle East), at the Diocesan Office, PO Box 87, Zamalek, Cairo; and, much nearer home, Mrs Vanessa Wells, Secretary of the Jerusalem and Middle East association at 1 Hart House, Farnham. I wrote to both immediately.

A warmly friendly letter from the Bishop's secretary regretted that their archives did not go back that far, as it was the early 19th century before the first missionary arrived in Egypt. In Farnham, too, the first record is dated

1889, but Mrs Bell suggested that Dr Hopwood at the Middle East Centre, St Anton's College, Oxford might be able to help. But no—their first record is 1840. However, he and his archivist pointed out that it was quite common for Anglican clergy to act as chaplains in cities and ports overseas where there was a resident British Diplomat or merchant community. They directed me to the Guildhall Library, as overseas chaplains came under the juris-diction of the Bishop of London.

A search there by the Keeper of Manuscripts, Mr Stephen Freeth, could find no mention of George Holme. The Assistant Archivist at Lambeth Palace Library also searched their indexes, but with no luck. Finally, I resorted to the Internet via Jo Smith, and had two replies. One suggested the Levant Company records are at the Public Record Office but, although copious, they are business documents useful only to traders and not relevant for our purposes. The second reply came from Eve McLaughlin, so well-known to family historians world-wide through her series of Guides to genealogy—her comments were helpful and thought-provoking. A 'factory' was a warehouse where goods were bought, sold and bartered—not a *manu-*factory. The Merchants of Algiers were probably English, trading in carpets, gold ornaments, embroidered slippers and the like, in exchange for English manufactured goods.

"Being mixed up with business men was a good place to come by the pickings," she says, and I must confess such thoughts had crossed my mind in trying to account for the 'poor child's' later prosperity. Indeed, as early as 1715 he paid for the marble pavement in Queen's College new Chapel, and in 1734 a silver Communion Flagon for Headley church.

***

And now, what of the man himself, and his background? Janet Woodger has for three months been searching every available source, starting with our Parish Registers. She has them on microfiche, so is still very much in touch with Headley. She has also consulted the International Genealogical Index (IGI) of the Church of the Latter-day Saints (the Mormons); Penrith Parish Registers; the Internet (which provided her with 27 possibilities); Penrith Library; the retired assistant county archivist (a member of Dick's congreg-ation); and the history of Queen Elizabeth Grammar School, Penrith. She remarks: "It is extraordinary to think that all our children attended the Holme School in Headley, moved 350 miles a year ago, and now attend the school that enabled him to go to Oxford and achieve so much in life."

One of the problems of her researches has been the number of Holmes in old Cumberland and Westmoreland, including two Richards. One was a schoolmaster/clergyman, the other a brazier (worker in brass). If the latter was George Holme's father, it might explain the grant that enabled the 'poor child' to go up to Oxford.

Finally, after a prolonged search of Wills in the Cumbria Record Office, Carlisle, Janet thinks that this branch is the most likely. If so, George was the third of six children, three of whom died in infancy, only the eldest, Margaret, and youngest, James, also surviving. But there is no further record of them in the Penrith registers, so perhaps they also moved away from the area.

NORTHCOURT,
The Seat of M.ʳˢ Bennet,
ISLE OF WIGHT.

George Holme was a bachelor of 42 when he came to Headley, but in 1724 he was married at Carisbrooke in the Isle of Wight to Catherine, the fifth daughter of John Leigh of North Court, Shorwell. Wondering how they met, I wrote to the island's Record Office, and am much indebted to Mr RH Smout, County Archivist, for a great deal of useful information, including the Leigh family tree and a print of the family mansion *(see above)*.

The small village of Shorwell has several imposing houses and a remarkable church full of unusual historic treasures and memorials to several generations of the Leigh family, who held the patronage there at the time.

It would have been very natural for Dr Holme to visit the island, as several incumbents were Queen's College men, and Cumbrians, probably his contemporaries—so we may presume match-making and/or a holiday romance. They were very happy together for thirty-six years, but as they had married in late middle-age there were no children.

By now the 'poor child' had become a generous benefactor, owning

94

property in Linsted and Whitmore Vale, and at Churt and Ash in Surrey. The rents and profits from these he used to make gifts and established several charitable trusts. In 1755, with his wife Catherine, he built and endowed the school at Headley—and in his Will, dated a month before he died, he left his Surrey properties to Queen's College in Trust for the benefit of poor scholars of the College who were not in receipt of any other grants. This Trust, called the Holme Exhibition Trust, still exists, as does the Holme Trust in Headley, which is administered by the Rector and Trustees.

We catch a glimpse of the man from Dr Holme's own words when he explains his generosity towards education: "in consideration of his natural love and affection for his said wife [she seems always to have shared in his beneficence] and for the liberal education which he received at Queen's College."

Extracts from the notes drawn up by the first Trustees are interesting:—

The school is to *continue for ever*, is to consist of 1 master and any number of children, but only 12 shall be upon the charity. It shall be called Headley Charity School.

In choosing the 12 children to be educated free, preference is to be given to children of the poor inhabitants of Headley, and the number filled up from the like of Bramshott and Kingsley.

Dr Holme is building a school-house on the said surrendered piece of ground and intends to build a schoolroom and house for the master.

The Foundation Deed stated that the children were to be educated "in such principles of learning and knowledge as are most proper for such young persons, that is to say, the boys in Reading, Writing and Common Arithmetic, and the girls in Reading, Writing and Arithmetic and in Sewing and Knitting."

The original school, built on part of the 'waste of the Lord of the Manor of Bishop's Sutton' (the Bishop of Winchester), finally closed in 1991 and is now an exclusive antique bedding centre. Headley children today go to the newer building on the western edge of the village—but it is still called The Holme School.

Catherine Holme died in 1760, and for five more years the old man soldiered on alone, faithfully carrying out his duties, and making entries in the registers in his usual firm handwriting. Then we see: *"George Holme, D.D. Rector was buried July 7th 1765. From thence till Mich. 1766 Tho Monkhouse M.A. supplyed the curacy of Hedley and had the care of the Registers of Baptisms, Burials & Marriages committed to him, in the absence of Wm Sewell M.A. the present Rector."* The next entry was not recorded until 18 Oct 1766—a lapse of some fifteen months.

***

At our Founder's Day Service in Alton each year, the pupils of Eggar's Grammar School used to sing some verses of the 44th Chapter of Ecclesiasticus from the Apocrypha: "Let us now praise famous men, And our

95

fathers that begat us … Such as did bear rule in their kingdoms, And were men renowned for their power." But it finished: "And some there be which have no memorial, Who are perished as though they had never been."

How many people living here now realise the significance of The Holme School's name, or know anything about the man who served Headley so well and for so long?

Inspired by this study of his life, and with the approval of the rector and the Church Council, on 29th October 2000, the Sunday nearest to All Saints' Day, a memorial tablet was placed next to that of his wife so that, after a space of 235 years, in the next millennium the name of Dr George Holme "will not soon be forgot."

This oval tablet was unveiled at a special dedication service. It was designed and executed by Paul Wehrle, and had been paid for by subscription, donation and fund-raising, both from within and outside the parish.

This stone was placed here in AD 2000 by Headley people in gratitude to

GEORGE HOLME
D·D
1676 ~ 1765

Fellow of Queen's College Oxford
Rector of Headley for 47 years
Founder of the original
Holme School
in 1755

Sculptor's sketch for the George Holme memorial

Edgar Kehoe—Racing Driver

Interviewed by Muriel Sherwood in 1999

Edgar Keyhoe driving at Silverstone, 20th June 1953

I have lived in Headley for 16 years and before that I lived in *Coopers Bridge House* in Bramshott. My wife died in 1984 and during my motor racing days she was a great help to me. I'll never forget, looking back from the comfort of my saloon car, seeing the rain dripping down her face as she sat in the race car while I towed her. Since she died I have lived alone here, but I have my younger brother living nearby who helps me with the garden. He is an international bridge player.

My mother was Anita Duggan and her forebears left Co. Longford in Ireland during the unsettled days in 1875 and sailed to Argentina. From Buenos Aires where they landed, my grandfather and his brothers travelled southwest to Ramallo and bought a house including 100,000 acres of land on which they kept sheep. As the families grew, so they built large estancias on the land and diversified into breeding cattle and polo ponies. Over the years, the activities of the Duggan family in racing, polo and cattle shows, etc., have resulted in an incredible number of trophies.

My mother married Dr Kehoe who was in charge of the British Hospital in Buenos Aries, and later my two brothers and I were born. I was the eldest, born on 10th November 1903, my brother Cedric was born two years later on the same date, and my youngest brother Alan three years after that. When I was seven, my father caught a bug at the hospital and died, so my mother decided to come to England. We lived in various places and were sent to private schools here. My brother Cedric became a Commander in the Royal Navy, but died in America after the war.

One of my mother's friends was a Commissioner in what was then Nyasaland, and when I was about twenty years old I was sent out there for a year. On the Commissioner's staff were armed police called Ascari—one or two of them took me to shoot big game.

I took a motorbike with me, landed in Beira, Portuguese West Africa, went up the Zambezi to Blantyre which was the capital of Nyasaland, and then rode the motorcycle from Blantyre to Crocodile Bay where the Commissioner's headquarters were. Having arrived there, I continued to ride my motorcycle around the area, but this caused great consternation among the natives who had not seen one before, and it came to an end when I ran out of oil and I had to leave my machine leaning against a tree. It took a couple of days to walk back to Crocodile Bay and I never saw my motorcycle again.

I took part in a lot of trials and won many awards, the first one in 1922, and as I had done reasonably well I was in a position to borrow machines and ride for different companies—Douglas and AJS for instance. That went on for some time before I started doing reliability trials in cars and then started to race cars. I did reasonably well, and eventually drove manufacturers' cars on 'competition loan'—which meant I kept the cars and they maintained them— in events like the Six-day Alpine Trials, the Monte Carlo Rallies and in Norway, Sweden, etc.

I raced at Brooklands and have several pictures showing me driving there—in one I am photographed in my Riley in the 1930 double 12-hour race during a violent rainstorm. In those days one had a riding mechanic on board, and in that picture it is my brother. We drove in 3 hour shifts and changed drivers and mechanics. We were not allowed to drive during the night, so drove 12 hours one day and 12 hours the next. We did well in that race. I also raced the Riley in the 1,000-mile race

I met my wife during the war when we both worked for Thompson & Taylor, an offshoot of Parnell Aircraft which was situated on the Kingston By-pass. While I was there, I worked in the experimental department developing a scanner which was fitted to aid night fighter aircraft. I was pulled into that job because the head of the company was Captain Arthur Frazer Nash who was the famous driver of Frazer Nash cars. His secretary was Mimi Helmore who became my wife.

I stopped motor racing when I was driving in an event at Silverstone in about 1953 or 1954. I had driven in one race and during the following 500cc Race, a driver called Headland spun and hit me. I was badly injured—particularly my legs and knees—and lost my competition licence for some time. I had to appear before a panel of RAC people, who asked me to sit and squat down and cross my legs, and I couldn't do it because of my injuries. From that time I virtually stopped competition riding or racing. I still suffer from the injuries I sustained whilst racing, including a damaged neck, right arm and knee, but it is what one must expect when motor racing, particularly riding motorcycles.

Having lost my competition driving licence, I was then made an 'Observer'—at race meetings around the circuit there would be half a dozen telephone boxes, and I would be there with one or two other people. I would report back to base if anything happened in my sector. That went on for quite a long time, and then I was elevated to being a 'Judge,' so I was able to throw my weight around!

Although that was the end of my taking an active part in racing I have continued to be very much involved. I have friends who race and I keep in touch with them. I go to all the meetings, mainly at Silverstone.

Among my other interests is polo. Two of my cousins in Argentina played polo a great deal, and with two of their friends made up the Argentine polo team which beat Germany in the days when polo was an Olympic sport. I now go to polo a great deal, and polo players come over here and stay with me.

A long time ago I was on a friend's yacht down on the south coast when I saw a Shetland pony, and as I love animals this little pony captivated me. I ended up with several. Then donkeys arrived on the scene, and there was a time when I had six or seven donkeys and Shetland ponies. I still keep some, but the numbers are now reduced to two donkeys and two Shetlands. I would also like to keep alpacas, as they are native to Argentina, and I am in touch with a man in Guildford who has some. Hopefully I will be able to have some here, but these particular alpacas come from Chile, so when the Argentine ambassador comes to see me I will hide that fact from him!

Interview at Hurland House, Hurland Lane, Headley—September 1999

Edgar Keyhoe died in 2004 aged 100

St. Francis Church, Headley Down

Hester Whittle—written in 1999

On a bright spring morning one Sunday in 1957, I walked for the first time down a shaded lane on Headley Down, then known as Sandy Lane. The unmade track led between high laurel hedges and there was only one dwelling, one *Quaint Cottage*, hidden away on the right hand side, although the converted laundry yard with its old cottages and recently-opened supermarket was much in evidence on the other side of the lane and the brick dwelling that had been Mr Eddey's shop marked the corner where the lane joined the main road.

I was suddenly aware of a group of people winding through the bracken-lined path and spilling out onto the lane through a wooden gate between the laurels. These were not people dressed for casual Sunday-morning country walking. The men were soberly dressed and many of the ladies wore hats, and as they dispersed I enquired about the event that had brought them to the lane, presumably to a meeting of some sort.

My companion, who much later was to become my husband, explained that these were people coming from their morning service at 'the little church,' at which point he paused to exchange pleasantries with a couple who had obviously been part of the congregation. I, meanwhile, scanned the distance looking for the said church, but could see neither tower, spire nor steeple and took little note of the small wooden hut which lay half concealed at the far side of the wooded site.

At that point our conversation took another turn, and for the time being the location of the little church was left unexplained.

It has taken many years for the situation of 'the little church' to be explained fully, and during the thirty-seven years that have passed since I married and moved to Headley, I have learned much.

I first discovered the little wooden building with its beautifully carved altar rails, reredos and priests chair—the loving work of a parishioner Louis Robinson—when I attended an Easter service in 1963. By then, Sandy Lane had become Eddey's Lane and the church, I learned, was officially Headley Down Community Church. A year later it was to be renamed St Francis on the suggestion of the rector of Headley, The Rev JS Tudor Jones, in recognition of the beautiful little stained glass window depicting the saint. This window, which today has been re-sited in the wall above the altar, had been designed by Viola Stenhouse and given to the church by Miss Robeson several years earlier.

I started attending the church regularly at about this time, in the mid nineteen sixties, when the demands of a young family sometimes made it difficult to get to services at All Saints' Church in Headley, and from my very first visit was struck by the warmth and fellowship that emanated from the small congregation. Although the congregation rarely exceeded two dozen people, the building itself was correspondingly small and was regularly, on festivals, filled to capacity. I well remember an Easter Sunday service with the congregation spilling out beyond the small porch onto the patch of grass beyond, as the Rector struggled to project his voice above the passing traffic.

The church first came into being back in 1921 when, the majority of people at that time being without transport, the journey to Headley became too difficult for some residents. In that year a small group of people living on Stone Hill (the name Headley Down only came into existence officially in 1923 when the post office installed a telephone exchange at Wilsons shop and decreed that it would be known as Headley Down) began to meet for Sunday worship in a 'church hut'. Led by Mrs Bessie Guy, the group erected their little hut in the garden of *The Nutshell* in Wilsons Road. Later in the same year, two hundred pounds was raised to enable the group to purchase two thirds of an acre of land from Mr Cotton who owned Beech Hill Garage, and the church was moved to its present site.

A Methodist minister, Mr LH James, lived at *Hurlands* and he was invited to conduct the services. The church was supported by the rector of Headley, the Rev WH Laverty, and in 1921 the Easter Offering from All Saints' was given to 'the church hut on Stone Hill.' Such was the good working relationship between the two men, that in June 1927 the Rev Laverty persuaded Mr James to be re-ordained in the Church of England, and since then the trustees of St Francis have invited the rectors of All Saints' to be their chaplain and have been served mainly by the All Saints' clergy team. The church also has links with the Methodist church and has input from visiting Methodist clergy. It is run by an elected committee and administered by a body of trustees and, despite many changes and some setbacks, it continues to thrive.

The wooden building was first extended in 1948, and the church hall built in 1964. In 1981, after months of deliberation, an appeal was launched to build the present brick extension. The Rev Harry Dickens, then curate at All Saints', was the driving force behind this initiative and I well remember the time of fundraising that preceded the opening of the new building. We held summer fetes and Christmas bazaars, jumble sales and coffee mornings.

Money was covenanted and donations made. As an act of faith, foundations were laid in 1981 to ensure that at some time in the future a wholly permanent church and hall will exist on the site, and meanwhile, in the autumn of 1982, the new extension was finally dedicated. The slogan "Raise the roof at St Francis" which had featured on so many fund-raising posters had been realised, and the laminated roof beams which had been specially made in Sweden soared above a light and seemingly spacious interior which continues to impress visitors today.

St Francis' continues to serve the community on Headley Down in the spirit of the little church of Stone Hill. I have been part of it for over thirty years and have watched it change and grow. Its Sunday School flourished for many years, and generations of children will remember the summer outings and the Christmas parties which filled the hall.

In 1977, Mr and Mrs Tom Prior, who lived in Pond Road, gave a bell to the church to celebrate the Jubilee. It was duly erected and for many years its single, insistent note summoned worshippers to morning service. I remember the way the children hurried to church in order to be first to ring the bell under Tom Prior's genial supervision and thus to ensure that no one on Headley Down was in any doubt that the service was about to commence! We no longer ring the bell, but little else has changed.

The site of the church is much more open than when I first peered through the bracken back in 1957. There is car parking space on the cleared area among the trees, and many new houses have been built on surrounding land. The church has welcomed new residents in recent years and there is a great sense of fellowship still among its present congregation. It continues today in the same spirit that encouraged Mrs Bessie Guy and her stalwart committee to erect that small wooden hut in the garden in Wilsons Road in 1921.

Reminiscences of Two Brothers

Interviewed by Ann Viney in 1999

Ted and Cyril Croucher were two of the six children of George Croucher of Binsted and Elizabeth Maria Burrows of Hollywater. Ted was born in Hollywater in 1908 and Cyril at Standford in 1913. When Ted started school at Conford, at the age of four and a half years, his teacher was Miss Tristan; he remembers learning to write using a tray of sand and a stick; after a while they used slates. They lived at Standford Hill for a while, in a cottage, where the rent was a shilling a week. Later they moved to No.1 *Gravel Cottages* at Standford and the children went to the Holme School. Mr Beck was the headmaster, Miss Taylor taught the infants, Mrs Beck taught Classes 1 and 2, Miss Hussey Class 3, Mr Fosberry taught 4 and 5 and Mr Beck 6, 7 and 8. In 1922 the family moved to No.4 *Mill Bungalows* and Cyril completed his education at the Deadwater Council School, which had opened in 1915, as the Holme School could no longer cope with the large number of children in the area.

Sunday was a full day for the children. After attending Sunday school and then the morning service at Headley, they went to Standford Mill Methodist Church (known locally as Warren's Chapel) in the afternoon and to the Iron Room at Standford in the evening. The Iron Room belonged to a sect known as the Plymouth Brethren. Some Sunday afternoons in summer, after Sunday School, their parents would take the family for a picnic tea on the Common. They took sandwiches and a milk-can full of tea, found a shady spot and enjoyed themselves. Some Sundays, father and the boys walked across the Common to the *Deers Hut* (at Griggs Green)—their reward was a glass of lemonade between the two of them. They used to put a finger up the side of the glass and say, "you can drink to there!" They would walk home through Conford.

As young boys they burnt the gorse bushes on Passfield Common every two years to obtain the furze sticks for burning on the fire at home—an age-old rite. They also used these in the ovens at the bakery in Conford. The small sticks were tied together and known as bavins. In those days there were no silver birches on the Common and you could see the houses at Hollywater from the Chapel at Standford. From Conford you could see Blackmoor spire.

At one time George Croucher tended the hop kilns at Hawkins Farm in Kingsley, a job that required attention both day and night. The children helped with the hop picking; they started work at 7am after having walked from Standford to Kingsley. Pay was a farthing a bushel, rising to three farthings. It was not all hard work—they enjoyed going to the hop kiln, taking the tea can, having a drink and sitting by the fire. The highlight was on the rare occasions when they bought fresh herrings from Fishy White, 12 for one shilling, made a fire of dry hazel sticks under the hedge, put the herrings on sticks and cooked them. Delicious!

Most of the children had nicknames. Ted was always known as Mouser and Cyril as Shun. One boy they remembered having a hole in his trousers, which revealed part of his shirt, and he was ever afterwards known as Shirty. The smallest boy was Tom Thumb (Tommy Chisnell) and others were Ginger, Monkey, Widdy, Nobby and Blanco.

During the first World War, for a time, Headley Green was out of bounds to civilians, as it was requisitioned by the Army. Some of the cooking took place there and Ted remembers the delicious smell of fresh-baked bread on his way to school. The field next to Lindford Club (now housing) was covered with white tents, which were used as accommodation for the troops. Many houses in Lindford and Headley were requisitioned and used as officer accommodation, including *Hope Cottage*, *Weydale* and *Elmside*.

Front and back of a
First World War ration book

Cyril recalled the first German Zeppelin which he saw, like a silver cigar floating in the air. He was passing Granny Black's cottage at Standford at the time (she was about 70 years of age). He asked her what it was and her reply was very positive: "It's an airship. Come inside. Don't let 'em see you or it will be bombing us."

When they lived at *Gravel Cottages* they remembered going to bed and, on hearing the clump, clump, clump of many men marching by, got up and watched from the window. These men went on manoeuvres to Weavers Down, and the columns of marching men included two G.S.s (General Service) wagons pulled by horses. One carried the food and the other was a mobile kitchen, including a stove so the troops could enjoy a hot meal.

During the War, Mr Bellinger's shop in Arford (now a house called *The Old Stores*) was registered with the Ministry of Food. Ration books were used and you could only go to a registered shop to use them. Ted accompanied his mother on a Saturday afternoon to help carry the shopping home. He remembers the queue, which stretched from the shop to the other side of the *Crown* Public House.

The ladies used to wear long skirts, cloaks and some wore huge hats. One or two were big ladies so they could hardly get through the door of the shop and had to turn sideways. Mr Curtis owned the *Church Gate Stores* and sold clothes and haberdashery. He lived at *The White House*, Standford, opposite the *Robin Hood*.

During wartime, they used to collect acorns and were paid sixpence a bushel. The acorns were fed to the pigs.

During the mid-day break from school they often played a game of paper chase. One day they stood outside the *Holly Bush*, with friends Stan and Chris Smith, and met two soldiers with a G.S. cart who were travelling from Fullers Vale, where a Colonel lived, to Bordon Camp. They told the boys that the war was finished; excited at such news the boys helped pull the cart as far as Garrett's shop in Lindford (now Broxhead Motors), school completely forgotten. When they returned late for classes, Mr Beck was going to cane them; however they said: "Sir, the war's over." "How do you know?" Mr Beck asked. They explained how they had met the soldiers and all they knew. Instead of the cane, everyone was given the rest of the day off as a holiday.

Behind the *Wheatsheaf* Public House there was a Blacksmith's shop, and at the bottom of Long Cross Hill there was a Builder and Undertaker's owned by Mr HR Chuck. Mrs Chuck was often to be seen leaning on the gate of the property, enquiring, "And how are you today?" A friendly greeting no doubt, but they never lingered there long.

Dr Crowther-Smith used to visit his patients using a horse and trap. Later on he had a Douglas motor bike. He had an orchard opposite *Gravel Cottages*; he lived at a big house just along the road. If the children had to visit his surgery at a certain time of the year, he used to say, "I expect you have been at my green apples again." Ted's father had a wisdom tooth extracted by the doctor; they had no chloroform so they tied him to the chair! He survived to tell the tale.

They always attended the Annual Flower Show and Fete. There was an Army tent-pegging competition, sports, dancing in the evening and the local band, known as "The Spit and Dribble", played. They also celebrated November 5th with a bonfire on the village green, and of course the fair came every year, both known as "a regular night out".

George Croucher worked for some years for Brigadier General Percy Brownlow at *Eveley House* (now *Standford Grange*). When Ted was about twelve, he worked there as a beater for the shooting season. There was a pond in the grounds and they shot ducks, as well as pheasants which they used to breed in special coots within the grounds. They used to go to Hollywater to pick up the beechnuts to feed the pheasants. When work was finished, they enjoyed home-made lemonade made by Mrs Lundy.

Artist's impression of the meeting outside the 'Holly Bush' (Mick Borra)

They also shot ducks at Standford Mill. They used to walk near the water meadows and always carried a stick to test how deep the water was—if the stick disappeared, they didn't walk there!

Another of Ted's jobs was to collect milk each evening from Mr & Mrs Dick Tilbury's cottage, which was the original public house at Standford. There was a notice board hanging outside the gate *The Little John*. There was a vine around the door. Mrs Tilbury was well known for her excellent home-made wine, including grape. The milk he collected was for their own use, but he also took some to old Mrs Blackman.

Ted played and enjoyed the game of cricket for many years. As a youth of fifteen or sixteen, a group including Tom Falkner, Chris and Stan Smith and Bernie Garnet played friendly matches with teams at Binsted, Blackmoor, Hollywater, Kingsley and Whitehill. They cycled to the villages, but they only had two or three bicycles between them, so they shared the travel, one cycling, one on the cross bar and one sat on a piece of wood at the back. The others would begin to walk, and then those cycling would drop the passengers off and go back for the others. They would take turns in this way until they reached their destination. The equipment would be tied to the handlebars. Most of them worked until four o'clock on Saturdays, so games would be played in the evening. If the game was not completed in one evening, they would return the next evening to finish it.

Later, Ted played for Headley, winning the I'Anson Cup twice and the Miller Cup three times; then he played for Lindford. He is the oldest living person to have played in the I'Anson cup matches.

Bill Moss had a horse and trap, also ponies; so did Cyrus Gates, and they kept them in stables opposite the *Holly Bush*. Cyrus Gates took his team to Shottermill to play cricket. He drove them in a horse-drawn open wagon and they sat on two wooden benches, facing each other. Cyrus had a few drinks at the match, and on the way home he took the corner at Fullers Vale too quickly; going on the bank and turning the whole team out of the wagon. It was said to be the only time they were all out in one over!

Ted remembers the team that day was: Colin Coles, Wally North, Percy Snow, Harry Blanchard, George Barlow, Bill Dunk, Ernie Nash, Charlie Courtnage, Ted Warner, Bill Webber, Percy Watts, Ernie Turner, and himself.

Ted left school at 14 and worked for Miss Verner at *Crabtree* which was a pig farm—he earned five shillings a week. At that time Captain Byng Stevens was in charge. He had been in the Rifle Brigade during the war and slept with a revolver under his bed. A kindly man, he gave Ted a telescope when he went away.

Miss Verner kept 90–100 pigs and about 20 cows. Tiptrees were black pork pigs and they used to be sent to local markets in Alton, Farnham and Petersfield. They were taken by horse and cart, starting early in the morning at about 5.30am. The Hurstwoods were the bacon pigs; they used to be sent to Salisbury via Bordon railway station. Doug Marshall used to take pigs to agricultural shows and it was Ted's job to clean them up ready for these. He used to put coconut oil over them, clean their ears and black their trotters.

Later Miss Dorothy Crowther-Smith joined the staff. She brought her special Jersey cow with her, called Mousey, and she took charge of the farm. When Ted was about 20, still working at *Crabtree*, around the time the buses had started to run from Haslemere to Whitehill, they had very high winds and many trees were blown down. An elm was down in The Street, an ash tree against the fence at *Pound Cottage* and also one against The Mill. Ted helped, with others, using a cross-saw to saw the trees into pieces and dispose of them.

Miss Verner retired to Chawton; the animals were sold and the ground sold to Mr Chadwick of Beech Hill. Sir Charles and Lady O'Brien bought

Crabtree and Ted worked for them for some time as a gardener. *Crabtree* is now known as *Yeoman's Place.*

Cyril worked for Headley Mill. One of his jobs was delivering the corn —his wages were ten shillings a week.

Some of the following tales were hearsay, such as the one about the bungalow in Hollywater Road, now known as *Woodview,* being a dame's school, where for a penny a week you could learn to read and write.

Their mother told them when she was young, Cranmere Pond near Greatham froze in the winter and the local gentry had skating parties, with lighted rushes on the side of the pond and roast chestnuts. The track which led to Cranmere Bottom went across the common on what is now the Longmoor Ranges. Their mother, always known as Liz, was born in what she called a 'half house' behind the public house in Hollywater.

Jimmy Hurlock worked at *Crabtree* and was an old man when Ted first began to work. He said it cost £1 to get your horse out of the village pound, which used to be in the Liphook Road.

Crabtree was an old coaching stop. The road from Grayshott to Headley went over the common to Fullers Vale, through the Patches, down by *Wodehouse* in the Liphook Road and then into the village by *Pound Cottage.* The roads were only tracks with deep wheel ruts so that you had to walk in the middle.

Their father told them he worked wherever he could before he was married, sometimes walking to Petersfield from Binsted to help with threshing on farms, and only going home for Sunday. Men cut the corn and the women tied it. Men dug potatoes and the women picked them up.

Interview at Lindford — October 1999

Essay on Headley (1925)

Mrs W.E. Belcher

From a report on Headley Women's Institute in the 'Haslemere Herald' of 21st March 1925: A pleasing feature of the gathering was the reading of essays on Headley, written by members, and it is interesting to record that of Mrs W.E. Belcher, who must have gone to a deal of pains in lifting the veil from some of Headley's obscure past and presenting some new facts connected with the parish. Her essay, which won the first prize, was as follows.

The parish of Headley covers a wide area, and until 1901 it included Grayshott. The district is remarkable for its abrupt inclines and irregular hollows. There are several little beauty spots, such as the winding piece of road at the bottom of Parfect's Hollow by Arford spring and pond, the hollow in Hearne Lane and Barford Hill, while the views from the churchyard, from the top of Beech Hill and Hammer Lane are most fascinating. The pine covered slopes and heather commons add to the beauty of the district, as do also several ponds, streams and the River Wey.

In olden days, this river served five corn mills within the parish. Now it serves two corn mills at Standford, and until quite recently one paper mill. Here until a few months ago paper money was made, giving work to many men of the district. Previous to the paper money, paper bags for shops were made, employing a large number of the women of Headley, also a few men. The water wheel of a disused corn mill on the Eveley estate is now used for making electricity for Eveley House, as is also the one on the Headley Park Estate for that house.

A stream near the Wheatsheaf Inn used to supply a sheep wash just below the Wheatsheaf meadow. It is now silted up. Two shearers at a time were given the privilege of using the sheep wash, the last two being James Marshall, of Parish House Bottom who is still alive, and the father of George Glaysher, of Barford. Farther on in the Hanger beyond the sheep wash used also to be some famous watercress beds. Many years ago this stream also supplied a tanyard, the site of which is now occupied by Brook Cottage. The cottages opposite, called the Fellmongers, take their name from their connection with the tanyard.

Until the Inclosure Act came into force their were no hard roads in Headley except the turnpike which passes the New Inn, on the Bordon side of which stands the old Tollgate house. Cart tracks passed across the common

*"Hop growing was one of the chief industries of Headley,
but has now completely died out..." (see Mrs Belcher's essay)*

in all directions, as there were no banks or fences. Banks came with the Act; the roads were then stumped out, but were not gravelled until some years later. When the open land was inclosed under the Act, portions of the inclosed land were allotted to the houses and farms of Headley. Some of the allotments were of little use to those to whom they were allotted, as they were at a great distance from the houses and farms, eg. a portion of land at the back of Mr Maynard's house was allotted to Eveley Farm, a portion on Beech Hill now owned by Mr Whitaker was allotted to Linstead Farm and some at Bordon was allotted to some houses at Grayshott, and were never claimed because of the distance.

Most of the oldest houses in the district were farm houses. On most farms may still be seen the remains of old lime kilns, eg. at the top of Toll's [Tulls] Lane, at the top of Bull's Hollow beyond Pickett's Hill, and at the top of Rooke's Hill. In olden days, each farmer burned chalk to make lime for his land, fetching the chalk from Seale and Butser Hill. Hop growing was one of the chief industries of Headley, but has now completely died out. Some of the dipping tanks still remain where the hop poles were dipped in boiling tar before being used, also several kilns where hops were dried.

Three or four generations ago some of the farmers of Headley owned wild ponies, which ran in part of the "New Forest" at Frith End. These were rounded up and marked at certain times of the year, and some were sold at Headley Fair and Farnham Fair. It was on one Farnham Fair Day that Headley Church was burned. Most of the inhabitants had gone to the fair. A girl was left at home in one of the cottages near the church, and to pass away the time gathered dry heather and made a fire in the church porch. The woodwork soon caught fire, and the flames spread, only the belfry being saved. During the re-building of the church, services were held in the Rectory barn, skylights being put into the roof for the purpose. The first baptisms after the completion of the building were George Cover and Mrs Edgar Beale, of Frensham. Dissenting services were at one time held in the barn at Crabtree, and also a dame school, the mistress being Mrs Bone, wife of a veterinary surgeon at *Birdsnest*. A dame school was also kept at Rose Cottage, now occupied by Mr William Heather, by a Mrs Parfect, from which the name of Parfect's Hollow originated.

At one period there was an unruly gang of men who built themselves cabins in the village on the uninclosed land. They were erected during the night to outwit the bailiffs of the Lord of the Manor. Trees were cut down to form the framework, the walls being made of turf and the roof thatched with heather. Before morning wives and children were installed. If discovered before completion, or unoccupied, by bailiffs, they were destroyed, but this seldom happened as the gang worked together, watching their opportunity and all helping to build. If the squatter had no children of his own he borrowed some, as the law would not allow the bailiffs to remove the roof of a house containing children. On being thus occupied for a certain time the cabin and land on which it stood could be claimed. Because of this, several houses in the district have no title deeds. These squatters were a terror to the neighbourhood, taking pigs from sties, potatoes from clamps, and even digging them from the ground, the surface being levelled to conceal the spot. Some ruffians found themselves in the stocks, the site of which is now marked by a chestnut tree in the High Street.

The chief fuel of the people of Headley in those days was heather, and the turf from which the heather had been taken. The heather was pulled up by hand and taken home in bundles, where it was dried and stacked. The turfs were cut in slabs and stacked in rounded heaps to dry where cut. It was no unusual thing for the turf cutters to find their dried heaps on fire when they went to fetch them home, this being one of the chief pieces of mischief of the boys of that period.

Headley has in its time attracted several notable people. Lord Salisbury once lived at *The Oaks*, Madame Patey, the celebrated singer, at *Sunny Bank*, Bret Harte, the American writer, at *Arford House*, and Tattersall at *Arford Cottage*.

The last sheep stealer, who lived in Parish House Bottom, was transported, while the ghost of a banker of London who was hanged for forgery *[Henry Fauntleroy in 1824—Ed]* is said to walk by the church.

The Watermills of Headley Parish

Joyce Stevens—written in 2000

This has proved to be one of the most difficult articles I have ever written, not because of lack of material. There is a superabundance of information provided by such knowledgeable men as Shorter, Simmons, and Crocker so that it seems presumptuous of me even to put pen to paper. In addition there is the River Wey Trust's own splendid publication of 1988—*The Southern Wey, a guide*—which encapsulates all the relevant facts, beautifully illustrated with maps, sketches and photographs, and written in language easy for the layman to understand.

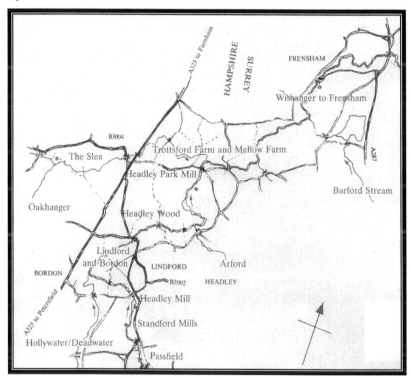

Rivers and streams in and around Headley
(from 'The Southern Wey, a guide' with permission)

So the only solution is for me to write as a lifelong resident of Headley, from a personal and very amateur point of view. For years the word 'mill' meant only one thing to me—a building by a river where corn was ground into flour. The nearest was Headley Mill, a mile from my home. As a teenager between the wars this was a place I visited every Saturday morning, not for flour, but to buy layers' mash for our hens, and to have our accumulator charged. Those were the days when 'the wireless' depended on its wet and dry batteries, and the wet one had to be recharged weekly. The mill generator supplied electricity to the business and to Mr Ellis's home next door, and I remember how the lights flickered and fluctuated with the movement of the waterwheel. Eventually, of course, realisation dawned that a mill is a building housing machinery: different machinery for different purposes and, as far as this area is concerned, the power to drive the machinery is water.

Except on the south-west boundary (Ludshott Common) the large Ecclesiastical Parish of Headley is surrounded by the Wey and its tributaries, as the names of the various hamlets show: Standford, Lindford, Sleaford, Barford and Arford. For centuries man had depended upon muscle-power, his own and that of his oxen and horses. The Romans introduced water-power to Britain, and in Saxon times every Manor had its cornmill which belonged to the Lord who exacted a toll from his tenants for its use. They had no choice, anyway! By the eighteenth century there were seven watermills in Headley Parish: three in a half-mile stretch of the Wey at Standford in the south, three equally close to each other on the Barford stream on the west: and one on a deep and slow stretch of the Wey at Headley Park in the north.

Headley Mill from the air, 1955

Of the Standford mills, Headley Mill has always been a corn mill, plus animal feeding stuffs in modern times, and Dr Richard Ellis has traced its

114

history back to the thirteenth century, further back even than Headley church. It is now the only working watermill in Hampshire and one of the few left in the whole country. A few hundred yards upstream, Standford corn mill was converted into a private house in 1929, but still retains some of the old machinery.

The third Standford mill was a paper mill for nearly the whole of the nineteenth century and was run by the Warren family, in conjunction with their larger Passfield mill just over the parish boundary in Bramshott. It was here that my great grandfather, William Suter, came from Portsea to work as a journeyman paper-finisher in the late 1830s and he spent the rest of his working life there, eventually becoming foreman. When he married he lived in the mill cottage and his wife is recorded in the 1851 census as a paper-sorter and in 1861 as a bag-maker. By 1871 she was dead, but his two sons aged 18 and 16 were described as paper-finishers. Only the coarser stuff was made here, like wrapping paper and the bags for the dry goods sold by grocers. This mill burned down in 1878, and although after repair an attempt was made to start it again six years later, it never prospered. For a time it was used to generate electricity, but finally it was demolished and the stones used to build a private house on the site.

Standford Corn Mill

The Barford stream which rises at Hindhead and flows into Frensham Great Pond is the county and parish boundary between Hampshire and Surrey, Headley and Churt. Of the three mills, which were on the Headley bank, only their ponds and two of the houses remain. The middle mill has always been a corn mill and is recorded as early as the thirteenth century, but the other two have had a more varied history, both for a time being paper mills. Some years ago I searched the Headley church registers for mention of people employed in this industry and found the names of forty-four families from 1738 onwards through the nineteenth century.

Richard Pym was one of the earliest described as a paper manufacturer and he insured one of his mills as 'corn and paper' under one roof. This prompted a waggish friend of mine to suggest that in the not-too-distant future some enterprising miller might make flour and paper and invent a third machine to bag the one inside the other and sell direct from the mill!

Painting of Barford Middle Mill circa 1832 [Mr F Swann]

The best-known name for the paper business in this area was Warren, and by 1823 there were 29 men and 40 women employed by the firm at Standford, Passfield and Barford. There were opportunities for skilled and unskilled workers, men, women and children: master paper-maker, journeyman, finisher, apprentice, machineman, engineman, layer, bagmaker, ragsorter, picker, cutterman—these are some of the terms used in census returns. But although providing employment for a considerable number of local people, the fortunes of paper mills were variable. By the very nature of the raw materials stored in great quantity there was always the hazard of fire, and when woodpulp began to be used, instead of rags as in the past, small inland mills were forced out of business while larger mills near a port prospered. Fortunately the buildings and the waterpower remained and so could be put to other work.

In the Middle Ages it is probable that at least four of the seven mills were used for 'fulling'. Home-woven cloth would be scoured to get rid of the lanolin then hammered in a suspension of fuller's earth to put a finish on the cloth to harden it—which sounds like just the sort of felting we try to avoid now when we wash our woollies. High-grade Fuller's Earth was plentiful on the north side of Fuller's Vale Road.

Following the decline of paper-making, the upper and lower Barford mills turned to making 'flock', a cheap filling for mattresses made from wool refuse or torn-up cloth. Another product was 'shoddy', a very inferior material using shredded wool fibres—so recycling is nothing new.

Headley Park Mill, sometimes known as the 'pepper-pot', served the Manor of Broxhead. It was an hexagonal building with two cottages for workers adjoining and was producing flour until the 1890s. From 1904 until 1929 a dynamo pumped water and generated electricity for the house and laundry. Jim Clark, just starting work as a postman, remembers delivering letters to the mill cottages fifty years ago, but now the buildings are derelict. They could have been saved had planning permission been given to an artist to convert the mill into a dwelling house and studio while it was still restorable, but no. What a wasted opportunity to preserve a place of English history dating back to Saxon times.

Fortunately Headley Mill remains. Thanks to three generations of the Ellis family this grand old lady is still going strong. There is a reference to her in the Woolmer Forest records of AD978, so it is fitting to say 'she has ground her corn, and paid her tax, ever since Domesday Book'.

This article first appeared in the River Wey Trust Newsletter

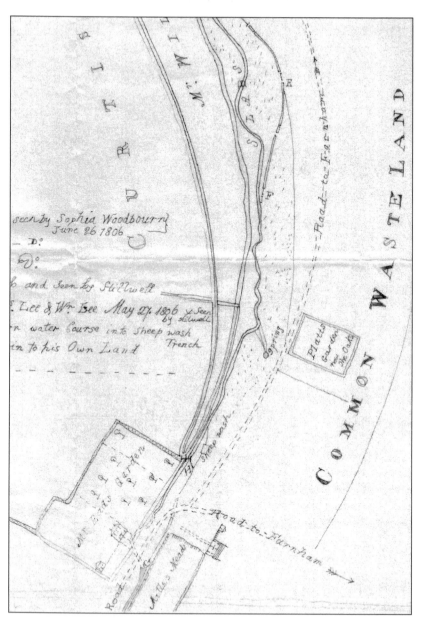

The upper (south) end of the valley below The Hanger, 1806/7

The Alderbed Dispute—1806/7

from the Headley Archives

In 1806, John Willoughby senior diverted water from the Ar stream over his 'new arch' close to the junction of Barley Mow Hill and the Hanger, and into his own meadow, thus robbing others further downstream of water which they regarded as theirs.

This brought complaints from William Bettesworth of Bayfields, and Edward Benham, both of whom had land below Willoughby's.

The dispute was settled the following year, as shown by the following document:—

William Bettesworth against John Willoughby (the elder) and John Willoughby (the younger); also, John Willoughby against Daniel Knight, Charles Lee and Edward Keen

It is agreed between the undersigned Parties that the above mentioned Causes shall be discontinued upon the following Terms, Viz:

Edward Benham shall continue to occupy and make use of the Water from the Watercourse Hatch opposite W. Eade's House down the old Watercourse leading through the Slabs and through the said John Willoughby's Field called the Alderbed and through Bilfords Mead to his Mead called Benham's Mead or Bilfords Mead during the first seven days of every calendar month without interruption, and that the said John Willoughby the elder shall make use of the Water over his new arch from the Watercourse Hatch opposite W. Eade's House to water part of Curtis Farm the next seven days in every month without interruption, and that the said William Bettesworth shall continue to occupy and make use of the water from the Watercourse Hatch opposite W. Eade's House down through the upper and lower old watercourses or either of them for the watering of Bilfords Mead during the remainder of every calendar month after the expiration of the first fourteen days of each month without interruption.

And with respect to the Cause Willoughby against Knight, Lee and Keen, it is agreed that the said John Willoughby's Fence of the Alderbed Field shall be put up by the said John Willoughby on the south side of the present watercourse leading to Bilfords Mead as the outside of the said John Willoughby's bounds of the Alderbed Field.

Witness our hands 4th March 1807

[There followed the signatures of the Parties, and also as witnesses: John Willoughby jnr, ?? Knight, Charles Lee, Thomas Clement and Thomas W Clement]

The text was accompanied by maps, two portions of which are shown with this article.

In the first portion (previous page) we see the following:—

Mr Eade's garden [later the *Wheatsheaf*] with Mill's Mead opposite; the position of John Willoughby's new arch (I); the sheep wash; Platts Garden (marked 'now The Oaks'); and the general layout of roads and watercourses at the top end of the Hanger valley.

In the second portion, opposite, we see the bottom end of the valley:—

Bilfords Mead; Benham's Mead; the River Wey; Mr Keen's Land; Mr Matthews Land; Mr Lee's Land; part of Mr Bettesworth's land; and the farmyard at Billford on Frensham Lane. *[This farmyard is no longer shown on a map c.1875—Ed]*

In the middle portion (not shown here) is Mr Willoughby's Meadow and Slabs Waste land.

Also on the map are shown the letters indicating:—

A= a piece of Waste Land that Mr Willoughby had enclosed

B, C, D= Mr Bettesworth's water course cut out by John Willoughby junior, seen by Sophia Woodbourn 26 June 1806

E= ditto, seen by Edward Keen, Charles Lee and William Lee, 27 May 1806, and seen by Stillwell

F= ditto cut out by Edward Collins, seen by Edward Keen, Charles Lee and William Lee, 27 May 1806, and seen by Stillwell

G= the place where the ? was placed in old water course to turn water course into sheepwash trench [opposite Eade's House]

H= where Willoughby cut trench to carry water over the arch into his own land [just upstream of the sheepwash]

I= the arch built by Willoughby [by the NE corner of Eade's Garden, just upstream of the sheepwash]

Of these, the letters from E onwards are shown on the map on p.118.

120

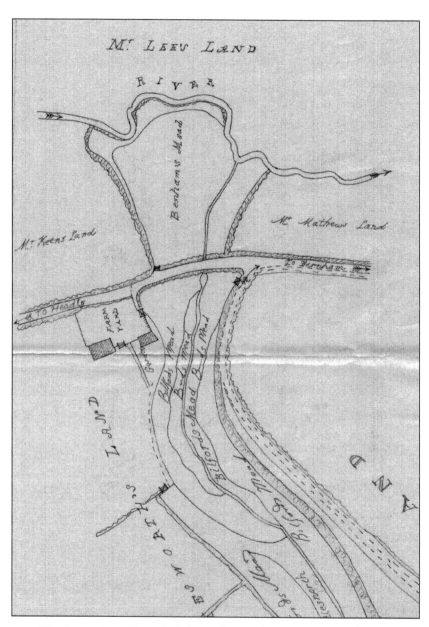

The lower (north) end of the valley below The Hanger, 1806/7

Henry Knight, 1805–1903

Sue Allden on her great-grandfather—written in 2000

Henry Knight was born on 27th November 1805 at Hearn Farm into a family which had been farmers for three generations in Headley.

In 1815, as a boy of 10, he stood in front of The Royal Anchor at Liphook and watched French prisoners of war being marched up from Portsmouth to London after the Battle of Waterloo.

Fifteen years later, in 1830, he was sworn in as a special constable to help the Parish constable quell the rioters who had attacked Headley Workhouse (now *Headley Grange*), and his truncheon still exists.

Top end of the painted wooden truncheon—the insignia is of George III, then dead some ten years—the letters 'TO' are part of the word ALTON

In 1833 he married Jane, daughter of Robert Parker of Wishanger, and they moved to Arford. They lived in what is now called the Corner House. He became a builder, but continued as a farmer. One granary still exists behind the house and another stood in front. He built houses and cottages, and also acquired old cottages. By 1901, he owned 40 properties in Arford.

He had a son and three daughters—and Ellen, one of the daughters, married James Allden of Aldershot who was my grandfather.

On Ascension Day 1836 when Henry was in the congregation, All Saints church caught fire, started according to one story by a little girl called Louisa playing with matches in the churchyard. Henry Knight organised a chain of men to pass buckets of water from the Rectory pond to where he was, up on the church roof—but the fire took hold, and the spire was destroyed. *[See the description given by him to Mr Laverty on p.24]*

Henry Knight was both an Overseer of the poor and a Churchwarden.

Even on his 94th birthday he was riding to hounds, on a grey mare by the name of Polly—his favourite hunter—and being presented with the fox's mask to mark the occasion. He died on 4th January 1903, in his 99th year, and is buried in All Saints churchyard.

Matthew Triggs and the 1830 Riots

Ann Viney—written in 2000

Matthew Triggs was born in Hollywater and baptised in Headley Parish Church on 23rd September 1792. He was the seventh and last child of Hannah and William Triggs of Stedham, Sussex. The family moved to Hollywater in 1786, when William bought a cottage from John Shrubb of Stedham.

By April 1802 William had died (probably in 1794) and in January 1804 his eldest son, also William, mortgaged the cottage with the outhouses, garden and orchard to Thomas Draper for £20. Interest not having been paid, for a further payment of £30 the cottage was sold to Thomas Draper in December 1808, with Hannah having dower rights for her lifetime. During the years 1800–1808 William (son) was serving with the South Hampshire Militia, mostly in Sussex, for the payment of one shilling and eleven pence per month.

Life must have been difficult for Hannah, but Matthew, working as a labourer and later as a bricklayer, would have been able to contribute towards the household.

Matthew married Mary Croucher of Kingsley in Headley Parish Church on 30th August 1820. Although his mother was still alive, she did not witness the marriage, but Ann his sister did and also James Shrubb. They lived in Hollywater and had five children, the last one being baptised on 23rd May 1830 in Headley.

Matthew enjoyed his pint of beer and this probably helped in his downfall, as on the 23rd November 1830 he was heavily involved in the riot at Headley when the workhouse was destroyed. It is recorded that thirty gallons of wine were found in the cellar and this was soon consumed by the mob. Matthew climbed onto the roof of the Poor House and was soon stripping the tiles.

For his part in the rioting he was sentenced at Winchester on 27th December 1830, to be transported to Australia for life. With 135 other convicts he sailed on the convict ship *Eleanor* on the 19th February 1831, bound for New South Wales.

According to the Medical Journal of Surgeon J. Stephenson, "no set of men perhaps under similar circumstances ever suffered less from disease." He considered it was due to the strictest attention to cleanliness, dryness and ventilation and, as far as could be done, the constant occupation of the prisoners. Also they were fortunate in having a delay of a week at the Cape where fresh beef, vegetables and soft bread were obtained. On 29th June

1831 the ship arrived in Port Jackson and on 11th July, all of the convicts were disembarked.

Headley Workhouse, built 1795—now Headley Grange

Matthew was one of the eleven convicts assigned to William Harper, who had 2,000 acres of land called Oswald, on the Hunter River near Maitland, N.S.W. Coastal vessels plied between Sydney and Maitland; the distance was 120 miles and it was about a 24 hour trip.

There was a lot of sympathy in N.S.W. for those convicted during the Agricultural Riots of 1830, and life for Matthew was probably a good deal better. Food and clothing was supplied by his master and, if he behaved well, he may occasionally have been given a coin or two, but would this have made up for the loss of his wife and children? Although he was pardoned by Royal Warrant dated 13th October 1837 (which he did not receive until January 1839), it was only a conditional pardon, which meant that he could not return to England. He could read but not write, and it is not known if he had any contact with his family.

According to the 1837 Convict Muster, Matthew was still working then at Oswald for Mr Harper. He died in the hospital on 30th November 1853 and was buried in West Maitland.

Life for his wife Mary was very different. She had a family to care for and times must surely have been hard. For some years the family lived with Mary's grandmother, Jane Tuckey, in Hollywater, but when she died in 1840, aged 90, the cottage was sold and Mary moved around the district. In 1851, her children then being married, she was a housekeeper in Frimley and noted as a widow. In 1861 she was lodging with Hannah Kiese in Headley and worked as a charwoman.

Later Mary moved to the *Crown Inn* at Arford and lived with her daughter Sarah and son-in-law James Upperton, who was the innkeeper. She died there of dropsy in August 1876, aged 72. She had lived to see four of her children married, and a son William killed in a war; she had 15 known grandchildren and had outlived Matthew by 23 years.

No doubt the riots of 1830, the distress felt by many people and Matthew's part in it were discussed within the family, as it is known that his grandson, Bill Triggs, made a search for information of events in 1899. I have certified copies of the baptism and marriage of Matthew, which Bill obtained from, and were signed by, the Rev. Laverty.

Mary and Matthew Triggs were the great, great, grandparents of my husband, Philip.

Matthew Triggs was the only Headley man to be transported as the result of the 1830 riots. For more information on this, read 'One Monday in November.'

Indenture 1862

In the days when young people were apprenticed to a Craftsman for a number of years to learn the trade, Indenture documents such as the one shown here were drawn up setting out the rules which the Apprentice should abide by for the Term of his Apprenticeship. In this document (full text shown below), Jesse Bone is to be apprenticed to Henry Powell to learn the art of the carpenter.

This Indenture Witnesseth that **Jesse Bone** of the Parish of Headley in the County of Southampton doth put himself Apprentice to **Henry Powell** of the Parish of Headley in the said County, Carpenter, to learn his Art and with him after the Manner of an Apprentice to serve from the Eighteenth day of August One Thousand Eight hundred and Sixty two unto the full End and Term of Five Years from thence next following to be fully complete and ended **During** which Term the said Apprentice his Master faithfully shall serve his secrets keep his lawful commands everywhere gladly do he shall do no damage to his said Master nor see to be done of others but to his Power shall tell or forthwith give warning to his said Master of the same he shall not waste the Goods of his said Master nor lend them unlawfully to any he shall not commit fornication nor contract Matrimony within the said Term he shall not play at Cards or Dice Tables or any other unlawful Games whereby his said Master may have any loss with his own goods or others during the said Term without Licence of his said Master he shall neither buy nor sell he shall not haunt Taverns or Playhouses nor absent himself from his said Master's service day or night unlawfully But in all things as a faithful Apprentice he shall behave himself towards his said Master and all his during the said Term **And** the said Master in consideration of the Sum of Ten Pounds of lawful money of great Britain in hand paid by his said Apprentice in the Art of a Carpenter which he useth by the best means that he can shall teach and instruct or cause to be taught and instructed Finding unto the said Apprentice sufficient Meat Drink Tools Lodging and all other Necessities during the said Term, (Clothing Mending Washing and Doctor's Bills excluded) and in addition to Meat Drink and Lodgings the said Master shall pay or cause to be paid to his said Apprentice the sum of one Shilling per week during the Third year of the said Term Two Shillings during the Forth year and Three Shillings during Fifth year of the said Term **And** for the true performance of all and every the said Covenants and Agreements either of the said Parties bindeth himself unto the other by these Presents **In Witness** whereof the Parties above named to these Indentures interchangeably have put their Hands and Seals the Twenty Second day of August and in the Twenty Sixth Year of the Reign of our Sovereign Lady Victoria by Grace of God of the united Kingdom of Great Britain and Ireland Queen Defender of the Faith and in the Year of our Lord One Thousand Eight Hundred and Sixty two.

Witnesses: Henry Howard Collins; W. Suter

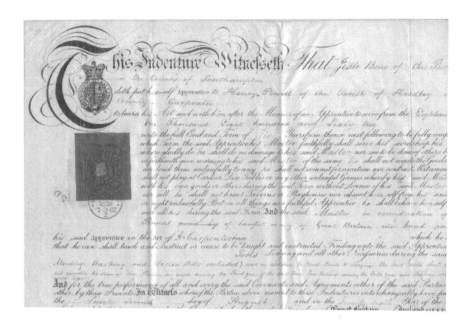

William Suter was the gt-grandfather of Joyce Stevens
who found this document.

A Piggott Descendant Returns

Trevor Henshaw—written in 2000

My mother Lillian Piggott was born in 1909 at Booleroo Centre, in the central north of South Australia. She arrived on a searingly hot February day, the latest resident of this small pioneering town, set in its folds of white-gold grasslands and parched, summer-dry hills. This little girl's grandfather, who had died some fifteen years previously, was Richard Piggott of Headley, in Hampshire.

Richard Piggott was born the eighth of ten children of John and Lucy (née White) Piggott, and was christened in Headley parish church on 29th Nov 1820. His father John was an agricultural labourer and, perhaps notably, some 55 years old at Richard's birth. Census records suggest that John and Lucy's home may have been towards the Lindford end of the village. The family would have all witnessed the momentous happenings of the Headley Workhouse Riots of 1830, and one can imagine a wide-eyed ten-year-old watching these events with a genuine mixture of fear and youthful fascination.

Richard can be found at age twenty in the 1841 Census, working as a man servant for William Swann at Moorhouse. Three years later he surfaces once more, marrying Susannah Harris on 21st July 1844, again in Headley parish church. Susannah does not appear to have come from the village. By 1848 they were living in Yorkshire, Richard working as an agricultural labourer.

Subsequent events show that the couple had begun to contemplate emigration—and so it was that Richard and his family travelled to Portsmouth in 1849 and set sail on 18th July at 8 o'clock, bound for Port Adelaide, South Australia, and a new life. They emigrated aboard the *Duke of Wellington* whose master was Capt RM Miller. By this time they had a daughter Martha (christened 31st May 1846 at Headley) and a son John (no certificate so far found, but almost certainly born in 1849, possibly in Yorkshire).

We have significant details of this ship, and also the full passenger list for this voyage, and it confirms the sad events which struck this family on the journey—the death of both small children at sea—Martha by diarrhoea on 7th Sep 1849 and John of pneumonia on 21st Oct 1849. How their parents coped with this double tragedy we can scarcely guess at. The parents arrived childless at Port Adelaide on 9th Nov 1849. Curiously, there is also an 11-year-old George H Piggott listed with this family group, who is recorded as surviving the voyage and doubtless went on to grow up in Australia. He may have been Richard's nephew, but within our family we have no record of this individual beyond this single mention of him. Nor is there an appropriate Headley census record for this youngster.

It is believed that Richard went to Australia to manage an estate bought up in South Australia by others from England. However, by 1853 he himself had bought land at Clarendon in the Adelaide Hills, a beautiful part of the State, and began to farm there. I believe he must have found farming profitable as during the Victorian goldrushes of the 1850s it was alleged that he was the only man left in Clarendon!

Fate had not finished with Richard, however, for his wife Susannah was to die at the pitifully young age of 29, on 6th May 1854, a victim of consumption. The probability is that she had been poorly in England and that there had been the hope of some recovery in the warmer Australian climate. It was not to be. Fortunately for me, of course, he remarried. He met Eliza Ann Beaumont, originally from St Mary's Hoo, near Chatham in Kent, and they married at Clarendon on 9th Aug 1854.

Richard Piggott with his eldest daughter, Sarah Ann

The rest, as they say, is history, leading ultimately to my mother, then me, and to my own little Richard, his great great grandson—at three-years-old, the first of his direct family to be born back in England since his own birth 180 years ago.

Richard and Eliza had seven children. His youngest was named Llewellin Herbert, born in 1871, and he was my grandfather. My mother gave me Herbert as one of my names. Grandpa lived until he was almost 93 and I am delighted to say I have some treasured memories of being with him on visits to his farm near Burra, South Australia. Here, my very old, very affectionate grandfather and his wonderfully warm wife Annie always made us so completely welcome. I especially treasure the cine film my father took of these days.

All the family were pioneering settlers in South Australia, and Piggotts still farm land near Booleroo Centre which Richard purchased in the 1870s. My grandfather Herbert's farm at Burra also remains in the hands of my cousin Ron Piggott and wife Jill. Burra is 80 miles north of Adelaide, not far from Clare—this should be a location readers have seen on bottles of wonderful Australian wine!

One cannot imagine the contrast between the beautiful wooded vales which surround Headley, and the sunburnt golden grasslands in which the Piggotts made their home in Australia. And yet within two generations, offspring of farm labourers had become established landowners, in my grandfather's case residing in the wonderful old farmstead that I remember so vividly from my youth. He had laid out a tennis court, and made a shady garden of fruit trees and flower beds to sit and relax in on warm evenings. Somewhat bizarrely, they even formed their own boating club on the stretches of nearby Porter's Lagoon—a salty, seasonal pool I remember being more mirage than waterway.

Returning to Richard's story, Herbert and Annie looked after him in his old age, until he died of acute bronchitis on 23rd Sept 1895. He is buried at Morchard, near Booleroo Centre in South Australia, close to where he spent most of his last years.

One other notable point is that the house, if one could call it that, which Richard first built at Clarendon in the 1850s is still preserved to my understanding, in much the original condition, although in some danger. It was written about in a book published in 1983 and the following was noted:—

"... Section 758 on which the buildings are situated was owned by Richard Piggott. Piggott appears in the 1865 Directory as a 'Farmer, near Clarendon' and in 1890 the property was occupied by EJ Masters, who according to the late occupier of the property Mr Keith Kieley, was the coachman to Captain Servante of 'Fern Hill,' Dashwood Gully. Mr Kieley's family has been associated with the property since about 1917. He maintained that Piggott built the house and Masters extended the original two rooms. This would appear to have been verified by the above.

"The two most significant structures to remain are unfortunately in poor repair. The cellar, typically built into the side of the hill, is most interesting since it retains a type of thatched roof in very good order beneath the present corrugated galvanised iron cladding. The cellar is approached from below, while the loft with the thatched roof is entered through an opening in the gable. Rafters are crudely shaped timbers with saplings as purlins. The house, in particularly poor repair, is interesting because of its quality casement windows set below timber lintels and the lath and daub internal walls. Internal timbers and roof structure would appear to be pit-sawn. Both the house and cellar are of rubble masonry with timber lintels over openings. The buildings are very original although dilapidated and threatened by natural forces. One wall of the house has fallen."

Grandpa Herbert would always say proudly how his father had been born in Hampshire, so it is wonderful to have found and become acquainted with this man's village for myself. I was in Headley for the first time in early 2000, and in the churchyard I was amazed to find the gravestone of a Mark and Maria Piggott. Looking at my records that night I discovered that Mark was

Richard's youngest brother. Their gravestone would appear to be the single last physical remembrance of this old Headley family in their village. Another of Richard's brothers, Steven, saw his son Walter become landlord of the *Robin Hood and Little John* pub close by the ford at Standford in 1885, but the building he knew is now demolished and the pub rebuilt.

Richard's elder brother Charles also emigrated to Australia. He and his wife Anne left the shores of England with their family on 5th July 1852. As yet, however, I do not know the name of their ship. They departed with three Headley-born children, and eventually produced another eight in Australia, further populating the Clarendon district with Piggotts. There is a road named after his family in this part of the Adelaide Hills.

[We have Pickett's Hill in Headley, the surnames Pickett and Piggott in various spellings being interchangeable within the same family—Ed]

In respect of Headley, readers may finally be interested to note that the Piggotts travelled out with another family from the village—that of George and Harriet Gardner—a fact I discovered when I thought to search for other possible Hampshire folk on that voyage of the *Duke of Wellington*. When one looks at the passenger listings, however, one finds that the father of that family, George Gardner, also died at sea. What a disaster it must have been for them. What on earth were conditions like on that vessel? Besides Gardner and little Martha and John, another three infants are recorded as dying aboard ship on their way to Australia.

That there were others from Headley on board the *Duke of Wellington* had not been known to my family before—in fact, I have to say very little has been known about Richard prior to his arrival in Australia until I began digging down Headley way. I live in England now with my family. Just as that part of South Australia to which Richard Piggott and his descendants travelled so many years ago has always moved and delighted me, so too a small piece of Hampshire has now become, in a real sense, home ground again.

The Canadians in Headley

War Diary of the Canadian Fort Garry Horse Regiment during their postings to Lindford and Headley, April 1942–June 1943

Their first week in Lindford & Headley:—

Wednesday 1/4/42: Cold and bright – Rain in afternoon. The Regiment left Aldershot and marched the 12 miles to their new quarters, arriving at 1500 hrs. Arrangements for their reception had been completed by the Advance Party and they were settled in quick order.

Thursday 2/4/42: Warm and bright. The day was spent in cleaning up areas. Sqn. locations were plotted. Officers get plenty of exercise walking between Messes and Orderly Rooms. The Auxiliary Services were already functioning with a show for the men at Hatch House Barn. The show "In Name Only".

Friday 3/4/42: Warm and bright with heavy rain in evening. Sqns continue work cleaning up in Sqn areas. Several keen gardeners have already put in small lots with various seeds. A Concert Party at the Headley Village Hall was very well attended and was pronounced a great success. Trooper Naylor of 'C' Sqn sustained injuries when he fell from a top bunk and was taken to 24th Fld Amb.

Saturday 4/4/42: Fairly warm with some cloudy periods. The Commanding Officer inspected the Sqn Areas this morning. Although a big improvement has been shown further attention is needed to bring them up to "Garry" standards. Trooper Jorgensen of 'C' Sqn returning to his lines across country mistook a river for a road and arrived home somewhat damp.

Sunday 5/4/42: Very bright and warm. Church Parade to churches at Headley (Prot.) and Bordon (Cath). The afternoon was spent by most members of the Unit in exploring the countryside.

Monday 6/4/42: Cloudy with some showers. Normal training resumed throughout the Sqns. Classes on Browning, 37 millimetre, M3 Tank and 2 pounder are being held. Dance was held in Headley Village Hall.

Tuesday 7/4/42: Cloudy with rainy periods. Troops are beginning to feel at home in their new location and general opinion appears to be that it is preferred to Aldershot. Normal training continues.

Selection of entries until 21st August:—

Friday 10/4/42: Cloudy but clearing in afternoon. Normal Sqn training. Advanced driving training (unditching vehicles, road repairs, etc) is being instructed. The Regimental Dance Band which has been practising assiduously recently played for a Dance at Headley Village Hall. Although there was a slight scarcity of partners the evening and the Band were both successes.

Wednesday 15/4/42: Bright and clear. Cool. Normal Sqn. training. Bicycling is fast becoming the hobby and means of transportation of a number of officers and other ranks.

Saturday 18/4/42: Bright and clear. Ground is drying and mud has disappeared. Afternoon allotted to Sports. Baseball and Softball is very promising. The local residents are very interested but find it hard to understand. An 'Alert' was sounded at 0215 hrs and Sqn guards turned out. 5 bombs were dropped at some distance away to the South-West.

Friday 24/4/42: Cloudy and windy. Cool in morning. Becoming warm in afternoon. Unit moved to Frensham Common at 0900 hrs. At 1500 hrs 'Stand To' was sounded by Garry Trumpeters on the arrival of Their Majesties the King and Queen. After the Royal Salute was given Their Majesties made a tour of the Brigade in the field. Their Majesties displayed keen interest in the many phases of Armoured Corps Training which were being carried out. After the Inspection the entire Brigade doubled over to the Circle around their Majesties car and three cheers were given led by Brigadier Rutherford. Then the Westminster Band played "Rule Britannia" and as the Royal Visitors moved off Lt-Col. Gianelli of the L.S.H. *[Lord Strathcona's Horse regiment, who were posted in Headley Down at this time]* led the Brigade in cheering.

Sunday 10/5/42: Dull and cloudy. Heavy rain during afternoon and evening. Softball game against 'A' Sqn had to be called off on account of heavy rain. Church parade to Headley for Protestants and Bordon for R.Cs. Regiment was ordered to stand by as result of fire at Grayshott early Sunday morning.

Friday 15/5/42: Misty and cool, warming and clearing in afternoon. All afternoon parades cancelled for Regimental Field Day. A real Success. Garden plots put in by different men are beginning to produce fresh vegetables.

Sunday 24/5/42: Cool and cloudy with intermittent showers. Recent rains greatly helped countryside as earlier dry weather had retarded growth and caused many heath fires. Church Parades to Headley and Bordon.

Tuesday 26/5/42: Cold and almost continuous rain. Range practices on Conford A/Tk Ranges with Browning. 300 Coax M.G. are being held for all tank crews on a basis of 65 per Sqn and 15 from R.H.Q. Coax practice is fired single shot as 2pdr as practice for when Unit goes on 2pdr ranges in Wales to fire.

Friday 29/5/42: Cool but mostly bright. Regtl Dance Band played to well-attended Dance at Headley Village Hall. Normal Training.

Wednesday 3/6/42: Very warm and bright. The Q.M. Staff have worked very hard arranging the Marquees for the Demonstration of all equipment on charge to the Regiment. 3 Marquees have been set up as well as the complete assortment of vehicles on charge to the Regiment, including their equipment. The Ministry of Information full length film "Next of Kin" was shown to all ranks and was very favourably received. The film made a great impression from the Security point of view.

Friday 12/6/42: Cloudy with intermittent heavy showers. The Hon. Col. of the Regt. Major Gen. P.J. Montague inspected the Regt. at 1500 hrs on Headley Green. Our escort met him at 1155 hrs and conveyed him to the R.O.R. where he was met by the Commanding Officers Lt. Col. R.E.A. Morton. The party arrived at R.H.Q. mess at 1315 hrs where the following officers were introduced:—

Troopers Kapitany, Livingstone, and Scott, 12 June 1942

Major E.B. Evans, 2i/c Regt. – Major H.C. Blandshard, O.C. 'H.Q' Sqn. – Major G.M. Churchill, O.C. 'A' Sqn – Major W.W. Halpenny, O.C. 'C' Sqn. – Capt. H.J. Peacey, O.C. 'B' Sqn – Capt. J.M. Bowie, Adjutant. – Capt. C.W. Bailey Ass't Adjutant – Lieut. H.M. Sleigh. – Lieut H. MacEwing, Paymaster – Brigadier J. Rutherford, O.C. 1 C.A.B. – Major Turnbull, B.M., 1 C.A.B.

Major Gen Montague was accompanied by Capt. Laury Andraine, Photographer who took pictures of the days proceedings. At 1400 Hrs he was taken for a drive in "Royal Betty" commanded by Capt. A.S. [Alex] Christian. Upon return he inspected the Regt. At approx. 1600 hrs a picture was taken of the General and the Colonel surrounded by the Officers perched on a couple of General Lees (see above and p.138). At 1700 hrs the party left for C.M.H.Q. escorted by the Regt'l D.R.'s. The General expressed his pleasure at the turn out of the Regt and addressed all Ranks while on Parade. The march past, led by the Regt'l band took place, saluting base being in front of old tree opposite 'A' Sqn orderly Room.

Monday 15/6/42: Clear and fairly warm. Normal training. The Unit was notified of a number of parcels and cigarettes lost by enemy action in transit here. Pay parade in evening for all Sqns. *[James Desaulnier signed "came from Canada" in the Church Gate Stores attic on this date]*

Wednesday 17/6/42: Warm and bright. Normal training. Permission has been granted for men to wear shirtsleeves on duty and to and from meals providing web belts are worn during the warm weather. *[Lieut. Squires of the Lord Strathcona's Horse regiment was killed falling from a tank in training on Ludshott Common this day — but not mentioned in the Garry's diary]*

Friday 19/6/42: Warm with some cloudy periods. Still a large number of men proceeding on various courses. The talk of the "Second Front" is main topic among the men.

Wednesday 24/6/42: Still remaining dry and clear. Crops in locality need rain. Inter Sqn ball games etc in afternoon. Regt'l tennis Doubles tournament started.

Wednesday 1/7/42: *[Dominion Day]* Cloudy, rather cool in morning. Proclaimed a holiday although training continued on Ludshott Common and firing parties were on Conford Ranges.

Saturday 4/7/42: Cloudy, showers. Training carried out all day on Ludshott Common and Conford Ranges. D38025 Tpr. Fine J. 'H.Q.' Sqn, was tried by Court Martial and found guilty by the Court of striking a superior Officer. Court held in Hatch House Barn.

Wednesday 8/7/42: Bright and warm. Occasional Clouds. The Regt paraded at 'H.Q.' Sqn Vehicle Park at 1600 Hrs and then marched to Bordon station. *[Arrived Pembroke 0630 Hrs. next day. R.C.A.S.C. Vehicles convoyed the Unit to Merrion Camp. Gun firing practice at Linney Head over the next few days.]*

Friday 17/7/42: Cloudy occasional showers. The Regt returned to Lindford and Headley leaving Pembroke in the Morning. Haversack lunch was carried and tea was obtained at Bristol. Regt'l Convoy from Bordon Station to Sqn Areas.

Saturday 18/7/42: Sky overcast, showers. Rear party returned from Merrion Camp. General settling down after return from Wales. Picture show Headley Village Hall in the evening.

Sunday 19/7/42: Bright not very warm. Church parades to Headley Church and Halehouse Chapel.

Sunday 26/7/42: Bright, warm. Church parade to Headley Church. After the Service a march past was held Lt Col Morton taking the salute. The saluting base was under the large tree opposite the Holly Bush Inn, Headley.

Wednesday 29/7/42: Bright, warm. Advance party packed and loaded ready to move to new location at Hove on the South Coast. Normal training for the Remainder of the Regt. Brigade Quiz on Map Reading, Field craft, Etc.

Saturday 1/8/42: Bright and warm. There was a Regtl Parade at St Lucia Barracks to-day — Lt Col R.E.A. Morton inspected the Regt and afterwards took the salute as the Regt marched past first in Column of Troops then in Column of Route. The officers held a garden party in the afternoon at Pound Cottage ('C' Sqn officers Mess) Headley. The was well attended by local inhabitants as well as a number of Officers and their Ladies from our own and other Units.

Thursday 6/8/42: Dull in the morning, clearing up in the afternoon. Reveille was early this morning also Breakfast. Kitchen vehicles and baggage was quickly loaded. Echelon Rdv at 'B' Sqn Tank party and proceeded to Frensham Common thence to Hove. There was one casualty enroute when an 'A' Sqn lorry turned over in the ditch. The driver suffered minor injuries.

Saturday 8/8/42: Dull with overcast sky. Some light showers in the late afternoon and evening. The Regt is pretty well settled down with only a few minor details to be seen to. Lt Col Morton spoke to all ranks this morning on the new phase of training that we are going into. An area on the South Downs Training area has been allotted to us. This evening there were several short Air Raid warnings. When the sirens went for the last warning immediately the A/A Guns opened up. This was the first time most of the men had heard A/A fire and there was plenty of excitement. It was reported that an enemy plane was shot down over the Channel. H26532 Tpr. Brooks R.A. was accidentally shot by B61419 Tpr. Mitchell W.E. at Headley where both men were on the Regt'l Rear Party *[Occurred outside the Church Gate Stores building]*.

Wednesday 12/8/42: Cloudy, light scattered showers. This afternoon H26532 Tpr. Brooks, R.A. was buried in Brookside Cemetery with full Military Honours. There was an alert this morning early and local A/A opened fire.

12 June 1942 – Fort Garry Horse Regiment on Headley Village Green
Gen Montague with Lt Col Morton on his left and Maj EB Evans on his right

Friday 14/8/42: Bright and warm. Sqn Training. There was a short Alert early this morning also one at noon today. The regt was paid this evening. A court of enquiry was held today at Winchester, Hants. for the purpose of inquiring into the circumstances surrounding the death of H26532 Tpr. Brooks, R.A. President – Major E.B. Evans, Members – Capt. C.M. McLean, and Lieut. W.E.A. McMithell.

Wed 19/8/42: Bright and Warm, light showers in evening. Normal training for Sqns. Great excitement throughout the Regt on hearing the news of Canadian and Allied Landings at Dieppe. Continuous stream of British planes over here on route to French coast. This afternoon one of our ships was bombed just off shore and our shore batteries opened up. The plane was brought down. Bde orders in at 1640 hrs for men to pack and make ready to move. Bde conferences at 1700 hrs. However no counter measures were taken by the enemy, but the general feeling of being close to action has proved a marvellous boost to the morale and the keenness of the men.

Thursday 20/8/42: Bright and warm. Normal training. Some enemy activity overhead in the evening and local A/A batteries opened up. The Garry Volleyball team beat the Westminster and LSH teams to win the Brigade Championship. *[Trooper J.L. Desaulnier F.G.H. D.R. signed his name again in the Church Gate Stores attic in Headley]*

Friday 21/8/42: Bright and warm. Some scattered showers in evening. Normal training. Rear party returned from Headley. The Regimental Volleyball Team carried on their record by winning the Divisional Championship.

The regiment moved on to Crowborough in October, and back to Hove in December. On 11th January 1943, they heard with disappointment that they were to be reassigned to a new Brigade, and were moved back inland to Aldershot. Then on 22nd February 1943, they were posted to Lindford & Headley again ... where they were to remain until June of that year.

We pick up the Diary while the Regiment was still stationed in Hove, and received the news that the Canadian Army was to be reorganised. This was not greeted with great enthusiasm, and made for one of the longest entries of any day in the Diary:—

Monday 11/1/43: There was an Officers' meeting in the evening when the Colonel delivered a momentous address. There had been a reorganization of the Canadian Army, modelled along the British lines. There will be only one Armoured Bde in an Armoured Division. The result is that this unit, with the First Hussars, leaves the 5 Armd Div. and becomes part of the 3 Cdn Armd Bde, along with the Sherbrooke Fusiliers of the 5 Div. Under Brigadier Bradbrooke.

Our present Brig – Brig J.T. Rutherford – takes command of the 11 Inf Bde in the 5 Div. The G.G.H.G. *[Governor General's Horse Guard]* become the Recce unit of the 5 Div. The R.C.D.s *[Royal Canadian Dragoons]* are Corps or Army Recce. The Officers mess is stunned by this news. Although they knew that the Cdn Army was to be reorganized, the completeness of the change was not visualized by anyone.

Why the unit which is by far the best unit in the Div, as can be shown by results of Div and Bde Inspections, by Linney head, by Sports results, by results of Officers and O.R.s on courses, by our reputation in the Canadian Army generally, by our reputation with the civilians where ever we have been stationed, by the fact that our leadership is by far the most able in the Div, by the fact that our men are head and shoulders above the general caliber, by the fact that we have managed by the sheer weight of our ability to make the Brigadier who at first did not favour us, claim that we were the best unit in his Bde and by the thousand other factors, why this unit was left paraded to Lieut. Gen. A.G.L. McNaughton on our behalf, our honorary Colonel Major Gen Montague did likewise and our Colonel went to see Gen McNaughton but Gen Montague saw him on his behalf. Gen. McNaughton's attitude was that this was not a kick in the pants but merely a change, that our new Bde under Brig Thomas formerly of the 3 Armd Bde (now deceased) was likely to see action as soon as the 5 Armd Bde.

The feeling in the unit is that although it is a blow to our pride, we can turn it into our favour. We realize that geographical considerations (one unit from the East, one from the West and one from the Pacific) had to be considered in the changing of the set-up of the Canadian Army. The Ld. S.H. stayed in the 5 Div because they were an excellent unit P.F. But there is also a feeling that questions of Political expediency may have been considered. We hope not–we hate to think that others have received favours out of line with their merits. So we take things on their face value and say that the 3 Cdn Army Tank Bde is just as important as the 5 Cdn Armd Bde. Besides, if it is not, the Fort Garry Horse and the First Hussars (past slight differences forgotten) will make it so. Our leadership is too good and ability too definite to be permanently set back by blows to our pride.

We still have our Rams *[a Canadian-built version of the Sherman]* which is a great help. For all and sundry we issue the warning that there were no better Armoured units than ourselves and there will be no better Army Tank Units and that includes the first Army Tank Bde (of which we were once a part, for about a month).

The attitude of the unit is that we have the ability and that we will display it on the field of battle as did our unit in the last war. We were the only Militia unit in the Canadian Army in the last war to keep its entity and that entity cannot be lost.

But the most interesting result of the reorganisation from our point of view was that the Regiment found itself posted back to Headley again:—

Monday 22/2/43: The Regiment moved off at 1000 hrs (from Aldershot) and arrived in the Lindford and Headley areas at 1130 hrs. The run was well handled and no accidents occurred. The remainder of the day was spent in doing maintenance and getting settled in the barracks. Offices were set up.

Tuesday 23/2/43: Tpr. Lalonde A.J., who won the British Empire Medal last November, and two of his friends, namely, Tpr Conway V.G.H. and Tpr Fidler C. left for Buckingham Palace this morning to attend an Investiture held there by the King. His Majesty shook hands with Tpr Lalonde and pinned a Medal on his chest.

Wednesday 24/2/43: A show called "Escape to Glory" was put on in Hatch House barn by the Salvation Army.

Sunday 28/2/43: There were Church parades to Headley Parish Church for the Protestants and to Headley Village Hall for the R.C.s. The afternoon as usual was free.

Monday 1/3/43: Lieut. H.E. [Harvey] Theobald took over the post of Regimental Intelligence officer today. Lieut R.D. [Bob] Grant was posted to the newly formed Recce troop.

Wednesday 3/3/43: In the afternoon there was a football game between our unit team and the Sherbrooke Fusiliers. Our unit won three to nothing. This evening there was a show ("Shall We Dance") put on in the Hatch House Barn by the Salvation Army.

Thursday 4/3/43: Four German airmen escaped in a Canadian Staff car from Crawley Sussex today. At 1600 hrs Capt D.S. [Buck] Whiteford of "C" Squadron saw a staff car which was thought to be the stolen car.

Friday 5/3/43: In the afternoon there was a Soccer playoff game at Daly Field in Bordon between our unit team and the South Alberta Regiment. The South Alberta Regiment won by a margin of 8–4.

Sunday 7/3/43: There was an R.C. Church parade this morning to Grayshott where Brigadier A.M. Thomas attended with his staff. After Church there was a march past of all Brigade R.C.s with Brigadier Thomas taking the salute. An English Armoured Corps Band played for this parade. The Protestants Church parade was to Headley Parish Church where they saw the graves of Canadian soldiers who died in the last war [Bramshott?–Ed]. During the night there was an air raid during which some new Anti-personnel bombs were dropped. Incendiary bombs caused heath fires on the London – Liphook road. There was also a high explosive bomb dropped near the Hindhead Hospital.

Wednesday 10/3/43: There was a Mobile Bath at HQ Squadron today. This evening there was a dance in Headley Hall.

Thursday 11/3/43: This evening there was a picture show ("Sergeant York") shown in the N.A.A.F.I. on Headley Green.

Monday 15/3/43: [Tpr Michaelis brawled with Tpr Gibbs near the *Holly Bush* – see 26 March]

Tuesday 16/3/43: Clear and cold becoming warmer on the day. On this morning's parade there were new mugs issued to the men. Normal training was carried out for the remainder of the day.

Friday 26/3/43: Corporal J.T. Gibbs died today from injuries received on March 15.

Saturday 27/3/43: At 1430 hrs today Lieut H.E. [Harvey] Theobald and Delores Irene Pidgin of Headley were united in marriage at St Joseph's Church at Grayshott. Immediately after the reception they left on their honeymoon. There was a range run this afternoon in which a number of competitors from each Squadron ran to Conford Ranges and then fired five application shots.

Monday 29/3/43: The Squadron O.C.'s and 2 i/c's plus the Intelligence staff proceeded to Hankley Common this morning to watch a demonstration on the handling of prisoners of war upon capture.

Tuesday 30/3/43: There were pay parades form 1230 hrs to 1800 hrs being paid in the following order "A" "B" "C" and "HQ". On these parades all men and N.C.O.'s turned out in light battle order and carried rubber boots.

Wednesday 31/3/43: This afternoon there was a group of personnel from each Squadron attended Corporal Gibbs's funeral

Sunday 4/4/43: The Regt advanced their time one hour.

Saturday 10/4/43: The Regiment went to "Martinique" parade square in "Camp Bordon" and practised Squadron and Regimental drill. There were marches past, first in line then in column. This was for an inspection by Major General The Hon. P.J. Montague our Hon. Col. After dismissal there was a Regimental "Victory Week" party. There were also races, rides in peeps and carriers and other entertainment for the children. The proceeds were 27 pounds.

Outside Long Cross Farm: Capt. H Peacey, Lt. John Whitton,
Maj. J.H. Wickey, Maj. Bob Grant, Maj. Alex Christian

Capt Peacey was killed in action on 25 July 1944, and Maj Wickey, who had served in the Foreign Legion prior to the war, was later transferred to Special Operations and parachuted into Normandy before D-Day to help organize the French Resistance.

Sunday 11/4/43: There was a R.C.'s Church parade to Headley Village Hall at 0900 hrs this morning. The Protestants turned out S.A.P. at 0945 hrs dressed in best battle dress, web belts, black gloves and berets. They were transported to "Grayshott" where they dismounted and marched to "St Albans" Church in "Hindhead". On the way to the Church there was a march past with Brigadier A.M. Thomas taking the salute. The party arrived back in camp at 1250 hrs.

Tuesday 13/4/43: This evening from 2100 hrs until 2200 hrs there was a steady stream of heavy bombers passing over head proceeding due South.

Friday 23/4/43: This evening there was an air raid alert about 2230 hrs. Explosions were heard in the distance and aircraft motors were heard over head, but there was no local A.A. fire.

Tuesday 4/5/43: The usual Tuesday morning Respirator period was held this morning. "A" Sqn went through the Gas Chamber and the Dental Clinic today. "C" Sqn was at Thursley Common training with #1 C.L.R.U. "B" Sqn carried out normal training all day.

Friday 7/5/43: There was a practice harbour scheme today in preparation for the coming Bde Scheme. Tanks were stowed in the afternoon and kits packed for the scheme tomorrow. Some of our Tank crews returned with some new tanks which were equipped with steel tracks and the new Stabilizers. The Regt left this evening on the Bde scheme.

Saturday 8/5/43: Broke harbour in the morning and proceeded to Basingstoke where another harbour was set up at noon. They remained there all day and slept there that night.

Sunday 9/5/43: Broke camp at 0300 hrs at Basingstoke and proceeded eastward where they set up a crash harbour four miles North of Farnborough at approx noon. Arrived back at camp at 1500 hrs.

Monday 10/5/43: Capt A.S. [Alex] Christian gave a lecture on his experience in North Africa with the first army.

Wednesday 12/5/43: In the evening all of the Officers and some of the N.C.O.s attended a lecture at the Sally Lund Café on "What to do if you become a prisoner of War".

Friday 14/5/43: Twenty all Ranks were invited to a dance arranged by the Women's Land Army.

Saturday 15/5/43: Part of the Regt this morning for Salisbury Plains to take part in a practice demonstration for the War Office. An ENSA concert was held in the Headley Village Hall.

Monday 17/5/43: The Regt with the exception of those at Salisbury Plains proceeded to Hankley Common today to practice for the coming inspection of the Bde by a distinguished dignitary of England.

Tuesday 18/5/43: Two more tanks were delivered to the Regt today bringing our total number up to fifty. This is the largest number that the Regt has ever had at its disposal at one time.

Wednesday 19/5/43: This morning His Royal Highness the Duke of Gloucester inspected the Bde at Hankley Common. First His Highness watched a tank demonstration by Bde tank crews and then he drove slowly through the lines of men of the Bde who were a file along both sides of the road. As he approached each Regt he was greeted with three rousing cheers. *[The Sherbrooke Fusiliers note that they extinguished fires on Ludshott Common this afternoon, started by their own mortars!]*

Monday 24/5/43: The Regt was issued orders to move to the Worthing area by June the first. The advance party left this morning.

Wednesday 26/5/43: Most of the day was spent in packing and preparation for the coming move. Maintenance and stowing was done on the tanks and other tracked vehicles.

Thursday 27/5/43: The tanks were loaded on transporters so as to be ready to move off early in the morning.

Monday 21/5/43: Final clean up and inspection and inspection and loading of equipment took place today. Tonight the personnel had to sleep outside so that things would be cleaned up and ready for an early start in the morning.

Tuesday 1/6/43: Bright and fairly warm with a few passing clouds. Reveille at 0400 hrs cleaning up of sleeping areas commenced immediately. All personnel were in "A" Sqn Vehicle Park by 0545 hrs ready to move off. The move began at 0545 hrs and the convoy arrived in Worthing at 0930 hrs.

So the Fort Garry Horse Regiment finally bade farewell to Headley. They were to embark for 'Juno Beach' a year later in support of the 8th Canadian Infantry Brigade as part of the D-Day landings.

For more information on the Canadians in Headley during WW2, read 'All Tanked Up.'

Memories of Fullers Vale Pond

Elsie Johnson (née Pearce)—written in 2000

My parents came to live at *Hillside* in Fullers Vale (the old shop) during March of 1914, when I was 10 months old.

I think one of my first memories of the pond was the use made of it by the ducks owned by Mr Hall, our nearest neighbour. Each morning they would waddle in view of our kitchen window to the pond where they spent the day. No assistance was needed to help them cross the road, for motor traffic hardly existed then.

Later I have happy memories of paddling on hot summer days in the cool, constantly running water.

A huge beech tree grew at the far end, on the edge of a field. From the bank below it a spring flowed continuously, keeping the water sparklingly clear. The tree had low, spreading branches on which, as children, we could sit dabbling our feet in the water, while watching the numerous beautiful dragonflies, and occasionally a kingfisher.

Tiny fish also were a joy to watch, and tadpoles to catch in their season!

Rushes grew abundantly around the pond's edges, which we made a hobby of plaiting and making into mats and tiny baskets.

In winter, when frozen, it became a great attraction to numerous children from near and far who would slide on it, and several young people from the larger houses came to skate and even ski from Mr Phillips' woods adjoining Hurland Lane, finishing their run on the frozen pond.

Accidents happened on the sharp corner of the road near the pond. I well remember my father being called upon to help rescue passengers from cars, trapped in the water. In 1935, for example, we heard, "The Rector's car is in the pond!" Great excitement. Actually it was Alec Alexander, the curate. His fiancée lived at Merrow, a long way to cycle, and he had just bought a car and was an inexperienced driver.

In those days, a stream always ran from the pond along the left-hand side of the road towards Headley, but entered a culvert under the road before the hill, where it continued down the valley to Arford.

Towards the end of the War, when Ludshott Common had been stripped of all vegetation by the tanks training there, Pond Road became the catchment area for water draining off the common land, and that caused the pond to overflow and flood really seriously, becoming a positive river flowing rapidly through to Arford.

My parents' shop suffered badly from the flood water, and I almost needed a boat to go to All Saints' for my wedding in October 1942—the 'river' had been running for 3 days! This happened repeatedly thereafter, and explains why the pond was eventually drained—but it completely changed what was once a delightful scenic corner of Headley.

Fullers Vale pond in 1912

Mr Laverty, the rector until 1928, had also taken an interest in the fortunes of this pond earlier in the century. The following entries of his are taken from the parish magazines of the time, and make interesting reading in relation to the problems of 1942 noted above:—

March 1910

I should like it to be remembered that up to about 1904 the pond No.1035 (number taken from the 25 inch Ordnance Survey map of 1897) opposite to Chatterton Lodge in Fuller's Bottom, constantly overflowed; the little stream crossing the road No.983 which is to the west of the pond, and flowing down the north side of Fuller's Bottom road No.968 into the lower pond No.976.

Sometime before the little stream ceased to flow, a pump had been placed in the east end of the pond No.1035, and the stopping may have been due to this. Or it may have been due to the addition of wells that had everywhere been dug. Or the spring may be of the nature of a siphon, and may again flow when the underground reservoir is once more full.

March 1914 *[Refers back to the 1910 entry, then]:*

For some months the water in the pond has been gradually rising; and now water is flowing from the pond; so that the siphon theory seems to be correct.

October 1921

The Spring and Summer of 1893 were very dry; and up to that time the pond at Chatterton Corner in Fuller's Vale constantly overflowed, the little stream crossing the road and flowing down the north side of Fuller's Vale into the lower pond. Then it ceased to flow for some years.

In the Parish Magazine for March 1914 it was noted that the water in the pond had been gradually rising; and was once again flowing from the pond. It will be interesting to see if there is a similar result this year or next, after the long drought.

June 1922

In the October magazine, I wrote that it will be interesting to see if, in consequence of last summer's drought, the little stream at Chatterton Corner in Fuller's Vale will cease to flow. It has ceased; and, judging by our last experience, it may not begin to flow again for 20 years.

In April 1973, a large pipe was laid under Fullers Vale road, leading from the bottom of the pond to an outlet further down the valley. This was intended to stop the flooding. Despite local protests, it also had the effect of permanently draining the pond, which then become a bit of an eyesore.

The Fuller's Vale Wildlife Pond Association *was formed in 2001 to secure restoration of the pond to its original habitat – as a wildlife preserve. By the end of October 2003 it had succeeded in this objective!*

See **www.headley-village.com/pond** for details of the restoration.

Inventory of The Wheatsheaf, Arford – 1864

We publish this in memory of 'The Wheatsheaf,' which was demolished in March 2001

Document made out when Francis Tipper transferred to Jonas Shrubb in 1864 —

An inventory of Mr Tipper's Goods and Stock at the Wheatsheaf Inn, Headley.

Garden:

All the Potatoes, Cabbage, Brocoli, Mangolds, Swedes, French Beans, Onions and all other things now in the Garden and all the Apples, Nuts and the Oats now standing, also the Potatoes in the Plot behind the Blacksmiths Shop—stack of Turfs, 2 store Hogs, Pig Trough, quantity of Dressing and heap of Ashes — (Slates, Boards, Slabs, etc to one pig pen).

The Wheatsheaf, Arford, circa 1908

Fuel House:

Quantity of Wood, Bavins and Poles, 3 Hurdles, Pig Trough, 4 Tubs, 3 Hoes, 1 Beck, 1 Rake, 2 Shovels, Garden line, Hand bill, Water pail, Ash box, quantity of Crocks and old Iron, 4 fir Stools, Ladder, Booth cloth and frame, Wheelbarrow, 18 wood Spitoons, Hand cart, Door in Stable with Hinges and Bolt.

Parlour:

12 Windsor Chairs, Oak pillar and claw table, window blind, Grate and fender, 24 Rummers *[large drinking glass]*, 14 Tumblers, 2 Water bottles, 12 Wine glasses, Snuffers and tray and water jug.

Tap Room:

Run round fixed to the ceiling, 2 deal tables and cottage grate.

Bar Parlour:

American Clock, Dresser and shelves, 5 pewter measures and funnel, 14 Quart, 31 Pint and 1 half-pint cups, 27 small Tumblers, 10 Beer glasses, 7 Rummers, 8 Dram glasses, 2 Mullers *[pulverising tool]*, Hand bell, 2 Trays and 1 waiter, 4 Bats, 6 Wickets and 2 balls, 9 Skittle pins and ball, Window shutter to room.

Wash House:

Circular meat screen, 3 Wash pans, Pork tub, 3 iron Pots and 1 tea Kettle, Meat saw, 3 Tins, 2 gallon Jar, 3 Pans and Colander, 5 iron and 1 brass candlesticks, 4 horse and carriage Brushes and 1 Comb, Sponge and Leathers, Deal table, 3 water Pails, American Oven, 2 frying Pans and 1 Gridiron, 80 ginger beer Bottles, 2 tin Warmers and 2 tin Saucepans, Dripping pan, 2 iron Saucepans, half-gallon Measure, pair of fire Dogs, 2 Trivets, 4 crane Hooks, pair of Tongs, 2 Pokers, Basket and 2 brushes, 1 fagging Hook, Dust pan and 2 Brushes, Paste board, Pipe kiln, iron Rod and meat Hooks.

Cellar:

A 6 gallon Cask, 3 barrel Stands, Mallet, Funnel, Gimblet, 3 drip Pans, 1 Stooper, 3 brass taps, Pincers, Salting trough and Stool and quantity of Coal.

Large Bedroom No.1:

Large mahogany dining Table, 2 deal Table tops and 4 Trestles, 12 Windsor Chairs, Warming pan, Night shade, Register stove and fender, 20 doz. pipes, large Cup, 3 Bowls, 1 Dish, 3 decanters and 2 Stands, 5 salt Cellars, 6 Cruets, Punch bowl and ladle, 8 blue and white meat Dishes, 11 large Plates, 18 Plates, 18 pie Plates and 12 cheese Plates, 1 pie Dish, 3 butter Boats, 5 vegetable Dishes, 6 Cups and Saucers, 12 knives and Forks, 1 carver and Fork, 12 Teaspoons, Scales and 8 Weights, window Curtain and Blind.

Bedroom No.2:

French Bedstead and Furniture, Mattress, feather bed Bolster and 2 Pillows, 3 Blankets and Quilt, Washstand and Fittings, Dressing Table and swing Glass, 3 bedside Carpets, Window Curtain and Blind.

Bedroom No.3:
Bedstead and Furniture, Hull bed and feather Bolster and Quilt, 3-leaf clothes
  Horse and 2 towel Horses, Clothes Basket, Window Curtain and iron Rod, 3
  pieces of Carpet.
Attic:
Stump bedstead and hull bed, 4 deal Stools and one fir Stool.
  Received of Mr Jonas Shrubb the sum of Sixty seven pounds for the
  above named articles. Sarah Tipper. August 6th 1864.

Original document supplied by Graham West, held in Headley Archives.

A Scandal in Wishanger – 1876

Pat Lawson tells us of her husband's gt-gt-grandparents' marriage

---

June 1936: "The King sends you heartiest greetings and wishes on your diamond wedding day"

This telegram message which was received from Buckingham Palace by Major Robert George Vining Parker and his wife Susannah, living in New Zealand after 60 years of marriage, hardly reflects the cloud under which their marriage occurred back in 1876.

Robert George Vining Parker was born in Wishanger in October 1855, the second child and only son of farmer Robert Parker and his wife Elizabeth Alice.[1] Robert senior is shown in the 1861 census of Headley as a 'farmer at Wishanger with 501 acres, employing 19 labourers and 3 boys', although the family is recorded as being absent on census day.

Elizabeth Alice died in 1865, leaving her husband to bring up a 9 year-old son and a 10 year-old daughter, Alice Mary. The 1871 census we see him as a widower age 61 at Pickett's Hill with 246 acres of land, and with him are his 31 year-old niece Louisa Piper and two servants.

From records later in his life, we know that young Robert was educated at St John's, Hurstpierpoint. Then in June 1876, according to family legend, he eloped with their 16-year-old parlour maid Susannah Mary Dare, daughter of Isaac Dare of Farnham—they were married at Kingston-on-Thames. Family legend also adds that he was given a trip to Canada as a 21st present, and the first his family knew of the marriage was when they found Susannah in his cabin when they went to see him off.

The reaction of Robert senior, apparently, was to disinherit his only son!

For two years the newly-weds lived in Canada, and we are told that Mrs Parker experienced 'the trials of pioneer life in the State of Minnesota' before returning to Britain at about the time their first child, Robert Vining Parker, was born on 2nd September 1878.

---

[1] *She is referred to as Elizabeth in Headley records, but Alice in West Meon records — she was a sister of Professor Thorold Rogers of West Meon, a famous economist and historian, and the daughter of George Vining Rogers, from whom the names 'George Vining' descended to young Robert.*

Maj. Robert George Vining Parker   Susannah Mary Parker

The Parker family, circa 1910, on the porch of 'Wishanger', Dunedin
(standing) Robert, Alfred, Lilian, David Lawson, Major & Mrs Parker,
Francis, Alice, Mabel – (sitting) Constance, Rose, Daisy (front) Gabrielle

Soon after this, Robert George joined the Royal Garrison Artillery in January 1879 and was stationed in turn at Portsmouth, the Isle of Wight, Channel Islands, Dover, Chatham and Lydd, and was awarded certificates of proficiency in laboratory work in Portsmouth and in gunnery at the School of Gunnery at Shoeburyness.

By this time they had two other children, Alice Isobel born in 1880 and Mabel Florence born in 1882.

Then in August 1883, Major Parker (as he now was) bought his discharge from the Army and left with his family for New Zealand on the sailing-ship *Lady Jocelyn*, landing at Wellington on New Year's Day of the following year.

For a time he was engaged in casual work, but in 1885 he was offered a position as artillery instructor with the Defence Department, taking up his duties at Auckland.

It was in this year that Lilian Edith was born, the first of nine children to be born to them in New Zealand.

The family transferred to Dunedin in 1889, naming their house there 'Wishanger' – and it was here in 1910 that Lilian met and married David Gilbert Lawson, my husband's grandfather.

Major Parker retired from the Army in 1919 with 40 years' service to his credit, and died in 1941 aged 85 years. His wife Susannah survived him by a year, and died in February 1942 aged 80 years.

David and Lilian Lawson had three children, two daughters and a son Ivan James Lawson, my husband's father.

Our interest in all this started following the deaths of my husband's parents in May 2001, two years after their own diamond wedding. When going through papers, etc, we found a typewritten tome entitled "A History of Our Family— Rogers of Westmeon 1451–1902" and references to Wishanger as a place in England. We searched the Internet for this name and discovered the Headley site. As a result we have found out a lot more information about the Parker family, which we will now add to the tome on the Rogers History. And we also intend to name our own house 'Wishanger'!

Headley Park & Headley Wood, 1945–49

The first of two reminiscences by Myra Treharne (née Pedrick) tells of her time with the McAndrew family

I was 15 years old in November 1945 when I got off the bus at Sleaford, after my long journey from Wales—the first time for me to be away from home. I was met by Elsie Stonard, the Headley Park cook, and my friend Gwenda who worked at Curtis Farm for Major & Mrs Powell.

It was pitch dark, and to me a never-ending road. We eventually arrived at the back entrance, up the steps, along a long corridor, through a large kitchen into a richly furnished room, where I was introduced to a lady with short ginger hair (Miss Wedge) and Percy Stonard who was the head gardener. He took Gwenda back to Curtis Farm.

Kathleen Wedge was a teacher at Bordon School and lived with Elsie & Percy at the Park.

I was tired and hungry. After a light snack and a drink, a lady came into the room and I was introduced to her—it was my first glance of Mrs McAndrew. She had blue eyes and a lovely smile. I was to call her Madam. She told me what I was expected to do in the way of my work. I had to start at 7am by taking a can of hot water to Mr McAndrew's dressing room for him to wash and shave, and a woman called Mrs Rose Marshall would be coming in to show me around and help me for a week. She lived in a cottage near to Lindford Garage, near the bottom of Curtis Hill.

I was shown to my own bedroom—it was a luxury to me—a single bed, wardrobe, side cupboard and a wash basin, and a fireplace. There were four bedrooms, bathroom and toilet, and a very nice sitting room for the live-in staff, Mr & Mrs Stonard, Kathleen Wedge, myself, and a spare room for visitors which we would be allowed to have. My room overlooked the road.

At the front of the house were the dining room and library, which was very large with lovely wood-panel walls, a drawing room with beautiful ornaments under glass domes, grand piano, television (rare at that time) and oil paintings on the walls, one being of Mr Gerald McAndrew in his tweeds and a gun hanging over his arm.

On the other side of the dining room was a study, and a music room where the children practiced their music when home.

The men staff were paid once a month in the study by Mr McAndrew, and the women staff were paid in the drawing room by Mrs McAndrew. I was paid £4 for the first month, and then after New Year 1946 it was raised to £6 a month. I asked to be paid weekly, and to everyone's amazement I was—the first member of staff to be paid this way.

Upstairs, the floors were wide polished oak. Mr & Mrs McAndrew's bedroom had white carpets and furniture, and overlooked the lake. Mr McAndrew's dressing room was adjoining. Then there was Geraldine and Antonia's bedroom, Constance and Caroline's bedroom, a nursery, guest rooms and a drying (laundry) room, lots of cupboards on the landing, plus the many bathrooms and toilets.

Mrs Patsy McAndrew (later Mrs Barnard) and her daughter Caroline in Headley Park library, 1946

On the next floor up, the furniture and carpets for the holiday house *Yellow Hammers* was stored.

The staff at the Park at that time were: Percy Stonard, head gardener; Elsie Stonard, cook; Mr Gould, butler; Mrs Gould, kitchen maid; Mr Fullick, gardener; Arthur Hayden, farm; Sid Ward, foreman farm; Jim Buchanan, chauffeur; Brenda Buchanan, laundry maid; John & Mary, footman & kitchen help; Mrs Marshall, house help; Len Marshall, farm; Bob Steven, gardener; Sylvia Steven, help.

Later on, when Mr & Mrs Gould retired, I took over waiting tables and the butler's duties and my cousin Sylvia came to work there.

We had shooting parties, gymkhanas; the girls had a pony each, and groomed them themselves when they were home from school. Geraldine and

Antonia went to Benendon, Constance went to Farnham until she was old enough to join her sisters, and little Caroline had just started at prep school in Farnham and I had to meet her from the bus at Sleaford to save petrol, as it was rationed.

We had some very nice guests to stay. Lady O'Brien, Miss Rosemund O'Brien and master Dick (when he was on leave from the Navy)—they were Mrs McAndrew's mother, sister and brother. Admiral Vian, Polly Vian and many more, especially young ones when the girls were home.

I introduced the family to fish & chips on Fridays. I begged Elsie to let us staff have them on Fridays, so we did—then Mr & Mrs McAndrew had them too. I cycled to Ewens Fish & Chip shop at Bordon for them.

I joined the Youth Fellowship at Headley with my cousin Sylvia. We met some nice boys and girls there—John Coombes from Openfields, John Warner the Churchwarden's son, Richard Gandy and Kathleen Amey, who I think were from Headley Down. The two Johns were very gentlemanly and always saw us home to Headley Park, which was a very long walk both ways for them. Oh, to be young again!

[In 1947, the McAndrew family moved from Headley Park to Headley Wood. According to Mrs McAndrew's notes: 'The family left Headley Park after the war because the course of the river altered and affected the supply of electricity and water, so it was not possible to continue in the house. We lived at the Swan Hotel in Alton for a month and then moved to the dower house – Headley Wood Farm.]

Just before the McAndrews moved, I went home because my parents were ill. Mrs McAndrew told me to come back when I was ready, and we kept in touch. When I returned in late 1947, they were in Headley Wood.

Headley Wood was much smaller than the Park, so there were a lot fewer staff—in fact I was the only 'live in' member, working as parlour maid, doing housework in the morning, laying table and serving meals in the afternoon and evening, besides meeting Caroline from school, serving her breakfast and sitting with her for mine (at Mrs McAndrew's request to make sure little Caroline would have her breakfast before going to school).

The main part of the house faced the fields and woods, and the back looked out over the gardens and lane leading up to the house. The garden was landscaped by a Mr Peter West, who lived with the Stonards whilst he worked at the Wood.

Starting from the back entrance, the house, consisted of porch, large kitchen, a corridor with a room on the left (which was at one time a nursery, but was then a sitting room for staff—me), a butler's pantry (me), a very nice dining room looking out on front garden and fields, and a drawing room which faced the lovely landscaped gardens at the rear of the house.

The front entrance hall lead to stairs. Just inside the entrance there was a 'boot room' for outdoor wear, and toilet-come cloak room, and the usual lot of bedrooms and bathrooms upstairs.

My bedroom and bathroom faced the lane, and Miss Mary McAndrew (Mr McAndrew's sister) lived in Linsted Farm, the house at the bottom of the lane.

Things were improving after the war. There were gymkhanas and shooting parties held at Headley Wood, and dances in the drawing room, and we started going to the holiday cottage in West Wittering—it was called *Yellowhammers*, and was a pretty thatched cottage with a garden path leading down to its own private part of beach.

I knew when we were there that Mr McAndrew was suffering with his heart because we had a visitor one day, a Mrs Tatton-Brown, she drove her big green Bentley car onto the beach and it got stuck in the sand. She could not push, nor could Mr McAndrew. He apologised and just looked on helplessly whilst we 'girls' pushed and shoved. *[Eventually he was to die in 1950 of a heart attack at the relatively early age of 58 — editor]*

Myra (left) visiting Elsie Stonard at Hop Kiln Cottages, Headley Wood in the 1950s

At *Yellowhammers*, I had to go to Chichester to do the shopping for the McAndrews, and the first time I was sent there I was asked to get buns and mushrooms besides other things. I remember her saying to me, "You must catch the 46 buns," instead of bus. I was in stitches laughing at her, but she took it in great fun.

The crest and motto of the McAndrew family was a sailing ship with 'Fortune Favours the Brave'. This crest was on all their silver and cutlery—in fact on almost everything, linen included.

When Headley Wood was eventually sold, the bedding people, Mayers Beds, bought it and the Stonards moved to Littlecote Cottage in Liphook Road. But by that time I had moved away.

At the end of 1947, I had met Dennis Nash from Standford, who worked at Lindford Garage as a mechanic. I left Headley Wood to marry him in my village church of St David's, Resolven in Wales on 20th August 1949, and after a few days we returned to Hampshire because of his work and went 'into rooms' with the two Miss Fishers, Emily and Daisie, at *Riverside Bungalow* in Hollywater. And what a change that was!

My time in Hollywater & Standford during the 1950s

Myra Treharne (née Pedrick) continues her story

After our wedding we returned to Hampshire. We had planned to live with an elderly lady who lived at a bungalow called *St Margarets* in Headley, where I was going to be her combined companion and helper. Unfortunately just two weeks before our wedding she changed her mind, thus leaving us with nowhere to live.

Before our wedding I had stayed with Ted Muff, his wife and son Barry in Lindford, who were very kind to me. Ted worked with my husband Pat [Dennis Nash] at Lindford Garage. Shortly after this Pat changed his job and went to work for Mr Meckiffe who had a business in Farnborough, where he looked after the fleet of vans and delivered goods to shops, hospitals, stores and even prisons. Pat's parents lived in No.1 Robin Hood Cottages near the Robin Hood Pub at Standford and Mr Meckiffe lived in the cottage next door.

The only place Pat could find for us to live was in two rooms of a cottage in Hollywater where two sisters, Daisy and Emmie Fisher lived. I had no idea what this accommodation was like, and knew nothing about the sisters. I wanted to cancel the wedding until I could see the place for myself, or found somewhere else to live. It was very hard to find accommodation after the war. My Father had died two months before the wedding so my brother Edwin gave me away. One reason we carried on with the wedding was because my Mother had already suffered by my Father's death and we did not wish to put her through any further trauma.

We received many presents from our family and friends, and one from Mrs Pester who kept the stores in Standford.

On our return from our wedding we first called on Pat's Mum. She gave us some milk and groceries to keep us going until we were straight.

When we arrived at the bungalow it appeared to be in the middle of a field with a long path up to it.

On knocking at the door a tall woman answered and said, "Oh come in Pat, and I presume this your wife Myra?" Pat introduced us, and Daisy Fisher said she would show us to our rooms as no doubt we were tired after our long journey.

I was shocked when I saw the interior of the cottage. Daisy opened the door of what was to be our living room. There was a primus stove for cooking, and she said that when we had registered with a coal merchant we would be able to do our cooking on the fire in the grate. She told me I would soon get used to cooking on the primus stove.

Also in the room was a table with an oil lamp on it, two chairs, an old sofa, and a little cupboard to keep our utensils in.

Off this room was a door leading to our bedroom. This contained an old iron bedstead with no bedclothes, a dressing table with a mirror, a small wardrobe for our clothes, and at the side of the bed a pail with a lid on it! I just did not know whether to laugh or cry.

I asked her if I could use the toilet. She said yes, and told me to follow her. She went out through her kitchen, which contained a dresser, a scrubbed top table, two old armchairs, two chairs around the table and a black leaded range. This led through to a room containing a big boiler that had to be lit underneath to warm water. The floor was flag stones. Daisy went on outside and showed me a small shed—the outside "loo". She said, "Here it is Myra, but in future you must use your own newspaper, and I will give you your own nail to hang it on." The loo was sited beside a small river (the Deadwater River). I could not believe my eyes or ears that people were still living like this. I had been so used to luxuries at Headley Wood and Headley Park, and even at home we had electricity, running water, washing facilities, and above all flushed toilets.

The outside loo at 'Riverside'

I asked Daisy where I could wash my hands and face. She said that as we were by the river I could use that, but to be careful in case I slipped in. She said that in the morning Pat could get me a bucket from the river to wash both myself and the dishes.

We unpacked some of our things so we could get at our bedding. Pat lit the lamps in both rooms. We checked there was enough water for our morning cup of tea, and then went to bed wondering what our first day in Hollywater would bring!

Pat still had a couple of days holiday left, so the next morning he fetched water from the river and then Daisy took him over to the people next door to show him the well where he could fetch water for making tea and for use in cooking.

I looked out of the window and the countryside around was lovely, but I could not imagine how I could possible manage living in such conditions.

Daisy would not allow us to bring the car inside the gate, saying it would cut up the grass! That first day Pat took me down to see his Mum at Standford and to see his boss next door. Pat's Mum took me to register my Ration Book at Pesters Shop in Standford and arranged for me to obtain fuel from

Mr Irvine. She was so good to me.

Later we went back to "Riverside" as the cottage was called and sorted out our belongings. Pat showed me all around the place. I felt I could not let him know how I felt about living there; I would just have to make the best of it. Daisy's sister Emmie was blind, and I felt sorry for her.

When Daisy came home from work she set the table for their meal. They kept their food down in the cellar. I heard her shout at poor Emmie because she had taken a tomato from the cellar. I found out later how she treated her poor sister.

They kept chickens, and I am terrified of anything with feathers. I was shocked to see the chickens running all over the kitchen. They would perch on the mantle-shelf, the chairs, and worst of all, on the table! Every time I wanted to leave the cottage, I had to pass these chickens. One day when I was leaving the cottage to go to Whitehill, I shooed them all out with my handbag. Daisy asked me what the problem was, and told me off for frightening her chickens. I told her I was scared of feathers and that it was not hygienic to have 'filthy birds' in the house. She replied that her birds were not filthy, but from that time on she kept them out of the kitchen.

I joined the midweek services at The Iron Room with Pat's Mum. I enjoyed going there. The members were all very friendly. Emmie was a member too, and sat near to me. Although she was blind, she knew all the hymns. As time went by Emmie told me how mean and nasty Daisy was to her, although by this time I had heard and seen for myself.

One day, I decided I really wanted a proper bath. I asked Daisy if I could have one, and she said I would have to fill the copper boiler with water from the river and use our own fuel to heat it. I had to bring a big tin bath inside the scullery and fill it from the boiler. I was told that afterwards I must be sure to empty the water onto our own waste heap not hers!

Soon after this, she stopped me when I was about to hang my washing on the line. She said she would give me my own line at the back of the cottage as she did not wish people to see knickers and men's underwear on her line – as this was visible from the road.

There were some very nice people living in Hollywater, who I met and spoke to quite often. I remember Venus Cooper and her sister. Her sister was badly disfigures on the side of her face, so she always wore a headscarf to conceal it.

When passing through the kitchen one day, I saw Daisy with a book in which she was writing something down. She tried to close it quickly so that I could not see it. I apologised for disturbing her, but she said it was alright, and she was just entering some dates.

When I got back, Emmie was sitting near the table holding Daisy's book. She asked me what it was, and I said it contained a lot of girls names, the dates of weddings and the dates of the birth of children. It turned out that it was so she could tell whether the date of the babies' births were long enough after the weddings! She was certainly a very strange person.

There were a lot of gypsies on the common land at Hollywater. I would pass them when going to Whitehill, and although they were not very clean in their appearance I do not think there was much harm in them. Most were quite polite.

We decided to go home to my Mother's for our first Christmas, as the thought of the home comforts were very appealing. I was looking forward to having a nice long soak in the bath, and having electricity and flush toilets! We had a wonderful time, but when we got back to Hollywater, Daisy was waiting to tell us that we had been burgled. This was a horrible shock, as our rooms were in a terrible mess, and our wedding presents were all scattered everywhere. The police came back the next day and told us they thought gypsies were responsible, but that they could not prove it.

Before very long I found I was pregnant. Pat was thrilled, but the thought of having a baby in the cottage horrified me. We tried putting our names on the housing list at Alton and Farnborough, but were told that many people were living in worse conditions than us.

My Mother wanted to come and stay with us just before the birth, but I did not want her to see how we were living. I kept making excuses to keep her away, but she was determined. Daisy said it would be alright for her to stay, so I had to give in, and two weeks before the baby was due she arrived. When she got to Hollywater she could not believe we were living in such a remote place, but I thought to myself wait until you see "Riverside". We got to the crossroads and I told her to follow me. We walked down the lane first of all, then reached the gate to the field the cottage was in. I thought she was going to run off. She said, "You are joking, aren't you Myra?" and I said, no this is where we are living and we have to make the best of it. I said it was alright because the people around were friendly. I warned her not to say anything to the Fishers when we went inside, as we would still be living there after she returned home. She told me that she had no idea of the life we were living—she thought it seemed like living in a cave.

My Mother settled down, and eventually my daughter was born and we called her Glenys. When I took her home, Daisy made a fuss of her, but it didn't stop her telling me that I could not wheel the pram through her kitchen as she did not want tyre marks on her lino.

Eventually, when Glenys was seven weeks old, Pat came home one night and told me he had found a flat in Farnborough. It had gas, electricity and running water! It was to cost £2.12.6 per week—more expensive than the £1.10s. a week we were paying Daisy, but I didn't need much persuasion to take it, even if it seemed a lot of money, so take it we did!

And so Myra moved away from Hollywater in the summer of 1950, and soon after that, in February 1951, back to Wales when her brother got a cottage for her and Pat in Aberdulais, 'next to the Falls'. She still lives in Wales, with her second husband Les, and has fond memories of the people and places around Headley.

Prologue

As dark succeeds to light and night to day,
So gloom now follows swift on gaiety,
For Cromwell's sombre men suppress by force
All levity of conduct and of thought,
Cavalier courtesy, lightness of heart,
Frivolity all quenched... ! swept clean aside
To give full rein to Puritan restraints.
All beauteous verse of James' Book of Prayer
All God-given loveliness decried as false,
And earnest Duty, overlaying all,
Stifles the merriment of yesterday.

The Roundheads, A.D. 1645

CHARACTERS :

Mr. John Fauntleroy of the Manor House, Hedleigh	...	J. S. TUDOR JONES.
Mrs. Fauntleroy	...	PAULINE BUCK.
Kathleen	...	KATHLEEN WILLS.
Jennifer } their daughters	...	ANN KING-HALL.
Isobel	...	VALERIE GATES.
Mary	...	JOYCE STEVENS.
The Rev. Averie Thompson, Rector of Hedleigh (1631-1670)	...	DUDLEY TEAGUE.
The Commissioner	...	D'ARCY CHAMPNEY.
1st Soldier	...	LEONARD ADAMS.
2nd Soldier	...	FRED GREEN.

SCENE :

THE MANOR HOUSE GARDEN.

*(Mr. and Mrs. Fauntleroy return from Church, carry-
ing Prayer Books. They are sombrely dressed, but
they are not Puritans. They are accompanied by three
of their daughters, Kathleen, Jennifer and Isobel. The
four women are arguing heatedly with Mr. Fauntleroy).*

Kathleen : But, Father, if the Rector continues in his course,
and it should come to the ears of Authority, will not the outcome be disastrous?

Mrs. Fauntleroy : And will not we all be drawn into the trouble
that will arise? That is what I fear for you, my love — *(to her
husband).*

Isobel : It is the possibility that we may lose the Rector's services which troubles me—so good to the poor, so kind, so truly
God-fearing. I think he would be irreplaceable.

Mr. F. : Have done! You women are all alike. You will discuss
and talk about things of which you have no understanding.

Jennifer : I understand only too well that any Rector who
makes use of King James' Prayer Book in any Church, or in any
way at all, must forfeit his living, if nothing else. So much the
Law makes certain in this "Protected" land.

Mrs. F. : My dear, be careful what you say.

25

*Scene from the 1951 Pageant of Headley
in which Averie Thompson is arrested—see p.17*

160

The Pageant of Headley, 1951

"But has Headley a history?" When the Pageant was first discussed, this question was asked more than once. It was anticipated that at some future date a short history of the place, which many of us have come to love, will be produced, but in the meanwhile this Book provides the answer.

So begins the Foreword to the published script of The Pageant of Headley.

The original idea for a parish pageant had taken root during a casual conversation at a Youth Fellowship summer holiday the previous year, and matured as a project for the Festival of Britain celebrations in June 1951.

The pageant told the story of an English parish from AD 894 in eight episodes, which included a reproduction of the parish's celebrations in the 1851 exhibition and a visionary look into the future—the year 2051.

The script for the two-hour staging was written by Mrs Eveline Clarke of Liphook, the musical director was Kenneth Adams of Kingsley, and the producer was Mrs Frances Paton-Hood of Guildford.

'Everything in the pageant could have happened, and quite half of it did,' said Mrs Clarke to a reporter at the time. 'I have tried to show the constancy of the land and all the changes that have taken place down the centuries.'

In an episode portraying the granting of Headley Mill to a Norman knight, two of the performers were John and Peter Ellis, the owners of the Mill.

Five performances were given in the garden of *Wodehouse*, then the home of the Thackeray family, and more than 100 players took part.

The eight episodes were as follows:—

1. The Saxons, AD 894—villagers ambush a party of Danes
2. The Normans, AD 1069—Eustace of Boulogne takes possession of Headley Mill
3. After the Black Death, AD 1351—medieval labour troubles
4. The Elizabethans, AD 1599—Fair Charter granted to Headleigh
5. The Roundheads, AD 1645—the rector is arrested
6. The Georgians, AD 1800—Cobbett and rural unrest
7. The Victorians, AD 1851—celebration of the Great Exhibition
8. Charles VI, AD 2051—a vision of the future

161

Characters from The Elizabethans

Characters from The Roundheads

The Theme of the 1951 Pageant was described by The Prologue:—

> Welcome, thrice welcome, in this festive year
> Which marks the twentieth mid-century.
> Welcome to Headley and this English ground
> Which Wessex was, and Hampshire is today.
>
> And, being come, you will be carried back
> From nineteen fifty-one to Saxon times;
> From Headley of today to Hallege then;
> From Headley Park as is to Broxhead Manor once;
> To watch events that happened in these parts,
> If not exactly on this very spot.
>
> Through centuries of change throughout the world
> We will transport you now; that you may feel
> What little change comes to the good green earth
> In little places set in the country-side.

The audience was seated in specially constructed stands, with ticket prices ranging from 2/- to 7/6d — on the last night from 3/- to 10/-.

One outcome of this very successful pageant was the founding of Headley Theatre Club in the following year, 1952, its prime objective being 'To unite the village in good fellowship'.

A second pageant, 'Salute to Elizabeth,' was run along similar lines to celebrate the Queen's Coronation in 1953—but we had to wait another 47 years for the next, held on the Village Green in June 2000 as part of the Millennium celebrations—Ed.

Characters from A Vision of the Future

Children who took part in the 1951 Pageant

Those shown in the photographs on previous pages are as follows:—

Characters from The Elizabethans (left to right):—
Michael Digby, Hilda Davis, Helen Tudor Jones (Rector's wife), Douglas Terry (head of Grayshott School)

Characters from The Roundheads (left to right):—
Fred Green, D'Arcy Champney, Joyce Stevens, Kathleen Wills, Valerie Gates, Ann King-Hall, Canon Tudor Jones, Pauline Buck, Dudley Teague

Characters from A Vision of the Future (left to right):—
Joyce Stevens, James Smart, Merryn Fairbank, Jeremy Calvert-Lee, Jennifer Pring?, Canon Tudor Jones, John George, Stephanie Phillips, Gordon Jones, Kathleen Tonkin?, Ann King-Hall

Children (as identified by Margaret Gauntlett, née Smith):
In the back row, left to right: Dorothy Clark, June Booley, Gladys Croft, Ann Jewell, Margaret Robbins, Sheila Hunt, Susan Burningham, Glenda Nash, June Able, Ivy Tubb, ?, Freda Taylor, Sheila Walsh, Jean Williamson, Margaret Fisher, Edith Goodyear and Jean Kemp.

Kneeling in the middle row: P Martin, Jacky Sinclair, June Marshall, Dorothy Keith, Iris Harris, Sally Woodford, Valerie Beecham and Margaret Smith herself.

In the front row: Diana Smith, Ann North, Patsy Goddard, Mary Fisher, Joyce Hillier, ?, ?, ? Leggett, Jean Tompsett, Valerie Cowie and ?.

According to the Programme, the other children involved were: M. Benham, K. Cain, B. Clarke, K. Harris, D. Johnson, M. McEwen H. Mortimer, R. Passingham, S. Rooney, D. Sarjeant, S. Tubb, J. Willshire and W. Woodford.

Photographs of the Pageant shown in this issue are courtesy of Joyce Stevens, except for that of the Children which is from Mrs Margaret Gauntlett (née Smith).

*The Producer of the 1951 Pageant, Mrs Frances Paton-Hood,
enjoying the show*

Notes on Headley, written in 1975

Beatrice Mary Snow

I was born in a bungalow at the top of Beech Hill in 1885. At the age of 3 years I attended the Holme School with 2d school money in my hand. At school I was taught Reading, Writing, Arithmetic, Botany, Cooking, Needlework. All these lessons have helped me through all my life. The great event of the year was our House Show. I got prizes at the age of 10 years. I have exhibited till I am 90 years old. The great attraction to visitors was the Rectory Field entertainment. We had free seating for 1,000 people and displays from the Aldershot Military, Musical Rides, etc, with the horses. It was lovely.

I remember Headley Fair outside the *Holly Bush*. Stalls of sweets, china, and always a whelk stall. Such funny old folks doing the selling. Our letters came from Liphook by pony trap in the morning to our Headley Office in Longcross Hill. The horse was put to graze till the return journey in the afternoon with our mail. Letters were delivered by our local postman. We had no gas, electricity, buses. We had to draw our water from wells 120 feet deep in places. To get to Grayshott or Bordon or anywhere it was just walk. If you wanted the Doctor, you walked down to Standford.

The Village Hall (see photo next page) is built on the village gravel pit. Alton used to buy the gravel for our roads, as there were no surfaced roads in those days. My husband was chairman of Headley Parish Council when the Hall was built and the council had a lot to do with it as it was on parish ground. My daughter Joyce presented Mrs McAndrew with bouquet of pink carnations at the opening and there was a hitch with the key at the unlocking. It was a very cold day too.

I have lived at *Heather View* for 60 years. When we came here Arford Common was lovely with heather of all sorts and butterflies and even corncrakes nesting here. Alas all is over now — it is not our common of years ago.

Now I close these few remarks of our village as it was. I loved my Headley and worked for it all through the years.

Headley Village Hall soon after construction, 1925.
Note addition of buttresses on side walls in picture below,
required after construction to stop subsidence into the gravel bed!

Headley Village Hall after extension, 1983

"Hartie"—Harriett Rowswell, 1879–1965

Cherry Forray of Seattle, Washington, USA—written in 2002

This is the story of my grandmother, who faced adversity with courage. From my childhood, I remember she had the name 'Grayshott' on her front gate. I never knew about her earlier life then.

My grandmother's name was Harriett Rowswell. She was named Harriett after her grandmother, but went by the name "Hartie" instead. Hartie was born on 9th January 1879 at *Arford Lodge* (now *Ivy Cottage* – see photo on p.173) in Headley. Her father was William Harnett, born in 1847, in Whiteparish, Wiltshire. He was a kind and gentle man. Her mother was Susannah Powell, born in Norfolk, in 1844. Susannah was said to have been adopted by a wealthy family. William and Susannah were married in 1868. After they married, Susannah, who was well educated, taught her husband to read and write. Susannah and William made sure that all their children went to school and received an education. In all, they had eight children, Hartie being their sixth child.

William Harnett is listed in the 1881 Headley census as being a "gardener and domestic servant". He apparently worked at that time for Mrs Elizabeth Windus of the publishing firm Chatto and Windus, who then owned Arford House. William and his family moved several times, but they must have lived in Headley for at least six years, since Harriett's name, along with three of her sisters, is listed on the Headley School's exam list for January 29th 1885. That year, Susannah gave birth to her last child. Hartie's parents then had five girls and three boys.

Every Sunday, William and Susannah would take their family to church in a small horse-drawn carriage. Hartie drew a lot of strength from her religious upbringing. It is what helped get her through the hard times in her life. The family apparently moved to Buriton in 1886. Arford House was advertised for lease that year. Tragedy struck the family in 1886. William, the oldest son and namesake of his father, drowned at Buriton. He was 14 years old.

Frederick Rowswell, was born in 1876. His family came from Somerset. He was the youngest of four children of Thomas and Jane Rowswell.

Harriett 'Hartie' Harnett in her twenties

William Harnett, Hartie's father

Around 1890 to 1900 the family moved to Hampshire. Fred's older brother, Arthur, opened a bicycle shop in Grayshott, and the family lived there, above the shop. Arthur Rowswell is listed in the 1903 Grayshott directory as being a 'cycle agent'.

Arthur married Hartie's sister, Annie. They moved to Petersfield, where Arthur opened another bicycle shop. Frederick then managed the shop in Grayshott, and continued to live there with his parents. Later, his sister, Helen, married Fred Lingley, who owned a sweets, tobacco and newsagents shop in Grayshott.

By then the Harnetts were living in Midhurst, where Hartie was working as a lady's maid. Fred liked his brother's young sister-in-law. He wanted to get to know her better. So every Sunday, Fred would ride his bicycle all the way from Grayshott to Midhurst to be with Hartie. Finally, in January 1907, Hartie and Frederick were married in Midhurst. Now that she was married, Hartie would move away from the countryside and family she loved so much to the town of Romford, Essex. Fred opened a bicycle shop there.

By August, 1914, Hartie and Frederick had four children: Fred, born in 1908, Win, born in 1909, Harold, born in 1911, and Edna, born in March,

1914. On August 4, 1914, England declared war on Germany. The First World War had begun. Hartie hardly had time to think what this would mean for them. In addition to having four small children to care for, her husband was ill with pneumonia. She had to take care of her children, nurse her husband, and try to run the shop as well. Frederick was getting worse. He needed to see a doctor, but there was a shortage of doctors, because so many had been called up for the war effort. Hartie managed to get Frederick to a hospital, but he never got to see a doctor. He died on 14 August 1914.

Hartie was 35 years old when her husband died. She had four small children, ranging in age from five months to six years. With no pension, or other income, how would she manage? Hartie was a strong woman, but she needed help. Her church came to her aid. Her landlord lowered the rent. Her neighbours helped her. So did her family. Her oldest sister, Em, who was married but never had any children, said she would take Winnie for a while. Her brother George, who was a schoolmaster, said he would take Freddie.

Frederick Rowswell, photo taken about 1900

Then Hartie's mother learned that Em and George were making plans to keep Win and Fred. They thought Hartie would not be able to care for all her

172

children. Susannah wrote to her daughter, "Whatever you do, don't let your children be split up." Hartie had no intention of letting her family be split up.

Since Hartie lived behind the shop, she could care for her children and run the shop too. She ran the shop for over twenty years, and raised her children herself. Sometimes, she would work until 11 o'clock at night, repairing bicycles or finishing other jobs. Then she would collapse on her bed and fall asleep in the clothes she had worn all day, too exhausted to take them off.

Hartie drew a lot of strength from her faith. Every Sunday she would take her children to church. It took a long time, when they were little, to get them all ready. They didn't always make it in time. When that happened, Hartie, pushing a pram and with her other children in tow, would walk around Romford until she found the Salvation Army band. Then she and her children would join them, and march around, cheerfully singing hymns as they went.

Arford Lodge in the 1900s, now Ivy Cottage, across the stream from Arford House

Although they didn't adopt Hartie's children, Em and George did help by taking them during the summer school holidays. Em took the girls. She lived in Datchett, near Windsor. George took the boys. He was now headmaster of Penner School, near Harrow. Sometimes the children would visit their cousins in Petersfield, and their grandparents in Midhurst. Fred sent his mother a postcard of 'Hindhead, Gibbet Cross', on 14 August 1916. He wrote, "Dear Mother, This is where we have been this afternoon. We have also seen the sailor's stone as well. We went to the Huts Hotel in a bus. Saw Ivy [his cousin] in the post office and then walked to the gibbet. Came back to the Cross Roads (or Huts Hotel) and came back in the bus. Love from Freddie." Three days later, on 17th August 1916, his grandmother, Susannah, died.

After Susannah died, William moved to Petersfield to be closer to his daughter, Anne. He would come by train to visit Hartie and his grand-children in Romford. He died in 1923. William Harnett is buried in Midhurst, alongside his wife, Susannah.

Hartie wanted her children to go on to grammar school, but school wasn't free then after the age of 12. Their only option was to earn a scholarship. All four children passed the exam. The headmistress of their elementary school was very impressed with Mrs Rowswell's children. She would tell people that Mrs Rowswell had four children who all earned a scholarship. Then she would add, "If Mrs Rowswell had ten children, they would all have earned a scholarship!"

By 1938, Hartie's children thought it was time to help their mother retire. A new chapter in Hartie's life would begin. Fred was now a language master at his old grammar school, and he liked to travel in Europe. In 1938 Fred took his mother on a trip to Switzerland with him. It was the first of many trips to Europe that Hartie made with Fred, who never married.

A year after that first trip, England would declare war on Germany, and all of Europe would be engulfed in war once again. In 1942, Hartie became a grandmother for the first time. Her oldest daughter, Winifred, gave birth to a baby girl. That baby was me. My grandmother had seven grandchildren altogether, and today there are nine great-grandchildren, six living in the United States, and three in England.

Harriett Rowswell died in 1965, at age 86. She is buried with her husband, Frederick Rowswell, in Romford Cemetery.

In researching my grandmother's story, I have been inspired by her. I have learned many things about her, including why she named her house 'Grayshott'.

Memories of Moor House Farm between the Wars

Edna Madeleine Morgan (née Hall)—written in 2002

Edna Madeleine Hall was born at 'Rooks Cottage' on the Churt Road and lived at 'Moor House Farm' (known at that time as 'Stream Farm') from 1923 until 1935.

John Azor Hall, my grandfather, had always rented farms but, although in 1923 he was only fifty-seven years old, he did not enjoy good health and was reliant on his three sons to cope with the heavy work of running the farm. His eldest son had remained at home during the First World War but his two younger sons had served with the forces. With two unmarried daughters still living at home and three married sons, each with one child, he needed a larger acreage for them all to get a reasonable living.

One property for sale in the area was just perfect for his requirements. It consisted of one hundred and thirty acres of arable land and water meadows —a fair stretch of the River Wey winding its way through lush grassland. There were cowsheds, stables and pigsties, a granary on staddle stones and various outbuildings.

The housing was even more ideal—one house and three adjoining cottages. He acquired a mortgage, and in September 1923 the family moved in. The farm was to have been a new beginning—but sadly, his illness worsened and in the following January he died.

During the 1920s and early 30s, making a living was difficult for people in all walks of life, and the farming community suffered considerably, often having to sell crops and livestock at a loss—no such luxuries as guaranteed prices and Government grants. However for we three children growing up in such idyllic surroundings life was fun and full of adventure.

My widowed grandmother continued to live in the 17th century parlour wing, which was always referred to by the family as 'Top End'. All the farm business was conducted by the three sons, Azor, Sidney and Stanley, in the kitchen where a huge roll-topped desk contained all the ledgers, invoices, receipts, etc.

The house was at that time divided into four—next to 'Top End' were three cottages, each with five rooms and a larder, occupied by the three brothers in order of their birth. The rooms at 'Top End' were larger and it had a front door which was never used. Mrs Hall senior worked and lived in

Edna's father Sidney Hall
walking between the woodsheds at Moor House Farm

the kitchen; the large back room was used only rarely, for family gatherings such as Harvest Suppers.

In those days all the water had to be drawn from a well *[as it still is today, but now by electric pump!]* and carried to the houses in buckets. The well was situated in the rick-yard outside the garden hedge. All the families had a woodshed halfway up the garden, and behind the woodsheds, discreetly screened by hedges, were the toilets. The 'bogs', as they were commonly known, were just buckets with a seat on top, housed in dark cobwebby shacks; and the door of ours never seemed to shut properly.

The General Strike of 1926 was a great talking point, but did not affect the family much as we always had home-grown vegetables available, and milk, eggs and poultry were plentiful, along with an abundance of rabbits.

During harvest time, anyone with a shotgun was welcome to shoot the rabbits both for sport and food. One particular occasion I remember well—a hundred and nine rabbits were shot from a ten acre field of oats. We carried them home on poles, and after everyone had taken all they could cope with, the remainder were sold to the local butcher for the handsome sum of fivepence each.

One uncle made 'bullets' from molten metal for his catapult—and many a pheasant dinner resulted from his accuracy! A keen fisherman, this uncle taught the children to fish with home-made fishing rods. They would catch roach, perch or occasionally a small trout. Freshwater crayfish were caught on wire mesh frames and, cooked alive like lobsters, they made a tasty meal.

Coal was usually used for the kitchen ranges as it gave a more constant heat, but during the strike wood was used instead, and that spring the mothers and children gathered wood for extra fuel.

The venue for 'wooding' was usually the Alder Bed. It was approached through the Little Meadow, a lovely tranquil place surrounded by trees and full of clover. Under one tree was a small dewpond and large green frogs could often be seen hopping about. The Alder Bed was wet and boggy, full of anemones, primroses and kingcups. In one place there was a spring where ice cold water bubbled out of clear sand and formed a small stream which wound its way down to the river. Part of the Alder Bed was considered too dangerous to set foot on—Delsey Hall (my aunt) remembered her parents telling her that a horse and cart had once disappeared in the bog—but the area was not fenced off.

At that time there was no electricity, and subsequently there were no milking machines. The cows were milked by hand and, when it was dark, hurricane lamps were hung in strategic places. In the dairy the milk was strained, cooled and strained again into the churns. The sterilising of the dairy was women's work, and my grandmother churned the butter.

Moor House Farm
*Above: Front showing 'Top End' on left and 2 of the 3 cottages
inhabited by the three sons and their families.
Below: Rear, with 'Top End' and its unused 'front' door to right.*

The milk was delivered to nearby village houses by ancient vehicles—I remember and old De Dion with a dickey seat being used—the milk being served from the churns in half-pint, pint and quart measures into the customers' jugs. My uncle Stan Hall had gained mechanical knowledge whilst serving with the Flying Corps during the First World War, and he kept the vehicles in working order.

Azor, the eldest son, ploughed the land using two of the three carthorses kept on the farm. A horse was also used to pull a horse hoe between the rows of turnips, swedes and mangolds. A colt was hitched to a cart which had seats, and the family would ride to the village or the more distant fields. My mother would take the grain by horse and cart to Headley Mill to be ground. Pigs were kept and, if cash was needed, they were the first animals to be sold off.

My maternal grandfather started a chicken enterprise in a field named 'Three Corners'. This field was only accessible through the 'Dipping Tank', which is an area up Smithfield Lane where at one time hop poles were dipped in hot tar to preserve them.

During the winter months there was always hedge trimming to be done, a laborious, time-consuming job; faggots to be cut and sold to the local baker for his bread oven; and, of course, endless 'ditching'. The water meadows were full of ditches and they had to be kept clean to avoid flooding. There was a weir on the river, but it was never used for flooding the meadows—natural floods were fairly frequent and to see the meadows turned to a huge lake was quite a sight. The houses and farm buildings were never in any danger as they were situated on higher ground.

Haymaking was much more enjoyable. The cut grass was turned, dried and raked into rows with the horse rake, then heaped into 'cocks' and taken by wagon to the rickyard and built into haystacks. The field perimeters were cut with a scythe and the sheaves were tied by hand. All available hands were expected to help stand the sheaves of corn into 'shocks' or 'stooks'. Harvest picnics were enjoyed by all in the hayfields. Later, the hayricks were skilfully thatched with straw by my father. How easy it is today to use a baling machine and cover with plastic sheeting.

In the autumn when the corn was dry, the threshing machine arrived. It was pulled by a steam engine along with a gypsy caravan—the two men who came with the machine lived in the caravan while the work was carried out. The grain was stored in the granary which was raised on staddle stones, supposedly to stop vermin getting to the grain, but somehow the rodents still managed to get in.

Some years the grain would remain in the granary for months—either there was no market for it at the time or the price was so awful it wasn't worth selling.

The farm was situated two and half miles from each of the three surrounding villages, Headley, Churt and Frensham. When my cousins and I started school, in Churt, our mothers walked with us the two and half miles on our first day, but after that we made our own way there and back. As there were no school meals, some children took sandwiches but I went to my maternal grandmother's house near the school for lunch. My grandmother was an intelligent woman who read the papers and liked to discuss politics. She kept up with the latest news listening to radio broadcasts through earphones on her crystal set.

'Top End' of Moor House farm from Frensham Lane

One summer an epidemic of diphtheria caused the death of several children in the district, so we three Hall children were kept off school and confined to the farm, since if one of us contracted the disease the retail milk round could have been affected.

The farming brothers rarely took a day off—they worked seven days a week, year in, year out. Our only visit to the seaside as children was the annual school outing to Bognor. Silent films were shown in the village hall near the school, and the cost of a ticket was minimal so occasionally we were permitted to go—a lady played music on the piano during the film, the more exciting the film, the faster the music was played. Mainly, we children entertained ourselves, playing on fallen trees or scrumping apples and plums from Grandmother's trees. On the 5th November a large bonfire was lit and neighbours would bring fireworks. The guy was made from old sacks.

Once a year the otter hounds would hunt the length of the river and the family would follow the hounds. There were large numbers of otters which were hunted to preserve the fish in the river. We never saw one caught, but I remember father shooting two one evening with a single cartridge. Such a killing nowadays would be considered a crime, the otter being a protected species.

A time came when the brothers held frequent evening meetings in 'Top End' —due to a serious cash crisis the retail milk round had to be sold. In future the milk would be taken in churns direct to the dairy which had purchased the round. Heavy tithe duties were no doubt due—a considerable sum had to be paid annually to the local Rector. I remember father telling me that in his grandfather's day, the Rectors had their own wagons and men to physically collect every tenth 'stook' in the cornfields, and store them in the tithe barns at their rectories. Farmhands would make sure every tenth 'stook' was a small one—and many a fight broke out if the Rector's wagons came into the field and went in the opposite direction to the 'arranged' route!

The farm had to be sold as the mortgage payments could not be met. Since the purchaser did not require the farm for his own use immediately, the brothers became tenant farmers for a while. However, after two years the owner decided to sell up, and in those days tenant farmers were not protected so notice to quit was given.

Our twelve years at the farm had meant hardship and misery to our fathers, and none of them were sorry to leave for 'pastures new', but to us children it was a terrible wrench. We walked the length of the river, and visited all our favourite haunts, taking our last sips of water from the ice cold spring in the Alder Bed, knowing we were going to miss it all. From our point of view, the beauty of the place had outweighed all its disadvantages and inconveniences.

Above: Mellow Farm.
Below: Huntingford Cottage and Forge.
Both pictures from the sales prospectus of January 1952

Early days at Mellow Farm

David Hadfield—written in 2002

It really started in 1952. I saw two or three farms before I came across Lower House Farm (as Mellow Farm was then called), which I think was in February. I wanted to be a dairy farmer; I *had* to be a dairy farmer because you got paid for your milk every month and I needed the income. At that time, all the farms around here had dairy herds. They weren't big; about 25 cows each. They all had them.

I came here when snow was on the ground and the house and the valley, which were very isolated or seemed to me to be so, looked perfect. We were welcomed by a Mr Sparey who was, had been, the batman for Brigadier Evans who lived at Wishanger. I suppose it just goes to show how life has changed, because Matthew Sparey had been with Brigadier Evans throughout the First World War in the trenches. They had been through hell together and had a great affection for each other, but although he had put water on for the cows he had not connected this house because he didn't think his erstwhile batman needed mains water; there was just the well and he recommended that if I ever wanted to make tea, the best water for that came from the river.

I bought it at auction at the Bush Hotel—Lower House Farm itself, 125 acres, the farm house and Huntingford Cottage for £11,250. I was signing the contract, and I hadn't actually signed when Brigadier Evans came up to me and said, "I hope you keep your ragwort down"—then someone else said, "£11,250! You'll never make a profit if you pay that much money".

Anyway, I bought it, and I set about the tremendous job of getting it running as an independent farm, separate from the Wishanger estate. There were commercial travellers in those days, who came—I suppose we must have had four or five a week—and, apart from the post and papers which were delivered every day, we had the laundry who came once a week; the Walls' ice cream man who came on Wednesdays at lunch time; a grocer, Kingham's of Farnham, who came on Monday to collect the order which would be delivered on Thursday. We also had a butcher who came, so we were well supplied.

The first thing to do was to get water in the house, which we did quite simply, and then to put in a bath, a loo, a Raeburn and a generator to provide electricity to milk the cows that we hoped eventually to buy. We applied for a grant, and in those days it was under the Alton District Council. The young man came and said, "Yes, you can get a grant to put in a bathroom and a lavatory, but I can't give it to you because this house is mainly made of wood and I have to sign a certificate to say that the house will still be standing in ten years time—and I can't do that; it's too old."

So I didn't get my grant, but I put it all to rights and then I employed a Mr Morgan, his wife and son, who was then about 7, and they lived in the house. Mr Morgan had been a policeman in London before going onto an agricultural school, and he and I first got rid of many of the poachers that were around, and then got round to cleaning up. This farm had been a dairy farm, but many of the cows had had tuberculosis and so everything had to be scrubbed and cleaned and painted and made ready for the herd.

At the same time, of course, we had a problem with Huntingford Cottage. The roof had fallen in and there was bracken growing in the sitting room. There was no water, no electricity of course, no bathroom, no loo and no cooking facilities; there was a ladder which went up from what had been the kitchen to the bedrooms. In those days we were only allowed to spend £250, and for that money I had the whole house re-roofed, bathroom put in, facilities for cooking, the fireplace built so it could be used, many of the walls plastered because the damp had got in, a new back door, the water connected and many other things—and I think I spent £275 to do all that and got into trouble for overspending the allowance.

Then Bill Grover came along wanting a job. I think he was recommended by his brother, another Mr Grover, who was the lengthsman. In 1952 there was a lengthsman who used to look after the road between the New Inn and the Frensham Pond Hotel. His job was the keep the drains beside the road open, and cut back various bits of hedge that might be growing over the road; he was also responsible for dealing with all the nests of wasps which might have bitten horses that were passing, and to cut back weeds beside the road. He would cut the weeds down once they had flowered and set seed so he was a very useful person to have around.

Anyway, Bill Grover came to me and he was about 76 then. He was retired and could only work for two days, otherwise it affected his old-age pension. He and I used to do a lot of work together, including hoeing kale and the sugar beet by hand. We had about 12 acres of that and it took quite a long time for the two of us to do it. I used to work like stink, but I could never keep up with old Bill Grover who used to get about 5 yards ahead, pause, light his pipe and then we'd talk about his life in which he had never been further than about 3 miles from here.

He'd worked on Headley Wood estate for all his life and the only time he ever left it was when they called him up and made him a stoker on a battleship at Scarpa Flow. He went to the Battle of Jutland. I asked him about the battle and he said he didn't know anything about it, apart from that he had to shovel faster! He came back from that and they decided that his place was on the land, so he came home again and I said, "Well Bill, you must have been to London, what did you think of that?" He replied, "I didn't think much of it. When I arrived at the station I took a taxi to Waterloo and came straight back."

He went to Farnham quite a bit because he and his wife used to walk the six miles there to whist drives. They would enjoy the whist drive and then walk back. He also told me, among many other things, how he saw his first motor car at the New Inn—and that the horse with a cart which he had loaded with coal was so terrified that it went into the ditch. He also reminded me of parties that were held after the First World War to welcome everyone home. Headley Park had its party under a cedar tree which stood in front of the house, and all the workers were there, but the people who lived in the house held posher parties down near a spring that used to be close to the river by Bayfields Farm. He also worked on altering the road by Headley Park for which a special Act of Parliament was passed. You can still see where road started to be dug into the bank, but it all came to an end on August 4th, 1914.

David Hadfield

Eventually, we got the place cleaned up and I bought a couple of short-horn cows. You don't see short-horns about now, but in those days they were much prized because they give both milk and meat. The first two cows weren't very much; I didn't have a great deal of money and so the first year we had a very mixed farm. We had oats, barley and a few pigs and some potatoes. The potatoes, of course, needed picking. We had a machine that spun them out of the ground and then people bent and picked them up and put them into sacks. To do that, I went to a family who lived on Arford Common and had to be interviewed by the grandmother. She asked me what I was going to pay and when I expected them to turn up and how long they would have for lunch. It was a good, long interview, and at the end she said her family would come. She was immobile herself, but the family came and we dug up all the potatoes and sold them.

The oats and barley were put into stacks and eventually the threshing machine came. There was only one threshing machine in the parish. In fact it went and did many parishes; Lynchmere and the other side of Liphook. It was owned by the Powell family. Since I was on my own I wasn't really expected to provide food for everyone. They all brought sandwiches, but it was quite a party because there was Mr Morgan, myself and about three people with the machine, and a terrier dog to pick up the rats—about seven of us in the end with this great big machine. I either had to sell the corn, or store it—I didn't have enough buildings, but I filled up the dining room with barley and it remained there until I got married some years later!

As for the pigs—well, there was Doris who was a sow and there were some to be fattened up. One became ill, and when I went down to do the milking one day, I found it had been slaughtered, butchered and hidden— ready for, as I since discovered, Mr Morgan to take to London. Well, he agreed that this wasn't quite on, and so he left. We have kept in touch ever since.

To take Mr Morgan's place, I had a herdsman who lived in Huntingford Cottage and I took on two land girls. One was called Angela and the other Marilyn. Marilyn was tremendous; she had been brought up in Burma and walked about in bare feet and very little else. She was quite a stunner and people used to come, really, just to see her. We used to have, on a regular basis, the OCTU from Aldershot, and one would find them in their army vehicles, parked in the yard. If they saw me they just asked the time, but if they saw Marilyn they passed the time!

Angela and Marilyn both got married. Marilyn also helped me with the hens because, to get income, we decided to keep hens both for eggs (layers) and to have capons which we would sell. I used to pluck them, she used to dress them and then I would sell them. One of the nice things about delivering the capons was when I delivered to the butler at the back door of a big house near here in the morning, and returned in the evening in my dinner jacket—in the morning he greeted me as David, but in the evening when he was also dressed up, he would greet me as Mr Hadfield!

Eventually I was made a JP, and shortly after that we had a tremendous fire here. It was arson; someone was seen on a motorbike in the yard before it went up. It was in September and all the harvest and silage had been gathered in. It burnt for 3 weeks and we had fire engines from as far away as Basingstoke, Aldershot, Farnham, Grayshott and maybe one or two other places. They changed over every three hours and used our kitchen as their mess room. It was quite an experience and a very costly one. We were insured, but of course we had to buy fresh in, in the winter, in very small quantities because we had no storage.

Then I got ill and had to go to hospital, but the farm was run very well by those left behind because one of the things I had organised right from the start of farming was that we had, and still have 50 years later, coffee at 10 o'clock where we look at the post and discuss what we need on the farm and the costs and where things come from—so everything went on as before.

It did, however, make me think about the future of small farms and I hatched a plan with three of my neighbours to form a co-operative which became known as Headley Farms. There was Tommy Whittaker, with a specialised pig unit with a lot of very poor land; there was me in the middle with my dairy herd; there was Sefton Myers at Headley Wood, also with light land; and there was Dick Barnsdale with his really good fattening land, next door to me in Dockenfield.

We hatched this plan so that the pig unit would stand alone but use the barley that we grew, and I and Sefton Myers, with our dairy herds, would provide enough animals for Dick Barnsdale to fatten on his really good fattening land and over-winter them on the poor land that Tommy Whittaker had at the Land of Nod. It was an ambitious scheme and it took a lot of legal advice. We even thought what would happen if one of us died because of Inheritance Tax. Anyway, it lasted for about three years and cut our costs very considerably and our output increased, but what we hadn't thought of was what happened if two of us died—and that is exactly what happened, so unfortunately it came to an end.

We built up the herd to 25 cows, but when we got to 25 we discovered that to make any money you had to have 40—and when we built up to 40 we found we had to have 75—so we got to 75, and then changed the breed from dairy short-horns to the Friesians which are now all over the country. Eventually, we got to 102 cows and my herdsman of 28 years, Fred, had reached the age of 67 and decided it was about time he retired.

Quotas then came in, and we would have had to get rid of many of our cows which would have made the thing unprofitable. So Fred retired, and I had done 37 years of getting up at 5.15 every morning, seven days a week, so probably I was tired as well—so the cows went. Then we had to think of diversification; what to do with the farm. When I came here I promised myself that I would never take out a hedge; that I would allow myself one building; that I would have electricity; and I would have one wife—and I did not specify to myself the order in which those came in. In fact my wife came before the electricity and we had just paraffin lamps, so she used to come down to the cow shed and beg me to get on with the milking so that she could cook the supper in the evening.

But when I was living alone here with paraffin lamps, I was something unusual. There were not many bachelor farmers living in such chaos, and frequently people would come on the way back from a party to show me off as this unfortunate individual. Frequently I was in bed, and would have to get up—and quite well-known people from abroad and all over the place would be shown this house with its paraffin lamps.

On one occasion I surprised some soldiers behind the barn, who were busy attacking or going to attack Bordon, or had got lost. It was a very cold night; I invited them in, and after a drink we loaded up the car with as many soldiers as we could get in (which was a quite a lot—it was truck actually) and all their weapons, and I took them to *The Cricketers* and told them that if they followed the electric cable they would find their way to Bordon—the electric cable being in the air, they could of course see it against the sky. What I didn't know was the enemy headquarters was also in *The Cricketers* and a Brigadier came out and lambasted me for not playing the game; it was against the rules.

We had quite a lot of trouble with poachers. You don't get them in quite the same way now. Poachers in those days were … well they probably needed the money. I can remember being rung up once by the butcher in Headley who said, could I provide him with a brace of pheasants urgently—and as I couldn't, he said he would have to ask this chap who also lived in Headley, who no doubt supplied him promptly. He was rather a nice man, this poacher, and one night he came to the house at about 2 o'clock in the morning and said he happened to be passing and was walking across the field—not poaching, you understand—and he came across one of the cows who was calving and badly needed attention, and so I got up and we both calved down this cow together.

On another occasion we had a lot of people poaching the fish. I let the fishing, and I had been asked to prosecute the next lot of people I found, so I got a policeman and we went into the field where there were four people poaching. The policeman knew the men well, and they were fairly violent—two ran off and he chased them, and I was left with another person, and I put my arm round him and lifted him off his feet slightly so he couldn't attack me, until the policeman came back. Later, much later, after the case had been tried, I met this man who eventually accused me of cracking his ribs—I met him in a queue in the local hardware store, and he was very friendly and said that he had had an awful lot of trouble with poachers himself recently; boys were trying to shoot his fish with an air rifle and he took exception to it.

In the days when we started, there was certainly a two-tier system. Brigadier Evans was always very friendly towards me. When he died his wife, who had been married before (her first husband was killed in the First World War and she had been a Gaiety Girl), invited us to tea at Wishanger. It was rather a polite tea and she said how she missed the olden days, the Edwardian days, because nowadays there was no-one in the locality to meet whereas when she came there were the Coombes who lived at Pierrepont, someone else at Frensham Heights and someone at Edgeborough, which is now a school, and so there were four of them who could meet and go to the races—but nowadays there was nobody. That's completely changed. Also what has changed is the fact that when I came here, to be a farmer was quite an honourable profession and there were many farmers in Headley—and now I can only think of four, and one is certainly at the bottom of the social pile. What the future is, I do not know. We are only allowed four beef animals and we have passports for each of them, and we have to remember their birthdays to alter the passport from one kind to another, and because we've kept the farm really as it was 50 years ago, the water company has taken advantage of that and we now have five bore-holes on the farm pumping out vast quantities of water for the public water supply.

Once I went with the Farnham branch of the NFU (it no longer exits because there aren't enough farmers) to see a Rex Patterson who farmed near Newbury. He was a very go-ahead farmer; he invented the buck rake, amongst other things, and he was telling us that he farmed his quite large farm for three years without paying any rent and without knowing who owned it. Nobody knew who owned it; everyone had forgotten who owned it in the late 1930s and it had just gone back to rabbits and scrub. He got rid of the rabbits and he got rid of the scrub and he set himself up as a dairy owner before the real owner came along and asked what was he doing there.

As I go round the countryside these days, I can see small fields being given up and it won't be long before bigger fields are given up as well, and maybe farming will be concentrated in those counties that have large fields and can take a combine harvester, because the days of mixed farming that I started with have definitely come to an end. One couldn't get the machinery into the fields and one would be producing in too small a quantity. Anyway, it's 50 years that I've been here now, which must be a record for this farm because people died much younger in olden days.

William Cobbett's experience in Headley
Sunday 24th November 1822

William Cobbett (1763–1835) was born in Farnham, Surrey, the son of a small farmer. In 1802 he started his weekly Cobbett's Political Register *which, with a three-month break, in 1817, continued until his death. His celebrated* Rural Rides *(first published 1830) were reprinted from the* Register.

Taking up the story of William Cobbett getting lost on his way from Headley to Thursley on Sunday 24th November 1822 as mentioned in *Headley 1066–1966* (see p.56), it is interesting to consider which path his guide may have taken.

Cobbett continues his story as follows:—

When, therefore, I had got some cold bacon and bread, and some milk, I began to feel ashamed of stopping short of my plan, especially after having so heroically persevered in the 'stern path,' and so disdainfully scorned to go over Hindhead. I knew that my road lay through a hamlet called *Churt,* where they grow such fine *bennet-grass* seed. There was a *moon*; but there was also a *hazy rain.* I had heaths to go over, and I might go into quags. Wishing to execute my plan, however, I, at last, brought myself to quit a very comfortable turf-fire, and to set off in the rain, having bargained to give a man three shillings to guide me out to the Northern *foot of Hindhead.* I took care to ascertain, that my guide *knew the road perfectly well;* that is to say, I took care to ascertain it as far as I could, which was, indeed, no farther than his word would go. Off we set, the guide mounted on his own or master's horse, and with a white smock frock, which enabled us to see him clearly. We trotted on pretty fast for about half an hour; and I perceived, not without some surprise, that the rain, which I knew to be coming from the South, met me full in the face, when it ought, according to my reckoning, to have beat upon my right cheek. I called to the guide repeatedly to ask him if he was *sure that he was right,* to which he always answered 'Oh! yes, Sir, I know the road.' I did not like this, '*I know the road.*' At last, after going about six miles in nearly a Southern direction, the guide turned short to the left. That brought the rain upon my right cheek, and, though I could not very well account for the long stretch to the South, I thought, that, at any rate, we were now in the right track; and, after going about a mile in this new direction, I began to ask the guide *how much further we had to go*; for, I had got a pretty good soaking, and was rather impatient to see the foot of Hindhead. Just at this time, in raising my head and looking forward as I spoke to the guide, what should I see, but a long, high, and steep *hanger* arising before us, the

190

trees along the top of which I could easily distinguish! The fact was, we were just getting to the outside of the heath, and were on the brow of a steep hill, which faced this hanging wood. The guide had began to descend; and I had called to him to stop; for the hill was so steep, that, rain as it did and wet as my saddle must be, I got off my horse in order to walk down. But, now behold, the fellow discovered, that he *had lost his way!*—Where we were I could not even *guess.* There was but one remedy, and that was to *get back* if we could. I became guide now; and did as Mr Western is advising the Ministers to do, retraced my steps. We went back about half the way that we had come, when we saw two men, who showed us the way that we ought to go. At the end of about a mile, we fortunately found the turnpike-road; not, indeed, at the foot, but on the *tip-top* of that very Hindhead, on which I had so repeatedly vowed I would not go! We came out on the turnpike some hundred yards on the Liphook side of the buildings called *the Hut.*

It seems that Cobbett's estimates of distance in this extract are unlikely to be accurate. For example, it is hardly possible to go 'about six miles in a nearly Southerly direction' from Headley without first meeting the turnpike-road, as it passed through Liphook which is only about half that distance away.

What seems more likely is that when they were as he says 'just getting to the outside of the heath, and were on the brow of a steep hill', they had in fact arrived at some part of the valley in which Waggoners Wells are situated. This would involve riding about two and a quarter miles south east from the *Holly Bush.*

From there one assumes that they back-tracked across what is now Ludshott Common before taking directions to the old road which ran across the common from Bramshott to Hindhead (now Headley Road through Grayshott) which emerges, as now, 'some hundred yards on the Liphook side of the buildings called *the Hut'*.

See map of 1776 on following page

191

192

Local Map of 1776

We can try to follow Cobbett's route on the map shown on the facing page, for which we have a date of 1776. This predates the Ordnance Survey and shows some glaring errors as well as some interesting versions of place names. *[Map supplied by Sue Allden]*

Headley and Thursley are both clearly shown, as is the obvious connecting road through Hern(e) and Churt (Charte). Waggoners Wells are shown as one lake (Pond) on the other side of Ludshott (Lidshot). The road from Bramshott through Ludshott is shown meeting the road which crosses the ford at the top of Waggoners Wells—we believe, on the evidence of other maps, that it continued through what is now Grayshott village and met the turnpike (shown prominently as parallel dotted lines) as it does today, a hundred yards or so below Hindhead.

Surprisingly, perhaps, Headley is spelt as we spell it now. However, note the following:—

- Badge Bridge = Bageants Bridge
- Picked Hill = Picketts Hill
- Sandhouse Green = Saunders Green
- Charte = Churt

We also find a Droxford Bridge—could this be the name of the bridge over the Slea by Trottsford Farm? Or is it a corruption of Brockford Bridge or even Trottsford Bridge?

Note that the River Slea is marked as the Wey River at Kingsley; also that there is a Boundstone Bottom where Bordon is now—and what is 'Lipput' near Hollywater?

There is a strange stream which appears to flow from Gentles Copse through Hilland and Arford down to the river—I assume this is supposed to be the stream down Fullers Vale but in the wrong place!

However, it is interesting to see where the routes of communication went in those days, however approximately they are shown here. There is, for example, no road where the A325 is today.

Extract from the Diary of Mabel Hussey

August 1940 – July 1941

Miss Mabel Hussey was a long-serving teacher at the Holme School in Headley. She is thought to have started at the school in the early 1920s and taught there until immediately after the Second World War.

On Friday 2nd August 1940 she writes on the first page of a chunky black-covered notebook: "Closed school for a curtailed summer holiday of two weeks, owing to the war. Decided to keep a diary".

This diary was passed to the Headley Archives by the executors of Elsie Watkins, also a teacher at the Holme, whose mother was a friend of 'Mabs' Hussey.

Although she kept the diary for no more than a year, it covers an interesting period from August 1940 to July 1941 when the area around Headley was being subjected to air-raids and the population was getting to terms with the onset of rationing.

In the extracts below we reprint some of the entries which give a flavour of wartime life in the village.

1940 —

Sun 18th Aug – Returned to Headley this evening after an exciting day— siren nearly spoiled our dinner midday. Norah nearly missed her 'canning' expedition. What a whirlwind of a day. Discovered Bordon had been bombed during my absence—a few casualties, among them poor old Mrs Chandler, where I used to leave my bike for so many years when I was week-ending and returning on the Mon morning—quite upset me. Mrs C had spent nearly the whole Friday in the dug-out, which Mr C made in his week's holiday.

Mon 19th Aug – It would happen to me. Miss Barrow sends a telegram to say she will be away from school—that means I have had her squad of 25 as well as my 50 today. There's a doctor's certificate to say she'll be away a week or two. Feel fed up about it, as we may not get extra help.

Tue 20th Aug – Enemy aircraft overhead during afternoon playtime. I had to dive into school shelters with two classes. Luckily we were soon out again.

Wed 21st Aug – Siren went this afternoon—in the shelters again. What a life!!

Thu 22nd Aug – A supply teacher from Basingstoke arrived at 3 this afternoon. It didn't take me long to hand over her class to her!

Fri 23rd Aug – Hot 'fireworks' display drove us to our dug-out last night, about midnight. So much continuous banging we began to wonder the cause—it appears to have been an ammunition train out the other side of Guildford. Jerry managed to get a truck or two, but the bulk was saved. We had visions of an enemy landing. Went to 'Sherwood' for the weekend to pick up more plums and the rest of my belongings left behind last weekend. *[Somewhere near Reading, where her family lived]*

Sat 24th Aug – Had intended buying a pair of shoes in Reading in case prices soar—but decided to invest in a pair of slacks instead—one needs them these days with the nightly trips to the dugout! Bought dark brown corduroy.

Sun 25th Aug – Arrived back here about 9—the plums were a dead weight—they nearly broke my back—but everybody was thrilled with them.

Mon 26th Aug – Played a game of singles with a Mrs Yeo this evening. I've had some nice games with her since she's evacuated herself from Portsmouth. Siren went just as we were sitting down to lunch—had to leave it and race back to school. Siren went at tea time—departed to our dugout with our cups of tea in our hands—stayed there ½ hour. Siren went again at 9.30—we finished our supper—nothing seemed to happen—many enemy planes making for London. Decided to go to bed. 'All Clear' signal didn't go till 3.30 making it a six-hour alarm—we were glad we went to bed.

Wed 28th Aug – Miss Brunton, my half section, came rushing into my room at 3 o'clock this morning—very distressed—quite sure Jerry was delivering a gas attack. She'd heard strange thuds and on looking out of the window saw gas. She was quite convinced that's what it was till I assured her it was 'mist'. This caused much amusement all round today, especially as I had to restrain her from wearing her gas mask.

Fri 29th Aug – Siren went at 11.45am—marshalled our charges to the dugouts—remained there for an hour. School reopened at 2 instead of 1.30. Stevey, our Assistant Master, went to Portsmouth for his medical today—passed Grade 1, and is down for the Air Force. *[Weston Stevens, who married Joyce Suter in April 1942 but was tragically killed in Service soon afterwards]*

Mon 1st Sep – Siren went at 5.15pm just as I was going off to Headley Down—had to postpone my trip—played tennis instead later on.

Fri 5th Sep – Siren went at 9.45am—no-one in school heard it—postman shouted to me through the window—lasted till 10.15. Again at 1.15, just in time to prevent me from going back to school.

Sat 6th Sep – Siren went while in bath last night—things seemed a bit 'peppery' so decided to follow the others to the dugout—rather scantily clad as I had to leave in a hurry. Quite a hectic night—bombs dropping all round—great display of 'fireworks' a long way off in a southerly direction. Siren went again at 2am while we were waiting for the 'all clear' to go—what a shock we got!! Finally went to bed at 3 during a lull in operations. Just as well as the siren didn't go till 5.

Mon 8th Sep – No Sunday paper yesterday owing to the raid on London. None again today. Siren went about 5.30—we actually saw enemy planes overhead in a 'dog fight', Spitfires intercepting them. We thought it advisable to take shelter. Four enemy planes brought down round these parts. Siren went again at 9, but we went to bed. 'All clear' didn't go till 4am. I never heard it.

Tue 9th Sep – Siren went at 9.15am—again at 5.30 and 8.30. Did the only sensible thing—went to bed and slept. Woke up at 2 to hear many planes overhead—but didn't hear the 'all clear' at 4.30. Weather suddenly turned colder.

Teachers at the Holme School (Mabel Hussey, sits second from right)

Wed 10th Sep – Siren went at 10.45am—lasted till 11.45—so not much work done. Siren went again at 3.45—what a rotten time, just as we were ready to close school—had to stay in the shelters till 5 o'clock. Did I enjoy my cup of tea? I'll say I did. Siren went at 5.30—short duration—again at 8.30 we were anticipating, but nothing doing at present (10.30) although we've heard a Jerry about. All the other have gone to bed so I'll follow suit. Bought some nigger-brown corduroy slacks when in Reading one weekend—put them ready each night with other stuff I take down in the dugout—just in case. Feel I have a slight cold about me—hopping out of that hot bath the other night, I guess.

Tue 17th Sep – Severe gale last night resulted in a balloon (barrage) breaking away from its moorings—possibly from Southampton. Put the electric light etc out of order—tore down the wires in the next village to Bordon—what a beano! Upset all the cooking arrangements and no wireless news. Mr C managed to put it right by 6 o'clock, just in time for the news.

Wed 18th Sep – Siren went at suppertime last night. Waves of enemy planes passed overhead—but heard no bombs—so eventually went to bed. 'All clear' signal went at 1.45 but didn't hear it—usually it doesn't sound till much later. Siren went again on our way to school this afternoon. We were in the shelters ½ hour. I've had several new children recently, bombed out of London I presume. Number on register 48—far too many.

Sun 29th Sep – Very disturbed night—bombs dropping all round. Miss B was away and the others didn't hear it.

Mon 30th Sep – Spent a very restless night—bombs dropping all round again—didn't go to bed till 2 o'clock. Terrific explosions took place at 1— we hurried to the dugout. I hadn't time to get into my slacks.

Tue 1st Oct – 'Fireworks' again last night, but not quite so close.

Tue 8th Oct – 75 incendiary bombs were dropped on Grayshott Common last night. Mr C woke up and saw the flares. Today he had to explore that part for damaged wires, etc—I brought home some of the pieces—evidently one of Hitler's 'bread baskets'.

Tue 15th Oct – Heard from Miss Letchford who used to teach at Headley School—retired 4 years ago and is now back in the Liphook district. She wants to meet me some time.

Sat 19 Oct – Met Miss Letchford at Grayshott and walked to Hindhead. I thought we might pay a visit to Haslemere pictures but she wanted to be home before dark, so it was a short but very enjoyable meeting. Country-side looking very lovely with its Autumn colourings—had see at the 'Golden Hind'—reached home about 6.30, so went along to Table Tennis in the evening.

Sun 20 Oct – Cycled to Liphook just after 1 o'clock after an early lunch— Miss L and I went for a two hours' tramp—had a lovely walk—back to her house to tea—reached home before lighting-up time.

Mon 4th Nov – Re-opening of school—minus two teachers. Stevey absent owing to visit to Oxford—exam for Air Force (pilot). Miss B not returning till after her brother's funeral. Our Head had a narrow escape while passing through Watford—Air Raid—25 incendiary bombs—spent night in hospital as a casualty.

Tue 5th Nov – Miss B returned at 4pm.

Fri 15th Nov – Enemy planes over all night—rather disturbing—no sleep for any of us—learned today big attack on Coventry—many casualties and much destruction.

Sat 16th Nov – Rotten wet day but went to Grayshott for some wool— supposed to meet Miss Letchford for tea at Hindhead, but she failed to turn up.

Mon 18th Nov – One foot of water in our shelters at school—unable to use them. Luckily we've had no sirens in the day-time—extreme wet weather the cause of it.

Tue 19th Nov – Our dugout is a young pond.

Wed 20th Nov – My equipment (on going to bed) in case of a hurried rush in the middle of the night consisted of my corduroy slacks, turned back to knee-length just ready to pop on—they look queer. I don't possess wellingtons and didn't want to get my trousers wet!! Hundreds of planes were going over from 6.30 to midnight—luckily no bombs dropped here—so no rush to the dugout. Baled out dozens of buckets of water from the dugout when we came home from school today.

Sat 28th Dec – My birthday.

1941 —

Sun 5th Jan – Returned to Headley.

Mon 6th Jan – Miss Brunton not returned—no news of her—no letter or wire.

Tue 7th Jan – Letter arrives to say Miss B is ill—doctor's certificate.

Mon 13th Jan – My usual luck—Miss Barrow away ill—I have her class to cope with—number on both registers 90 children.

Tue 14th Jan – Feeling somewhat irritable with such a big class.

Wed 15th Jan – Weather bad—frost and snow. Miss B and Miss B both still away—Mrs Maloney going home to bed—looks lively for tomorrow.

Thu 16th Jan – Arrived at school to find I'm the only member of staff to turn up. The Head ill in bed. Rector sends word to close the school for the rest of the week—so two days holiday. Jolly glad to get rid of my 90—for a spell.

Mon 20th Jan – All staff back at work.

Sun 26th Jan – Spent weekend indoors—weather miserably wet and foggy. Seem to have started smoking again—only just realised it.

Sat 1st Feb – Went into Farnham—saw 'The Great Dictator', quite enjoyed it—bought a pretty knitting bag—about time—also a new umbrella.

Sun 16th Feb – Things keeping very quiet still—nothing of any importance to relate. I have spent most of my spare time reading and knitting. Am making a pair of socks—Air Force blue—for Mrs C's brother.

Sat 22nd March – *[Away from Headley]* Severe cold in head—stiff neck etc—couldn't move in bed—Norah has vision of mastoid—rings up doctor—a form of muscular rheumatism—get a medical certificate.

Mon 31st March – Returned to Headley.

Tue 8th Apr – Had the misfortune to break off a tooth at breakfast time—luckily not in the front. New Budget taxes—pretty big increase in Income tax—this would happen after taking out an Insurance (a War Bond £100) connected with Alton's War Weapon week. This will be a drain on my cheque each month—but daresay I'll survive it.

Wed 9th Apr – Leaving tomorrow for Easter Holiday. Only getting a long weekend this year—our week's holiday to come at end of April. Terribly cold weather again—had thought of buying a Spring costume, but weather not very encouraging.

Tue 15th Apr – Had a visit from the Prudential Insurance Inspector. Took out a War Bond to aid Alton's War Weapons Week. Shall be stony broke —broke each month now.

Fri 25th Apr – Start of my week's holiday (instead of Easter week). Wore my new woollen frock made by Mrs Cleare.

Mon 5th May—Started tennis in Headley—weather very cold still.

Mon 12th May – Managers meeting at school—chief item being the over-crowding due to so many children (some evacuees). Some talk of an extra teacher on the Staff—hope so anyway—give me a breather, perhaps!!

Thu 22nd May – Inclined to rain this evening so no tennis.

Sun 1st June – What a bombshell in the papers!—clothes rationing!!! Got my leg well pulled for not buying anything *[while visiting Reading]* yesterday, being in need of many things. It was a great surprise to us and the secret had been well kept—everybody talking and counting in 'coupons'.

Tue 3rd June – A visit from our Drill Inspectress—seemed thrilled with my squad—so much so that another teacher was invited out to watch.

Sat 7th June – Took a trip into Aldershot with Miss B who wanted a new coat. 14 coupons went in one go (out of 26).

Fri 27th June – Closed down for summer holiday of three weeks.

Sat 28th June – Grand weather—wearing brown shorts—sun bathing—played tennis.

Sun 29th June – Heat terrific.

Thu 3rd July – Trip to Reading—saw 'Virginia', a lovely coloured film—still no shopping—waiting for a drop in the 'coupons'—badly in need of sandals but don't want to part with 5 coupons.

Tue 8th July – Really did shopping in reading. Bought two dresses—5 coupons for a bluish cotton dress and 7 for a more expensive one (claret and white), and 5 coupons for some nice Coolie sandals—so bang goes 17 out of my 26 coupons!!

Wed 9th July – Saw 'Philadelphia Story' (K. Hepburn) and enjoyed it very much.

Sat 12th July – Mater celebrated her 80th birthday—doing a Highland jig with Jane in the lounge!!

Sat 19th July – Saw 'Comrade X' (Clark Gable and Margaret Sullivan)—quite good. This finishes our little stints to the pictures. Raspberry season very disappointing—too dry.

Sun 20th July – Returned to Headley—arrived at Bordon 10.20. Some drunken Canadian vomited all over me in the bus—so the end of a perfect holiday.

Perambulation of the Bounds of Headley Parish in the year 1890

with [corrections from 1895] and {additions in 1919}

1. A cross and stone, E. of the road from Sleaford to Greatham [Bordon Camp to White Hill], about 4 chains E. of the stone (W.D., No.24) which is at the S. apex of the Government triangular piece; the cross and stone being on the S. side of the driftway.

2. Thence, in a straight line very nearly S.E., to a point in Mr Lemon's S. hedge, about 8 chains from the Deadwater and Walldown road.

3. Thence, in the same straight line, to a point in Lady Erle's S. hedge about 3 chains from the same road; a cross being made on the S. side of the hedge in Mr Lemon's firs.

4. Thence, in the same straight line, through Mr Lemon's firs and across the road, to a cross by the roadside, 1 rod from the S. fence of Mr Chalcraft's piece.

5. Thence, in the same straight line, to a point in this S. fence 2 rod from the road.

6. Thence, in the same straight line, to a cross on Walldown just to the right of the clump.

7. Thence, in the same straight line, between Mr Dixon's two buildings.

8. Thence, in the same straight line, to White Hill cross on the S. side of the road, opposite the E. end of Mr Lawrence's house.

9. Thence, in the same straight line, to a cross by 1 oak in Headley and 13 oaks in Selborne [an oak in Headley, there being 13 oaks in Selborne] on the N. side of and near to another road leading to Hollywater Village.

10. Thence, slightly curving to the E., to a cross on the S. side of this road about 3 chains from the N.W. corner of Mr Fisher's ground.

11. Thence, on the same curve, to a point in Mr Fisher's W. hedge 9 rod from the same corner.

12. Thence, on the same curve, to where "Eade's chimney" was.

13. Thence E. through a big stump to the stream at the bottom of the field, where the more Northern of the two water-courses runs in.

14. Thence in the same straight line to the S. corner of a fuel shed belonging to Mr Huntingford; cutting off a very small piece of Mr Greenaway's plot.

15. Thence, still in a straight line, across the road to the corner of the hedge

on the N. side of the road.

16. Thence in the same straight line along the bottom of a ditch to another road.
17. Thence in the same line, and 25 feet from the hedge [ditch], to where the bank again projects.
18. Thence up the common, 3 feet from the bank, right up to the Farnham and Liphook road, and across the road with the drain.
19. Thence, up the S. side of the hedges to Westlands.
20. Thence in the same direction down the watercourse on the W. side of Westlands.
21. Thence in the same direction, 20 paces, to the head of the old course, thence down the course to the hedge, taking in one paine, and down the centre of the course to the river.
22. Thence across the river nearly in the direction of an oak tree, and across the meadow between the streams to where the rails were.
23. Thence E. (after crossing the stream) up to Mr Warren's road; by a course, and then 12 paces.
24. Thence across the road, and up the S. side of the hedge of several fields (one meadow and four fields) to the pond opposite Mr Tilbury's.
25. Thence, without going into the pond, up the W. side of the road to the corner of the hedge opposite the limekiln, [noting on the green the cross showing where James Luke Hack was killed].
26. Thence across to the E. side of the road, and up the E. (and afterwards S.) side of the road to Golden Cross, (sometimes called Reden's Corner) by a gate leading into what was Little Common.
27. Thence through the gate up by the S. hedge of what was Little Common, this S. hedge being out of the parish, (crossing a new hedge after a while, so as always to keep to the S. side of Little Common,) to Hurland's Cross on the road leading to Bramshott; Hurland's Cross being about 21 [25½] rod S. of where the above "new hedge" strikes this road.
28. Thence across the road to the end of the stone wall opposite, and N. up that wall, and (through the gate) round by the N. hedge of Gentel's coppice, (keeping to the N. of the hedge), to a stone at the head of Fuller's Bottom road. {Stone gone in 1919 but will be replaced by Trust}
29. Thence, crossing the road at right angles, to a point about 5 chains up the bank, noting an old mound and cross 2½ chains up. [The small pieces outside the bank here and in Nos. 31 & 32 are supposed to have been left so as to give access to the common. The boundary in 29, 31 & 32 is taken from the Inclosure Map.] {Cross and mound re-cut 1919}
30. Thence, up the E. side of the bank, nearly to the top of the hill to within about 5 chains of a tree on the bank where the bank bends. {National

Trust stump and cross found 1919}

31. Thence, leaving the bank, to a cross 1 chain to the S.W. of the tree in a line with that part of the bank which is to the N.E of that tree. {Cross not found in 1919}

32. Thence, in about the same direction, to a cross which is 12 paces to the right of the tree. {Cross renewed 1919}

{33 to 36 The Military trenches made during the Great War have obliterated the old marks}

33. Thence, in about the same direction, up a sort of little hollow, 100 paces to a cross.

34. Thence, in a straight line (which produced backward would meet the bank 39 feet N.E. of the tree of No.30) 150 paces to a stone on a mound, set with its point uppermost. [see below]

35. Thence in about the same direction, another 150 paces, to a cross and stone at the beginning of a ditch and bank.
[1835 correction to cover both 34 & 35: Thence in a straight line, some 300 paces, to a cross and stone at the beginning of a ditch and bank.]

36. Thence up the bank to a cross which is just beyond where a road crosses the bank.

37. Thence, up the bank to the bend, 20 paces from the road, where the road into the manor should be.

38. Thence, up the bank some 2½ chains, to a cross a little beyond the existing wrong road into the manor.

Note: the Proposed Boundary with Grayshott diverges here to rejoin at 67.

39. Thence, still up the bank, some 400 paces or thereabouts, to a cross W. by S. of Greyshott Hall.

40. Thence, [just] across the road into the manor, to a cross some 2 rod from Greyshott Hall bank [now levelled].

41. Thence, by some crosses from 2 to 4 rod from Greyshott Hall bank, to the cross and stone and thornbush W. of where the firs were.

42. Thence, in about the same direction into the enclosure, (passing in about 1½ rod N. of the point), and by a cross to the curved bank.
[1835 correction to cover both 41 & 42: Thence (for the most part up a little hollow, some 2 rod from the old bank) about 105 paces, to a cross; and on to the end of a deeper hollow which is a chain from the Hall bank and is near where the bank bends to the E.; thence in a straight line about 9 rod to a point a chain from the bank (cross not found in 1895); and thence in a straight line to the S.W. point of the acre inclosure near Mr Woodthorpe's house.]

43. Thence, round by the curved bank, to the road.

44. Thence, down the W. side of the road to Wagner's Pond head.

45. Thence, by the stream, to the ram, and afterwards where the stream runs, ie. up the lowest land.

46. Thence through the penstocks. Note: sluices.
47. Thence in the ditch on the N. side of the road, below Mr Vertue's property, up to the further end of 1282 on the Ordnance map.
48. Thence up the middle of the road as far as Miss I'Anson's land goes [to the hedge on the east of Miss I'Anson's field].
49. Thence to a point in the S. hedge of the road 20 paces up.
50. Thence up the new fence passing through the W. gate post, to a point in the W. hedge of Morrey's land.
51. Thence to the E. hedge passing about 1 rod from the front of the house.
52. Thence again up the centre of the road.
53. Thence diagonally through the middle of the small field belonging to Mr Mowatt, striking it at the new fence.
54. Thence out into the road about 2 chains up, and up the S. hedge of the road to Wagner's Wells Bottom head, at the corner of the hedge by the apple tree.
55. Thence nearly N. across the mouths of the two roads to a cross at the bend of the bank not far from the pathway.
56. Thence in a straight line parallel to the direction of this path to the Greyshott and Hindhead road [the whole of the Boundary Road being in Headley Parish].
57. Thence, crossing this road, in the same straight line to a bank which meets the N. side of the road.
58. Thence, down the W. of this bank and 3 feet from its top, to the head of Whitmore bottom, a distance of some 7¾ chains.
59. Thence down the S. of the bank; taking the S. hedge where there are two parallel hedges.
60. Thence down the centre of the bottom.
61. Thence through the pond and over the hedge and down to the end of the centre hedge.
62. Thence [up the low land] to where the pond is on the other side of the further hedge.
63. Thence, over the hedge and through the pond, and down the lowest land of the meadow to a point in the S. bank a chain from the W. bank.
64. Thence through the S. hedge cutting off a small piece of Lord Sackville Cecil's [Mr Leuchars'] meadow.
65. Thence over the hedge and along the S. side of the hedge.
66. Thence across the hedge of the next field where the stream crosses it, and down the centre of the bottom to meet the stream.
67. Thence, along the stream to [the fish bar above] Barford Upper Mill Pond; [thence along the centre of the meadow into the Pond; (but excluding a piece of pasture on the West)].
68. Thence through the centre of this Pond to a cross at the head.
69. Thence, through the cottage under the chimney, [two bedrooms of the

cottage being in Headley Parish,] and by the front of the other cottages to again meet the stream.

70. Thence, by the stream, to the lowest pond.
71. Thence, through the pond and by the E. side of all the buildings, and therefore by the W. side of the road, to again meet the stream.
72. Thence, by the stream, to Frensham Pond; [but following the Ordnance Map at Simmondstones].
73. Thence through Frensham Pond, as on the Ordnance Map, to the sluice which is some 4½ chains from the N.W. corner of the White Horse Inn.
74. Thence through Beale's mead down the centre of the stream to the centre of the river (the island at this point being in Dockenfield).
75. Thence (passing through the rushes on the Headley side of the island, from 3 to 5 yards from the island) up the centre of the river in Mr Whitaker's meadow called Little Moor.
76. Thence, leaving the river near the beginning of Wishanger mead, at a point in the river in a line with the ash tree and stone, straight to the ash tree and up a drain to the stone.
77. Thence N.N.W. to the river.
78. Thence again up the central line of the river, passing by the same and another of Mr Whitaker's meadows.
79. Thence into Lower Stream mead all up the middle of the river, to a point in the mead W.S.W. of a gateway in the mead, and E.N.E. of a gate in the opposite meadow belonging to Mr Watts.
80. Thence across the river to this latter gate.
81. Thence W.S.W. up a ditch by the side of the road to the end of the field.
82. Thence across the road diagonally in a N.W.ly direction where the old hedge was.
83. Thence nearly N. up the E. side of Mr Watts' field (and therefore to the W. of the plantation); the boundary being the ditch in the plantation.
84. Thence, still outside the field, S.W. down the other side of the same field to the gate and road; the ditch being the boundary.
85. Thence S. up the road to the S.W. corner of Mr Watts' field.
86. Thence across the road and over the hedge in a line with Mr Watts' S. fence.
87. Thence in nearly the same direction across Rock field to a mark in the field near the further corner, 50 yards from the W. hedge and 40 yards from the N. hedge.
88. Thence N.W. [parallel to the West hedge] to this last hedge.
89. Thence in the same direction, over the five-acre field to the junction of 2 hedges, and over the hedge.
90. Thence, nearly in the same direction, up the S.W. side of the hedge of the seven-acre field (anciently Rack field) to the edge of the hedge: i.e. to the corner S.W. of the cottage.

91. Thence round the same field, by 2 short hedges, to a corner.
92. Thence W. (but over the hedge at the corner) still round the seven acres.
93. Thence by the N.W. hedge inside of Long meadow (anciently Holt mead).
94. Thence by the S.W. hedge half-way down the meadow to a stone by an ash stem nearly opposite (i.e. S.W. of) the corner of the seven-acres.
95. Thence W. across Cradle Lane field to a drain which [a point where a drain] crosses Cradle Lane.
96. Thence down the N.E. side of the road to the middle of the river (noticing a boundstone, near the river, a short rod from it, just inside the hedge of Cradle Lane field).
97. Thence up the river to a cross, showing where the river originally ran; the cross being S.S.E. of two gates in the opposite meadow [in the S.W. corner of the bend.]; and 110 paces from the rails on the W. of the meadow.
98. Thence up this old river bed, round an old tree, about 60 paces in all again to the river; (all this being in Bajeant's [Baigeant's] meadow).
99. Thence up the river to the bridge on the road between Trottsford and Groome's farm.
100. Thence still up the river to where the Holt stream runs in. [It is better to go the N. side]
101. Thence N. and W. up the Holt stream ([over which there is a bridge]) about 100 paces.
102. Thence, leaving the stream, W. up the ditch to the stile on the Farnham road.
103. Thence in the same direction across the road.
104. Thence up the ditch in the same direction about 13 paces[: viz, in a line between the bridge and the oak tree].
105. Thence S.W. to the E. end of the pond[: so as to strike No. 106].
106. Thence W. through the pond and up the central ditch of Beggar's mead, some 11¾ chains from the E. end of the pond, to a point about 40 feet beyond a hedge new since the Ordnance survey.
107. Thence S. by E. up a little ditch almost obliterated, 138 feet to a point in the S. hedge of Beggar's mead, 24 feet from the corner.
108. Thence on in about the same direction across the next field to a boundary post by the hedge, some 15 rod W. of the main road.
109. Thence down the ditch to the road.
110. Thence across the road and down the ditch [and in the same direction] to the river [i.e. leaving the ditch at the bottom].
111. Thence up the river to Sleaford bridge on the Alton road.
112. Thence under the Southern arch of this Sleaford bridge (noticing the boundary-stone fixed in the bridge on its W. face).
113. Thence, leaving the river, about 43 paces up the water-course which lies

to the S. of the river.

114. Thence along a straight line between the most Southern elm tree on the road-side hedge of the meadow and 9 or 10 withies on the bank of the river (about N.W. by W.), to the said withies, treading in about ¾-acre between Nos. 113 and 114 and the river.

115. Thence up the river round Sleaford meadows to the further (the W.) end of the 2nd meadow.

116. Thence S., 2 chains, towards the Forest stream.

117. Thence up the S.E. or E. side of Mr James Gardener's hedge as far as Oxney stile.

118. Thence, still under the bank, 4 chains.

119. Thence, nearly due S., out into the middle of Oxney marsh.

Oxney Pond around 1900

120. Thence up the centre of the ponds and marsh, about 5 furlongs to where two banks project out into the marsh, one from each side, in a straight line with one another. (That on the W. shore is 1 rod to the S. of where the W. hedge of the marsh turns off at right angles to the W).

121. Thence 2 chains further S. to a point in the marsh W. by N. of Ogmoor great pond head.

122. Thence E. by S. up the marsh-centre and up the drain to a cross at Ogmoor great pond head where the penstock was.

123. Thence up the middle of the great pond to the S.E. bay [S. corner].

124. Thence up the trench to the Long pond. [Thence S. or S.S.E. about 80

yards to a Boundary Cross.]

125. Thence S. up the middle of the lowest ground where the Long pond was to its S.W. bay. [Cancelled]
126. Thence N.W., between 2 and 3 chains, to a cross on the end of a bank. [Thence S. or S.S.W., about 65 yards to another Boundary cross.]
127. Thence W. up the side of the bank by the old watercourse (crossing the new bank after 5 rods) about 4¾ chains to a cross on the bank.
128. Thence on by the same course to a cross a short rod from the corner of the new Priory Farm Inclosure.
129. Thence up the bank of this Inclosure (built over the old course) to the road.
130. Thence in the same direction across the road.
131. Thence by the course to a cross at the "100 yards road".
132. Thence by the course, rather more than 3 chains, to a cross where the course bends to the W.
133. Thence by the course, 2 chains or less, to a cross where the course again goes S.
134. Thence by the course, a short 3 chains, to a cross by a road.
135. Thence still by the course 4 chains to a cross [2 chains to a cross; then (by compass 18 degrees E. of S.) on by the new straight ditch, 2 chains 17 links, to a cross (not renewed in 1895) which is 1/3 chain south from the junction of the aforesaid ditch with another branching to the West].
136. Thence, leaving the course [ditch], S. through the lowest land 2 chains to a broken tree, and then S.S.W. 9 rod further to a cross by a road; this [9 rod] being in an old much defaced watercourse.
137. Thence S.W. 20 paces to a cross where two watercourses cross almost at right angles.
138. Thence diagonally across the larger course and still S.W. about 107 paces to a cross by [on the W. side of] a water-course.

(135 to 138 are the treading shown to us by Mr G Lemon which he had from his father. The Ordnance map gives 5 or 6 roods more to Headley; and would thus read: 135A. Thence still by the course 2 chains to a course which branches [ditch which goes] to the S. 136A. Thence up this latter course [ditch] 3 chains to a trench. 137A. Thence over the trench. 138A Thence S. some 190 paces to the "cross by a water-course".)

N.B. The difficulty lies in connecting the cross of No. 135 with that of 138. The Ordnance Surveyors have taken a straight line, noticing at the North end of it what looks like a part of the original course. Mr Lemon takes what certainly on the whole looks like lower ground, and which strikes the nearly defaced watercourse of No. 136.

See correspondence from Mr Henry H Coventry to Mr Laverty next page.

139. Thence by this watercourse some 5½ chains to a cross (passing a cross a short distance from the starting point).
140. Thence on by the watercourse another chain to a road.
141. Thence in the same direction across the road.
142. Thence through the centre of the bathing pond to a cross about 12 feet to the E. of the old junction of the two trenches [E. of the big trench, and S. of the pond].
143. Thence up the W. trench about 14 chains to a road.
144. Thence in the same direction through the water tank.
145. Thence in this same W. trench to a new road.
146. Thence by the trench to [a stone on the bank by] an old road 7 chains from the water tank.
147. Thence again by the trench some 3½ chains to a cross by a road.
148. Thence another chain on by the same trench to a cross by a tributary trench.
149. Thence (about S.S.E.) in a straight line to a point (on the E. side of the Sleaford and Greatham road) 5 chains to the N. of stone W.D. No.24.
150. Thence in the same straight line to the starting cross and stone.

As noted, there were some problems in determining the precise line of the boundary between Nos. 120 to 142, and these were the subject of a detailed letter from Henry H Coventry (a Civil Engineer living in Lindford) and the rector WH Laverty, which also sheds some interesting light on the use of this part of the Parish in past times:—

Dear Mr Laverty,

Of the various knotty points in the boundary which you brought under my notice, all except one yielded a ready solution when confirmed with range rods and tape, but that one was certainly a knot that seemed of Gordian complication. However I think that I have hit on the right way of untying it. This point affects the boundary from 120 to 142 of this year's treading. I should say at once that I consider the recent treading, 123 to 126, to be quite wrong. The description, 90 to 92, of the 1873 treading agrees with the Ordnance boundary and seems to be correct. That the party here went wrong or were led wrong by Mr G Lemon is scarcely to be wondered at. The boundary for miles had followed streams, rivulets or marshes—always, that is, the lowest ground: and the description given of the old treading of 1772 is in part apparently confused that it is only with difficulty that one can arrive at its true meaning.

Article 52 of the 1772 treading says, "Thence up the middle of this great Pond to the tail of the lesser or Long Ogmoor Pond which falls *or is emptied* into the greater". The italics are mine. Please also observe that the long pond is only touched at the tail of it. It is art: 53, however, that is the puzzling one. It says, "Thence from the tail of the lesser pond along the cut or canal or

208

watercourse by which it is supplied to the great morass or marsh". Along the *cut*:– it must be something artificial then: *canal*:– something also of considerable dimensions: or *watercourse*:– a work then capable of water flowing along it; fairly level, that is, though by no means on the lowest ground: *by which it is supplied to the great morass.* Now really this is too bad. Either the old perambulator—I apologise for the epithet for I mean him no insult—wrote nonsense or I am lacking in insight. We shall see, presently, that it is the man of 1890 who is at fault, not he of 1772.

It is clear that the parish boundary does leave the lowest ground and does follow something, very indefinite now, but called nevertheless a cut, canal or watercourse. The fact is clear, but I am not quite satisfied unless I can see the reason why. Allow me, then, to go back; first to go back a very long time— to a time when artificial works, Ogmoor ponds, cuts, canals and watercourses did not exist here. Undoubtedly at such a time the parish boundary would keep to the lower ground and follow up Oxney Marsh, as the most striking feature of the ground, to its source in the great morass, hidden now by fir woods until one comes on to it, boggy still, but rendered passable by deep and well maintained drainage from which flows a copious and perennial stream. This morass is of some extent and abuts on the Portsmouth Road at the level piece between Deadwater hill and White hill.

Now there came a time when Ogmoor pond was formed by banking in the lower end of the depression of which the pond forms the lowest part, abutting nearly on to Oxney marsh. I say "was formed by banking in" for this, like every pond—and they are very numerous—in the district, has been artificially formed. This certainly was not done without a definite and practical objective. The object, I firmly believe, was the obtaining of water power by an overfall for the working of tilt hammers in connection with the extensive iron industry which was formerly carried on in this neighbourhood, or for fulling and other mills required by a population probably far in excess of that now occupying the district. On examining Ogmoor pond, however, it at once strikes one that the natural drainage flowing into it is from not more than about 200 acres, and that its outflow would be insufficient to effect a result commensurate with the cost of formation of the pond and erection of wheel, buildings, etc. Here perhaps our old perambulator of 1772 may help us, and his article 53 may, like the old barbers sign[2], so tempting but misleading, be very much altered by a little punctuation.

I'll make a little—a very little—alteration and put a comma after "supplied". Now we find that the watercourse or canal or cut supplied water from the Great morass to the lesser pond which falls or is emptied into the greater. This then is the secret. The copious stream now flowing out of the

---

[2]   What do you think   What! do you think
       I'll shave you for nothing   I'll shave you for nothing
       and give you a drink.   and give you a drink?

great morass was caught at its source and led along a higher level so as to run into the ponds. Here then we have a first rate water privilege.

We can now go back to a period, the commencement of which I am not antiquary enough to date, but which terminated not so very long ago—a period when the iron railing round new St Pauls, erected after the great fire of London and completed in 1710 was supplied from iron works in Sussex. At this time the surroundings of Ogmoor pond must have presented a very different aspect to their present ones. Oxney marsh, now so impassably swampy through the water being dammed up to work the water wheel pumping water to Broxhead Court, was then drained, at least below Ogmoor, by a deep cut to obtain the utmost benefit of probably a 14 foot fall from Ogmoor pond. The pond itself was dammed two or three feet higher, making its water surface very much more extensive and causing it to reach, at its southern bay, a point very near the long pond, now a mere swampy hollow, but then an extensive and striking piece of water. The roads, now embracing the ponds between them, had then no existence but tracks trodden by frequent trains of pack mules and horses laden largely with lime for use as a flux with the iron ore, would cross the marsh by the hard that exists here and, coming direct from Selborne, would here divide, one track leading by Lindford or by Hungerford to Frensham, the other passing by Standford and Passfield to Headley and Bramshott. This traffic with the buildings and works at the foot of the pond (miscalled "head" in all the perambulations) and workmen's cottages on the rise above would make the scene a busy one—very different from its present desolate and heron-haunted aspect. At this time too the enclosures and fir woods were not [there], so that the ponds and watercourse would form a very striking and visible feature.

As to how this feature became the parish boundary, which I have supposed originally to have followed the lowest ground, is not difficult to conjecture. Here was something of value—something that is, in an otherwise improductive region of heath and bog, [which] could pay rates. Though this valuable property lay wholly in Headley, it was a thing for which Selborne would fight, and the more so that she had in her hand a very effective weapon for the purpose—a very small cut on the Selborne side of the swamp would easily tap the great morass and lessen, if not cut off, the supply of water flowing through the canal to the ponds. The great morass, too, being equally in either parish, the water supply would be as much from Selborne as from Headley. It would therefore be equitable and natural that the user of the water should pay a rate to both parishes and, the land being of itself valueless, the water course or canal should have a peculiar and distinctive character, rendering it quite distinct from the drainage ditches and enclosure banks which have been formed in recent times. Its purpose being to lead water from the great morass to the ponds, it should be nearly level with a slight fall northwards. It would be irregular in direction following the contour of the ground. It would be banked entirely on one side, that is on the downhill side and, as its object was to deliver water at as high a level as possible, it would not generally be deep. All these characteristics it has. Its very shallowness causes its present indistinctness. At the end nearest the ponds it was necessary to pass through somewhat higher ground here therefore it was deeper and is consequently quite distinct.

Placing myself now at the boundary cross mentioned in paragraph 126 of the recent perambulation, the "cross on the end of a bank", one is at the point where "the cut, canal or watercourse" ended and delivered its water at will to either the long pond for storage or to the Great pond for immediate use. There are yet visible on the ground traces of a runnel to the long pond—a very short one as this pond, when full, would rise very nearly to the point at which we are standing—and of a longer one towards the great pond. About three chains off, along this runnel, is the boundary cross shown on the Ordnance boundary, and a few yards further on yet, barring the way as it were, is a low bank, vertical on the hither side but sloping on the side towards the great pond. This I take to be the remains of an overfall weir and am confirmed in this opinion by finding immediately on the vertical side of the bank a deep groove about 5 inches wide and 9 deep. This, I think, must have been the seat of timbering, now rotted away, but of which the form has been preserved by the roots of heath and swamp grasses.

Now turning round we can follow the cut, canal or watercourse without a hitch in accordance with the successive paragraphs of the recent perambulation from No 126 on to 136. Here to 139 the ground is swampy, encumbered by tall tufts of hummocky grass, and cut in many directions by drainage grips, newer and older. At this part the cut, canal or watercourse is not traceable and, indeed, may never have existed in a definite form. The ground to the right, being somewhat higher, may have acted as a natural dam, taking the place of the bank which is found on the downhill side of this cut everywhere else in its course. Here, in fact, the water may have been allowed to widen out to its natural limits forming a sedgy pool. Of the two treadings given here in the perambulation notes I should prefer Mr Lemon's. He seems to me to have taken about the middle of the sedgy pool, while the other treading takes the somewhat higher ground to the right.

From here (139) the water course is quite easily traceable and bears the characteristics I before mentioned, on to 142 where it originally tapped the great morass. At this place the swamp leading from and forming the natural outlet of the water from the great morass is quite narrow, firm ground coming up on either side to form a narrow neck. At this place there would have probably been a low dam. I could see no traces of one: the large ditches and bathing pond, recently constructed, and occupying this part of the ground quite account for the disappearance, however, of a work which need never have been more than slight.

Before leaving the subject I should like to remark on the rapidity with which the works represented by these ponds and this canal, works of considerable extent and much interest, have become almost obliterated and the very tradition of their existence died out. The whole organization was in working order, probably, well into the last century. The canal still carried water to the ponds in the last quarter of the 18th century (as shown by the treading of 1772), probably even to its very end. When Suttons enclosure (which includes the great morass) was formed and the drainage works carried out—and this I think was about 80 years ago—then first would water have ceased to flow through the canal and its rapid decadence to have commenced. I think one may assert with truth that the very careful way in which the Headley boundary perambulation has been carried out has been the one thing that has saved from utter oblivion this record on a not uninteresting past.

    I am Dear Mr Laverty
        very faithfully yours
            H H Coventry

Wood Engravings & Lithographs of Headley

Five illustrations of Headley have been discovered, made by the late Norman Wilson probably in the 1960s. We reproduce them in miniature here. Full size copies may be obtained from The Headley Society.

		Arable			Pasture			Wood		
		A	R	P	A	R	P	A	R	P
66	Adams										
50	Alder Peter	0	2	27	3	1	17	—	—	—
52	Annett Henry	0	0	12	—	—	—	—	—	—
71	Alfield George	0	0	26	—	—	—	—	—	—
98	Aylen Widow	0	1	2	—	—	—	—	—	—
2	Balhe Robert Glebe	50	2	19	0	1	19			
3	ditto Curtiss	58	3	19	3	3	5	—	—	—
7	Barnard	0	1	17	—	—	—	—	—	—
9	Benham	0	1	5	—	—	—			
9	Blunt Jno Esq., Headley Park	80	3	0	138	3	29	3	1	24
11	ditto Ricketts Hill	115	1	30	35	2	10	16	0	7
18	Bennett Jno Pt of North Farm	15	1	0	5	3	6	—	—	—
20	Baker Thos, Hatch House	44	2	12	12	3	32	0	0	14
21	ditto, Crabb Tree	42	3	38	2	1	2	—	—	—
22	ditto, Dunces	29	2	35	—	—	—	—	—	—
22	Bell	4	1	10	—	—	—	—	—	—
40	Bettsworth Wm Barfields	93	3	27	0	0	13	15	1	1
41	ditto Bilfords	14	2	3	3	0	20	—	—	—
51	Bartholomew Jno	1	0	5	0	2	13	—	—	—
52	Brambley William	0	1	0	2	2	36	—	—	—
55	Bridger J	0	0	6	—	—	—	—	—	—
58	Birmingham	0	0	7	—	—	—	—	—	—
59	Burrow James	0	0	27	—	—	—	—	—	—
62	Burrow Thomas	0	0	14	—	—	—	—	—	—
63	Bailey William	0	2	15	—	—	—	—	—	—
64	Burchett Richard	0	0	27	—	—	—	—	—	—
65	Bridger J	1	1	20	1	2	16	—	—	—
71	Button J	0	1	30	—	—	—	—	—	—
74	Barrett Thos	0	0	28	—	—	—	—	—	—

A page from the 'Valuation of the Parish of Headley by Mr Cull & Mr Comely, 1822' which was rescued by the husband of Mrs Barbara McCardle when he cleared out Rogers' shop in the 1950s.
(A transcription of the entire ledger is on the village website)

Charlie Payne 1901–1992

(C.A. Payne of Wey Valley Farm, Tulls Lane, Standford)
by his son, Denis Payne—written 2004

Charlie Payne, born in 1901 and the youngest of the four children of Harry and Flora Payne, came to Liphook as a three year old when his father took up a position as foreman at Griggs Green brickyard. The family had moved from Wokingham, Charlie's birthplace. He attended Bramshott school, at that time under the headship of a Mr Crowther, a strict disciplinarian who believed in the maxim 'Spare the rod and spoil the child' as Charlie would testify when recalling his schooldays.

Nevertheless the no nonsense approach of the staff brought results, and Charlie having passed the leaving examination at the age of twelve was able to start work, initially as an errand boy for W.A. Coyte of Liphook. He later worked for W.A. Stoneman & Co. of Haslemere as a lorry driver, delivering building materials to sites in the area. His vehicle was an American built Pierce Arrow two ton truck with solid tyres and a top speed of sixteen miles an hour. (This vehicle's handbook is still in our possession.)

In 1921 the family moved to Hollywater Farm, and in 1934,having had a grounding in farming in partnership with his father he decided that he would make it his life's career and he and his wife and young son, (his daughter was born two years later) moved into a new bungalow at Wey Valley Farm, where on a holding of thirty acres they managed a herd of a dozen dairy cows and some three hundred chickens.

Before leaving Hollywater Charlie and his father had already started selling their home produced milk and eggs locally, and following the move to Standford the business grew rapidly. By the start of World War Two in 1939, Charlie was delivering over three hundred and fifty pintas daily, as well as fresh eggs and cream. Initially the means of delivery was by motorbike and sidecar. Soon however the combination was totally inadequate and was replaced by an Austin Seven van, to be superseded in 1939 by a much more aerodynamic looking Austin Eight.

Incidentally the motorcycle combination figures in a great story concerning a runaway pig! Charlie was taking the pig to Farnham market with the pig secured by netting in the sidecar. However the pig overcame the restrictions and made a bid for freedom in Alice Holt Woods. He (or she) was only recaptured after a lengthy chase and with the help of the local constable who fortunately enjoyed the whole incident immensely!

The Payne family in 1910
Front: Charlie; Centre: Harry and Flora, his father and mother
Back, his brothers and sister: left, George; centre, Nell; right, Fred

Charlie, assisted by his father who was now living in semi retirement in his cottage at Standford Hill, rose at 4.30am daily, and after helping with the hand milking of the herd would set off at 5.45 on his delivery round. The route was as follows: Standford Hill (although during WW2 his first delivery was to Passfield Mill which had been taken over by J. Sainsbury as a distribution centre after their depot at Blackfriars in London was destroyed in the Blitz), Hollywater Road, Whitehill, (including Sandy Lane), Bordon, down Chalet Hill, (including the numerous side roads), Headley Mill Road, Branson's bungalows and then back to Hollywater crossroads, up to Standford Hill (top road) arriving home around 9am.

After a breakfast of either a boiled egg or fried egg and bacon (no cholesterol problems for Charlie!) he would set off on the second leg of his round, which included the Headley Mill area, Lindford and Headley.

Meanwhile the deliveries in Standford village were being made by his one full time employee, an Irish girl called Betty (who later married and settled in Standford). Her transport was a sturdy bicycle, the handlebars of which supported four large and strong leather bags containing quart, pint-and-a-half and one-pint capacity bottles (a very hazardous operation on the icy winter roads!)

During WW2 the round continued to grow, and the supply of home produced milk soon became insufficient to meet the demand. The answer was to buy in additional supplies, which were brought on the 'milk train' from Petersfield and collected from Liphook station around 6pm each day. This came in ten-gallon churns and had to be bottled by hand, a process taking a good part of the evening. The washing of the 'empties' took place in the morning after the round had been completed, another task which took up to three hours to complete, and was carried out by a young woman called Ruth from Hollywater.

With the influx of Army families into the area trade prospered, and while the majority were as honest as the day is long, there was the odd occasion when a customer would 'disappear' without paying the bill. This was considered to bring shame on the integrity of the British Army and on more than one occasion a word in the appropriate regimental ear would result in the defaulter paying up.

Petrol was of course in short supply during the war and Charlie found great difficulty in managing on his 'ration'. Fortunately he had several good friends whose supplies of the precious fuel were more generous, and he was grateful for the additional 'coupons' that sometimes came his way. There was one morning though when a kind benefactor had left two cans of petrol on his doorstep for Charlie to collect on his rounds, but which he was unable to appropriate as an officer of the law was in the vicinity. The donor was mystified by Charlie's apparent non interest in the gift until the reason for his non acceptance was explained later!

In spite of Charlie's business being a fourteen hour, seven day a week job, (which increased to eighteen hours at haymaking and harvest) he still found time during WW2 to serve as an A.R.P. (Air Raid Precautions) warden, although he was once branded as 'unpatriotic' by the area organiser, a retired WW1 colonel, for failing to turn up for practice drills at haymaking time.

Charlie and Irene Payne on the occasion
of their Golden Wedding anniversary, 29th May 1979

Haymaking in those days was very labour intensive and Charlie was able to call on several locals, 'strong men and true', to help. Among them were Jack Gardner (who married the aforementioned Betty), Charlie Brand and Roy Harding. However although plenty of refreshment was provided it was all of a non-alcoholic variety as Charlie was a strict teetotaller. Abstinence was not a way of life shared by all and it was fortunate that the route from the hayfields to the farmyard passed close to the 'Robin Hood' where those who wanted something stronger than tea or lemonade were able to satisfy their needs!

Two regulars at the farm for much of the war were Neil Ross and Harry

Coventry, members of the Canadian Forces stationed at Bordon Camp. They were fortunate to have spent much of their service life in Bordon, except for a period after D-Day when they served on the continent, and they never missed an opportunity to get away from camp and relieve the monotony and discipline of army life by spending time at Wey Valley Farm. Charlie was glad of their help, and for Neil particularly it was really 'home from home' since he came from a farming background. They became lifelong family friends, and although Harry died some ten years ago, Neil, now a sprightly 90 year old, still rides his beloved horse 'Patches' in the local agricultural fairs in his native Prince Edward Island.

As a member of a devout Christian family Charlie even found time to conduct services in local churches and chapels as a very acceptable lay preacher. In 1986 he, and his brother Fred (who had a jewellers shop in Liphook for many years)[†] were presented with certificates marking sixty years as lay preachers in the Methodist Church.

Charlie was on the Headley Parish Council in the 1950s and 60s, including a period as chairman. He could become very firm in his control of the members, so much so that he had many heated exchanges with certain councillors, but it was a measure of the respect in which he was held that he remained firm friends with them in later years.

Back on the farm, Charlie had sold out the milk round to Farnham Dairies in 1946, installed a milking machine to speed up the process of getting the milk from the cow to the dairy, and from that time until his retirement from farming in 1976 all the milk produced at the farm was collected daily by lorry and taken to a creamery at Guildford.

Charlie spent his retirement in his bungalow at Standford Hill. He had many visitors, including former customers, and they always received a warm welcome. He always had a story to tell, and his recollections of life in a country parish in bygone generations were always illuminating and informative. His wife of 58 years, Irene, died in 1987, and Charlie continued to live alone until the final few weeks of his life when he moved to live with his daughter near High Wycombe. He was blessed with a long and healthy life (and this following an accident with a horse and trap when he was a boy which resulted in severe injuries causing fears for his recovery. Indeed there was even a rumour circulating widely at the time, clearly false, that he had succumbed to his injuries!). He was a fund of local knowledge, and as is so often the case with such characters, so much more could have been gleaned of that long and happy life in a country parish.

He died on the 27th of March, 1992, four weeks after his 91st birthday, and as a committed Christian who believed in the afterlife, who is to say he isn't at this moment enjoying talking over old times with his many friends?

[†] See pp40–43 of 'Liphook Remembers' published by the Bramshott & Liphook Preservation Society, 1987

Mystery Mugs

These mugs were the property of James Herbert and Mary Ann (née Harding) Gardner (both born 1880) who were married in 1903. We do not know what they commemorate. Can anyone identify them?

James was the son of Richard Gardner of Hatch House Farm, Lindford and became a farmer himself at Bramshott and East Liss, before taking over Bramshott Post Office for about five years in the 1930's. He played cricket for Headley and, with his brother Thomas, played full back for the local football team.

Mary was the eldest daughter of Thomas Harding of Grayshott. Her family came from Lion Lane Shottermill, she was apprenticed to a dressmaker in Haslemere and later began her own business in Grayshott.

Photo supplied by their granddaughter's husband, Austin Harland of Chesham, Bucks.

Grayshott in the 1870s

as described by the son of Grayshott's first schoolteacher

Mike Powell writes (in 2004) "I have in my possession an old exercise book in which my grandfather (Ernest Arthur Clark, born 29th August 1869) has written down his experiences on coming to Grayshott in 1871. His father had died in Brighton when only 26 years old, leaving a widow (Esther) with two young children and no means of support. Apparently the daughter of the vicar of St Marks, Brighton knew Miss I'Anson and arranged for her to move to Grayshott as the first teacher at the new school there."

The following is an edited transcript of Ernest Clark's notes, written presumably towards the end of the 19th century:—

Now Miss I'Anson had just built a school but had difficulty in obtaining a teacher and so, finding my mother had had a good education, offered her the post, which she accepted. This school was just finished but there was no proper approach to the door except by a gap in a bank covered with furze-bushes and which gave to a very primitive cart track which led in one direction, to the Headley Road (now a street!!!) and past the school, in a straight line to a concave cart track, with deep ruts, made, I should think, by the Ancient Britons, about the early part of the Year 1, which led to the lane which leads past what is now the Church Corner, to Whitmore Bottom and on to Churt and Farnham.

After a long journey, at least to my sister and I, being mere babies, ie. from Brighton to Haslemere via Havant, and a drive in the carriage from the station to Greyshott, we were put to bed. Now Miss I'Anson had no house for us and so she had hurriedly arranged with her coachman's wife to set apart a spare room to accommodate us until our house was built. We arrived at our new home in the late evening and I well remember the dank and farmyardy smell of the air which surrounded the place. We, my sister and I, were put to bed in an unfurnished room.

A good fire was burning in the grate, but there was no fender. I saw a piece of red hot coal fall from the fire and burn its way through the floor boards. It set fire to the roof of the harness room below. Shortly after we were hurriedly removed to safety. The alarm spread rapidly. Mr John Tullock, the general foreman, rushed up the steps to the hay loft in order, I suppose, to see he extent of the fire. Presently we heard a succession of loud yells, and on investigation, discovered John suspended from the ceiling of the harness roof by the large hook used to hold the straps while being polished. Now John had a voice as powerful as a fog horn, although his stature was short and his circumference great. Eventually he was released, but the damage to his attire necessitated an unsightly patch before he could sit comfortably.

Our house was soon furnished and my mother secured the services of Lucy Crawte of Whitmore Bottom to care for my sister and other domestic requirements, I being allowed to go to the school—so that I was the first pupil. There were few children at first and my mother had to be somewhat strict in order to command attention, as none of them had ever been to school before. On one occasion she had to cane a boy and the result was a rumour that some of the fathers had threatened to hang her on a tree!! This sprit, however gradually died out and one of the mothers said "She's strict but anyway my girl can read like a parson".

Shortly after commencing duties as a teacher, my mother, although fully able to teach, was not in possession of the Certificate required by the Education Act recently passed in Parliament, so she had to attend the necessary examination—and passed. The children each paid one penny per week, which however Miss I'Anson returned to them in proportion to the number of attendances made during the year. The schooling, therefore, to those making full time was free.

The Government gave a "grant" to those schools able to show a certain percentage of passes at the annual examinations, conducted by H.M. Inspector. The highest class or "standard" as it was termed, was at first Standard V as it was considered at Westminster that that would be about as high as the common people's capacity would reach. However these "Commoners" passed so well that nearly all these schools earned the full amount granted. In order to reduce the public expense "Standard VI" was introduced. This alteration, to their surprise, was not as successful as they had anticipated for, to their astonishment, they discovered that these common people had brains!! As a last endeavour to check the cost, Standard VII was added together with, I believe, a smaller grant to be earned. This latest standard contained, among other difficulties, broker's stock and averages—a subject rarely understood by the teachers themselves. It was also found that there was a shortage of teachers able to cope with the requirements of the profession and in consequence teachers colleges were instituted.

Boys, as well as girls, were taught needlework! All H.M. Inspectors were men and many women teachers did not like the idea of their work being judged by a man. That reminds me of an incident that occurred on one occasion. The Inspector asked one of the pupils, a girl, what the garment was which she had made, and on being told it was a shirt was praised by him for her fine needlework but, with a sly glance at the lady teacher, he said to the girl "button it up, please". She endeavoured to do so but was unable as the button holes were too small, or, if you like, the buttons too large. "Ah!" said he with a smile, "even a man can sometimes detect an error in needlework"—

he gave her full marks for her good work though.

An afternoon service was held in the schoolroom each Sunday, the Revd. W.H. Laverty driving over from Headley in his dog cart for the occasion. Most of the men, some of whom came from a considerable distance to attend, were dressed in their best smocks, a loose garment with the upper part gathered in lines of sewing and usually dispensing *pro tem* with the customary straw between the lips. One man nearly always entered the room just before the service began although he had arrived early. We always knew when he came in as he had a club-foot and walked very heavily with the defective member. He could read and followed the instructions given in the church prayer book as to the responses, especially the Amens, with the greatest power at his command.

There was no Chancel at the time of which I am speaking, that was added some years later, as was a small classroom to accommodate the younger children as the number increased—many came from Bramshott and Headley Common and others from a considerable distance. My mother presided at the harmonium except when, on occasion, Miss Emma I'Anson would volunteer. Her performance at that instrument however was somewhat erratic as her touch was unsuitable, being too brief to allow sufficient air to enable the notes to sound unless sufficient pressure was obtained by extra pedal work. She was an expert at the piano—that was perhaps the explanation of her poor performance on the slower-speaking instrument.

One of the natives, Mrs Rogers, was employed in scrubbing and cleaning the school room. Her husband I saw only once was a man who was, I suppose, a frequent visitor to the Royal Huts Inn, Hindhead—close to the Punch Bowl—now a Trust House hotel! And very often he would pass the time after the closing of that place in beating his wife. We always knew when this happened as the few neighbours filled their tea kettles with small stones and rattled them so vigorously that the noise could be heard at least a mile away.

Sound at night travels a tremendous distance in that otherwise silent valley. Mrs Robinson's voice calling her son home "Hen-re" well above an ordinary pitch of voice was audible at a radius long enough for the whole of Greyshott. Mrs Robinson's shop, I remember, was one room of a fairly large house and across the ceiling on strings hung a number of rush lights, tallow candles and a few wax ones which latter must have been there years as few of her customers could afford such luxuries. Tin candle-sticks with snuffers to trim the cotton wicks and an extinguisher were among her wares. Black treacle in drums with a tap to each stood in a row at the back of the counter, also a row of glass jars filled with bulls eyes, sticks of toffee bars twisted and "hundreds and thousands"—little balls of hard sweetmeat, about the size of small shot and various colours. She sold marbles, too—the cheaper sort were of brown baked clay, but she also sold glass ones which, at least locally, were called Taws and in a game a Taw was counted as worth five to ten of the common sort as its value was dependent upon its internal colouring and size.

Wallis Hay Laverty, rector of Headley 1872–1928

(see page 63, among many other references in this book)

A very large oven was in another room. It was like a dome-shaped cavity, the sides and roof were brick lined and the floor of large flat stones like pavement slabs. On baking day a long row of dough-loaves were placed on a wide plank opposite the oven. To heat the oven, faggots were placed in the dome and set alight. Sometimes the heat was so great that the bricks looked red hot. After the wood had burned out the ashes were removed with as long handled heather broom and the loaves put, one at a time, upon a shovel-like tool—called a "slice"—also with a long handle because of the great heat— and by a jerky movement the loaf was deposited in its place on the stone floor. When filled, the big iron door was closed and the baking began. The bread at that time was very good indeed—practically "home-made"—and would keep fresh a long time. Mrs R. made a small loaf for each of us—Ada and I—at times.

Shop toys for children were non existant and hand-made by the boys themselves. Among them were bows and arrows, and as woods of all kinds grew in profusion within a few yards anywhere at Greyshott the bows and arrows were excellent in quality and the strings were often of real cat gut, thicker than the G strings of a violin. Another toy was a "hummer" which consisted of a piece of oak or other hardwood about two inches long and a quarter of an inch thick. The edges were cut with V shaped notches as in a coarse-cut saw. Near the top end a hole was made through which a length of whipcord was fastened and the other end—at a suitable distance—formed a handle. The "modus operandi" was to swing the wood in a circular direction until it revolved and it would give a loud hum, varying in pitch with the speed with which it was swung.

Then pop-guns were made. They were pieces of elder wood, about one and a quarter inches in diameter, perfectly straight and cut between knots and about ten inches long. The pith was removed and the inside cleaned out. This formed the barrel. Then a piece of wood, smaller than the barrel was made to form a ram. Next a small quantity of tarpaulin string was chewed in the mouth (the boys!) until by mastication it became malleable. Two lots like this were required unless a suitable cork was handy. The length of the ramrod was about as long as the barrel plus a length over this size to form a handle. To use the gun you first put the piece of tarpaulin or cork tightly in the end of the tube and then force another plug into the other end of the tube. Now by smartly pushing the ramrod through the tube, thus driving the plug inwards, the air being compressed caused the plug (or cork) to fly out as a bullet a good distance (if well made) and with a bang.

Some of the boys were quite expert in the making of slings. They consisted of a strip of soft leather with a length of whipcord attached to each end. A chosen stone of suitable size was placed in the centre of the leather— one end of the cord was wrapped around the hand to prevent it slipping and the other end just nipped with the thumb, in order to release it at the moment the stone was to leave the sling. The sling was then swung around until its velocity was judged to be sufficient to impact the stone with sufficient force to travel the distance required. Much practice was needed to become proficient as to the direction aimed at, as the moment of the release of the end held by the thumb determined the success of its flight.

Whistles also must be mentioned. Some, giving a single note, were made from a short length of wood cut from a branch in the Spring, while the sap was fresh. The mouthpiece cut to shape and also the slot, before removing the bark. This latter act was generally easy to do by merely twisting it off, but in some cases it required a gentle tapping all round with the handle of the pocket knife before it could be removed. A longer whistle, with holes for the different notes, as in an ordinary commercially made tin whistle, were occasionally attempted and as to appearance were quite good looking but were rarely successful owing to the difficulty of deciding the correct position of the holes, a point essential to its usefulness as a musical instrument.

Catapults, many capable of killing a rabbit at ten yards or so, were quite a common possession with the older boys.

Ernest's mother Esther remained in charge of Grayshott School until June 1885, when she left to marry a fellow Grayshott teacher Mr F.E. Child. When the school started in 1871 there had been just 7 pupils—by the time she left there were 51.

Ernest Clark won two silver medals with clasps engraved Transvaal, Relief of Ladysmith, Orange Free State, Cape Colony and South Africa 1901–2. He married Edith Agnes Woods in Essex in 1903, but after the birth of a daughter (Mike Powell's mother) in March 1904 he seems to have disappeared. Mike recently discovered that he died in Leyton in 1953 aged 83, a retired locomotive driver, but is still trying to find out what happened in between, as it was never discussed in the family.

Counting Heads in Headley

The first two censuses in 1841 and 1851, by John Owen Smith

While writing the story of the Headley Workhouse Riot of 1830, I kept coming up with questions which seemed to have no immediate answer.

What happened to the family of Matthew Triggs, the only Headley man to be transported for the affair? Did his uncle 'Tuckey' get out of the work-house and go to live with his sisters? Was the workhouse repaired and used as a poor-house again? Can we find any trace of the James family who lived in the forest? Who was the malevolent Richard Rook, and why did he testify against Robert Holdaway?

I thought that perhaps some of the answers might lie in the census returns of the time, but the first detailed census didn't occur until 1841, eleven years after the event. However, since there seemed to be no other source of infor-mation, I decided to spend a few hours looking through the handwritten lists to see what I could get out of them.

The photocopied sheets were not easy to read and, to make it easier to reference them later, I started typing relevant parts into a computer—and I typed and I typed—until some days later I found I had transcribed so much that it seemed a pity not to complete the job. Not only that, but I had also begun to look at the next census, of 1851, in order to try and decipher some of the more illegible names in the first. And once I'd started ....

So with two full census returns in the computer, I not only had printouts which were considerably easier to read than the originals, but also the means of doing some analysis on the information, and in doing so I found a number of stories based on the results; some happy, some sad, some conjectural, some corroborated.

The Parish Boundary

In the early nineteenth century, the parish of Headley was bounded by the parishes of Bramshott to the south, Selborne and Kingsley to the west, Dockenfield to the north and Frensham to the east, the last of these being in the county of Surrey (Dockenfield was in Hampshire until 1895).

At that time the parish included Lindford and the relatively unpopulated districts of Grayshott, Bordon and Whitehill *(see map on next page)*. Only in 1902 did Grayshott become an independent parish, and it was not until well into the 20th century that Whitehill civil parish (covering Whitehill and Bordon) was carved from areas of Headley and Selborne parishes. The small civil parish of Lindford is a relative newcomer, dating from 1982.

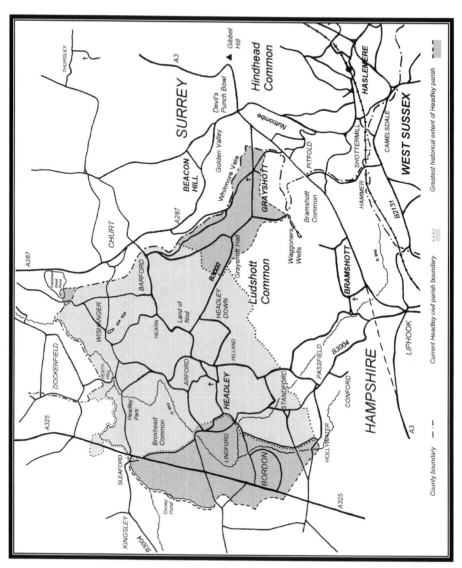

*The parish of Headley, showing today's civil parish (light shading),
and the greatest extent of the parish as it was up until
the start of the 20th century (darker shading).*

Population lists prior to 1841

There were no regular lists made of population in England and Wales until 1801 when, at a time of growing concern about the rate of population increase, the Government decided it needed to take a simple count of heads every ten years, analysed by sex and, later, by age. The enumerators chosen were local men, and generally made a list of householders in the parish by sex and noted their dependents. They were also asked to record how many houses were inhabited and uninhabited, the number of families occupying them, and the trades or occupations of the people in the parish.

Censuses were taken in 1801, 1811, 1821 and 1831 with minor changes in the information recorded. In 1821 the first attempt was made to grade people by age. The ages quoted were not intended to be precise—a 'five year banding' or 'quintuple' system was used, whereby ages were rounded down to a figure ending in '0' or '5'—thus a 29 year-old would be recorded as aged only 25, but a 31 year-old as aged 30—a significant difference.

The totals were sent to the Government by way of the High Constables or Clerks of the Peace. They were then published as summarised Census Reports, the original notes being usually destroyed. Some original manuscript schedules still exist among the records of certain parishes, but we cannot find them for Headley.

In some parishes there are a few even earlier lists. When Napoleon was expected to invade in 1798, a list (*Posse Comitatus*) was made nationally of all men from 16 to 60 with occupations, and these were kept by the Lord Lieutenant ready for the call to arms, and at various times lists have been made of property owners (for Land Tax assessments), householders and the number of fireplaces they had (for Hearth Tax), of paupers, bachelors, aliens, and any number of other lists, nearly all for the purposes of imposing national taxes or local rates. Those for Hearth Tax and some for early ratepayers have survived relating to Headley.

The 'Modern' Census begins

It was hardly surprising that when, with the Population Act of 1840, the Government decided it needed more information than it had collected hitherto, reaction was "sharp and unfavourable". Some objected on religious grounds, believing that 'numbering the people' was blasphemous, but most objected on the more practical grounds that it was probably a ploy to extract more taxes. For this reason the Government continued using local residents as enumerators rather than sending in strangers from London, and decided to restrict the amount of information asked for to what they considered the bare minimum. Hopefully local men would get more co-operation, and would be more likely to know if they were being deceived.

The Method of 1841

In 1841, the country was divided up into 2,193 Registration Districts, based on the existing Poor Law Unions, and these were further divided into about 36,000 Enumeration Districts, none with fewer than 25 or more than 200 inhabited houses. Headley parish was split into three Enumeration Districts, within a greater Registration District which also included Bramshott and Kingsley under a Superintendent Registrar at Farnham.

Towards the end of May 1841, the enumerators sent to each household in their Enumeration District a form to be filled in on the census night of 16th June. They then collected these, checked them, and copied the information into printed books of blank forms. These Enumeration Schedules, or Census Returns, were sent to the Registrar of the Registration District for further checking, and revision if necessary, then to the Superintendent Registrar of the District before being sent finally to the General Register Office in London.

Thus the population of each city, town, village, hamlet, and even isolated farm, or travellers' camp, was listed, household by household. There was a separate section to be filled by the enumerator for his best estimate of the number of "persons (if any) who, on the night preceding the day of enumeration, have slept within the Enumeration District in boats or barges, mines or pits, barns or sheds, or in the open air, or who from any other cause, although within the District, have not been enumerated as inmates of any dwelling house." Nobody was recorded in this section for any of the Headley districts.

For each person included in the main body of the census, the following six pieces of information were supposed to be recorded: Location, Surname and one forename, Sex, Age (using the 'five year banding' principal for adults, but exactly for children up to 15), Occupation, Birthplace (but only whether they were born 'in this county' or not, unless they came from Scotland, Ireland, or 'Foreign Parts').

Households were normally set out in 'natural order' with father first, then mother and the children, then other relatives, servants, employees, lodgers and visitors—but no relationships were stated, and one can sometimes be misled by unusual combinations, of brother and sister, nieces and nephews, etc. The example opposite shows the information transcribed from the 1841 census for a part of Headley High Street.

The *Location* given is very general. Even where a property is obviously identifiable, such as a pub, a shop or a rectory, no indication was normally written down. The second column has a '1' entered against each Head of Household, or a 'U' if the property was unoccupied, and can be used to count the number of families visited in the census. It does not necessarily equate to the number of buildings, as families (households) often shared a property— *Suters* in the High Street, for example, was sub-divided into at least three parts at one time, and some of the entries shown may in fact relate to that building.

Surnames and *Forenames* can be difficult to read—not only because early nineteenth century handwriting is different from ours in style, but also because some of the writing is now so very feint. For instance, I had read Hampton as Bampton until I checked with the 1851 census where it was written more clearly, but this was of no help when it came to the family below them, whose name remains unknown to me (my guess is 'Parfect').

Ages were put in separate columns for males and females, and this is sometimes the only way of telling a person's sex if you can't read their Christian name. They should all have been rounded down to the nearest 'multiple of five' for adults, but you can see from the example that this particular enumerator did not always stick to the rules. Sometimes the figures are difficult to read, and it is easy to mistake '6' for '8', '0' for '9', and so on when transcribing—so beware if you see any 'impossible' ages.

Location		Surname	Forenames	Age M	Age F	Occupation	Born in County?
Headley	1	Hampton	William	35		Carpenter	n
		Hampton	Mary		32		n
		Hampton	Mary Ann		13		n
		Hampton	Rebecca		9		y
		Hampton	Emma		6		y
		Hampton	George	5			y
		Hampton	Charles	1mth			y
ditto	1	Curtis	Mary		71	Ind	y
		Slade	Eliza		13		y
ditto	1	?	William?	40		Ag Lab	y
		?	?		15		y
		?	William	11			y
		?	?	7			y
		?	George	7			y
		?	John	4			y
ditto	1	Chalcraft	Thomas	55		Grocer	y
		Chalcraft	Mary		50		y
		Chalcraft	Mary		25		y
		Chalcraft	Ann		22		y
		Chalcraft	Thomas	20			y
		Chalcraft	Elizabeth		15		y
		Chalcraft	Frances		12		y
		Chalcraft	Sarah		9		y
ditto	1	Wheeler	William	30		Clergyman	n
		Turner	Thomas	35		M S	y
		Turner	Mary		30	F S	n

Example of the 1841 census for the centre of Headley

An *occupation* was supposed to be entered for all, but this was not consistently applied. Abbreviations were used for common occupations, the most familiar being Ag Lab for 'Agricultural Labourer'. Others shown here are: Ind for 'Independent Means', M.S. for 'Male Servant', and F.S. for 'Female Servant'.

The column for *Born in County* is neither particularly accurate nor, in this area next to a county boundary, very useful. The 1841 enumerator implies that Mr and Mrs Hampton and their eldest daughter were all born 'out of county'—however the 1851 census tells us that while he was born in Farnham, Surrey, his wife and daughter were born in Headley.

The three Enumeration Districts for Headley in 1841 broadly corresponded to the south-east, south-west and north sections of a 'pie' centred at Bayfields Farm. They were numbered Districts 5, 6, and 7 respectively by the supervisors at Farnham and had the following populations:

District 5   84 inhabited houses, 201 males, 222 females (423 total)
District 6   117 inhabited houses, 315 males, 275 females (590 total)
District 7   35 inhabited houses, 120 males, 94 females (214 total)
Workhouse   19 males, 19 females (38 total).
Total 237 inhabited houses,   655 males, 610 females (1,265 total)
– an average of 5.2 per house (excluding the Workhouse).

We can see from the handwriting on the forms that three different enumerators were selected for Headley, but we only know the name of one of them, Charles Collins, taking the south-east district. The names of those taking the south-west and north districts seem to have been lost, but we do know that a fourth man, Edward White who was Master of the workhouse at the time, was responsible for recording the occupants and inmates of the workhouse on a separate sheet.

It is interesting to note that, although census night was supposed to be 16th June, Charles Collins signed his schedule as complete on 10th June, and passed it to Charles Berry, his Registrar, on 12th June—a full four days before the census night! It was delivered to Mr WJ Hollest, the Superintendent Registrar, on 18th June. This was evidently not an isolated instance, as the neighbouring Kingsley schedules were signed off on 11th and 14th June, and Edward White's schedule for Headley Workhouse was signed as early as 7th June.

The Method of 1851

When the second general census took place on 30th March 1851, the amount of information demanded was increased. Additions were:

- Full forenames
- Relationship of each person to the Head of the household;
- Marital status;
- Exact age in years;
- Details about employees, and how many acres owned;
- Parish and County where born;
- Whether people were blind, deaf or dumb.

The example shown is a transcription for the same area of Headley High Street as before.

Instructions to an enumerator in 1851 included the following:–

"He should in the 1st column write the No. of the Schedule he is about to copy, and in the 2nd column the name of the Street, Square, etc, where the house is situate, and the No. of the house if it has a No., or if the house be situate in the country, any distinctive Name by which it may be known.

"He should then copy from the schedule, into the other columns, all the other particulars concerning the members of the family (making use if he pleases of any of the authorized contractions); and proceed to deal in the same manner with the next Schedule.

"Under the last name in any house he should draw a line across the page as far as the fifth column. Where there is more than one Occupier in the same house, he should draw a similar line under the last name of the family of each Occupier; making the line, however, in this case, commence a little on the left hand side of the 3rd column."

../cn.	Surname	F/names	Reln.	St	Age M	Age F	Occupn.	Born Cty	Born Place
	Chalcraft	Thomas	Head	M	65		Grocer	Hants	Headley
	Chalcraft	Mary	Wife	M		59		Hants	Headley
	Chalcraft	Elizabeth	Daur	U		25	Dressmaker	Hants	Headley
	Chalcraft	Frances	Daur	U		21		Hants	Headley
	Chalcraft	Sarah	Daur	U		19		Hants	Headley
	Slade	Edward	Head	M	60		Butcher	Som.	Yeovil
	Slade	Susannah	Wife	M		56		Hants	Headley
	Slade	Eliza	Daur	U		24	Dressmaker	Hants	Headley
	Slade	Henry	Son	U	21		Butcher	Hants	Headley
	Slade	George	Son	U	19		Butcher	Hants	Headley
Holly Bush	Keeling	Abraham	Head	W	62		Victualler	Staffs	Br...ley
	Keeling	Thomas	Son	U	23		Carpenter	Hants	Alton
	Keeling	John	Son	U	21		Blacksmith	Hants	Selborne
	Keeling	Ann	Daur	U		18		Hants	Selborne
	Keeling	Mary	Daur	U		11		Hants	Selborne
	Court	John	Lodger	U	51		Blacksmith	Surrey	Thursley
	Courtnage	George	Lodger	U	27		Ag Lab	Hants	Headley
	Ballantine Dykes	Joseph	Head	U	47		Rector of Headley	Cumbs	Bridekirk
	Couthard	Mary	Servant	U		29	Gen Servant	Cumbs	Whitehaven
	Woods	John	Servant	U	24		Groom	Hants	Headley
	Curtis	Mary	Head	W		80	Annuitant	Hants	Bramshott
	Slade	Robert	Grdson	U	16			Hants	Headley

Example of the 1851 census for the centre of Headley

Each household was given a sequential number in the leftmost column, but in Headley the *location* column was even less well completed than for 1841, and the instruction to draw a partial line between the families of occupiers in the same house seems to have been ignored. Some of the farms were named, and in the example so was the Holly Bush, but our knowledge of where other families lived comes chiefly from noting the locations recorded for them in the previous census, and assuming that they stayed largely where they were for the next decade.

In the 1851 census forms the *names* are generally more legible than in 1841. *Relationships* of all residents to the head of the household were stated for the first time, combined with marital *status* (married, unmarried, widow/er). *Ages* were recorded to the exact year, rather than to the nearest 5 years.

Occupations were given somewhat more thoroughly. Tradesmen were defined as 'master', 'journeyman' or 'apprentice' and the number of employees of a master stated. Farmers gave acreage and number of employees by sex. Children at school or not employed were 'scholars' and this occupation is sometimes even given for infants of a few days old.

Birthplaces were given by parish and county.

Compared with 1841, Headley parish was divided differently this time into four Enumeration Districts numbered 2a, 2b, 2c and 2d, and broadly corresponding to:

- 2a: all that part west of what is now the B3004 through Lindford;
- 2b: the rest of the parish (except as below);
- 2c: the Grayshott area;
- 2d: the centre of Headley and Arford.

Four enumerators were chosen, respectively: 2a, William Bayley (64), parish clerk, farmer and ex-schoolmaster; 2b, Henry Powell (57) a carpenter in Hollywater; 2c, John Bayley (22), son of William; 2d, John Dawes (57), a land surveyor born in Devon, then living in Headley.

Interestingly, apart from Mr Dawes, the enumerators did not live in the area they were given to count.

This time the Superintendent Registrar was at Farnborough rather than Farnham, but he was the same man as 10 years previously, Mr William Hollest. The Registrar for Headley District was a different person, Harvey Hoare. The schedules were all signed off by the enumerators on 7th April, eight days after the census night, then signed by Mr Hoare on 10th April, and passed to Mr Hollest on 17th April.

Comparison of the 1841 and 1851 censuses

So what do we find when we compare the two census lists? Well firstly, we can fill in a few of the entries where the 1841 documents are virtually illegible by referring to details of the same families in 1851. For the technically minded, I merged the two lists and sorted by surname and then Christian name, looking for the same individuals appearing twice. This allowed me to double check on spellings of names, on ages, occupations and locations where these were doubtful. Generally I was able to add corrected names to the 1841 entries, and locations to the 1851 entries.

I also looked at the parish records for baptisms, marriages and burials for the 10 year period, as well as a number of other sources such as Mr Laverty's notebooks, and added relevant information when I found it.

If I identified duplicate entries, I made them into one. In doing this I reduced the two individual census lists of 1,265 and 1,424 names respectively down to one of 2,049 names. From the arithmetic, you see that I identified 640 people as being on both lists.

Population Movement

Do these figures mean that only 640 people, about half the population in 1841, remained in Headley parish during those 10 years? I expected to find a much higher number. A few extra could possibly be accounted for by the handful of names which we are still uncertain about on the 1841 census, but I wondered if perhaps the main difference was to be found in considering those girls who married and stayed within the parish. They would be shown on the second census under their married surname, and therefore appear twice in our merged list, but I found only 84 marriages recorded in the parish during the whole period, and for only 36 of these were the wives included in the 1851 census—presumably the others moved away.

On the face of it then, according to our best information from both census and parish records, only 676 people remained in the parish between the two censuses, which means that some 589 either moved out or died.

We know that 185 burials were recorded, but only 101 of these relate to people who we can find on the 1841 census. So we are left with the conclusion that 488 people, or 38% of the 1841 population, seem to have moved out of Headley to some other parish, or at least were not recorded as being in Headley in the 1851 census. This is considerably more than most of us thought likely, for in those days the Settlement Act, restricting movement across parish boundaries largely to the wealthy or the skilled, was still in force.

Location of Houses

I had hoped to use the comparison of the two censuses to give a better indication as to where particular individuals lived. However, the enumerators were not very specific about naming locations—especially in 1851—and usually the best you get is an indication that a property is in a general area such as Arford, Headley, Lindford, Hollywater, etc; and even then we know of some inconsistencies, particularly in the areas of Barford/ Whitmore Bottom/ Grayshott/ Waggoners Wells, where a number of families put in one location by the first census are very definitely put in another by the next.

Overall, very few house names are mentioned, and we cannot even be sure that the entries are written in a logical sequence. For example *(see previous transcriptions)*, where we think we can identify specific properties, in the middle of Headley, the 1841 census lists them in the sequence: Slade's *(later Wakeford's)*, Holly Bush, other, other, other, other, other, Chalcraft's

235

(now Crabtree House), Rectory; while the 1851 census has them in the sequence: Chalcraft's, Slade's , Holly Bush, Rectory.

Neither order seems particularly sensible. The 1841 version puts Chalcraft's out of sequence, but at least includes properties between the Holly Bush and the Rectory (perhaps Suters and Church Gate Stores); the 1851 version has them in the correct order, but misses out the other properties. If we cannot even identify locations in Headley High Street, there is seemingly little hope of identifying specific properties in other areas of the parish.

The Farms

The main exception to this is with the major farms. Farmers holding large acreages were some of the most important people in the parish in those days, as can be seen from a 'Poll of Headley' list produced in 1836 showing the 20 most significant men in the parish at the time. Of these all but six are farmers, the exceptions being the Rector, two mill owners, a wheelwright, a publican and an absentee landlord. Perhaps it is not surprising then that their farms are generally identified by name in the censuses, although this is by no means always the case—some which are named in 1841 are not named in 1851, and vice versa. In the latter census all farmers' acreages are also shown (along with the number of labourers they employ) even if the farm itself is not named.

Names of People and Places

It is only comparatively recently that we have come to spell the names of people and places consistently, and even now we don't always agree—take the local spelling of Whitmore Vale, or is it Whitmoor Vale? Between the two censuses I found several variations in the spelling of place names, for example Slaford for Sleaford.

When we look at the names of people, the situation is even worse. If you are a Combes, not a Coombes, and think the difference significant, I have to tell you that your ancestors were probably spelt one way in 1841 and the other in 1851, and the spelling you ended up with was likely as not a pure accident. In merging the two censuses I had to decide which spelling to use, and opted for the 1851 version where there were differences.

There were about 200 surnames recorded in each census, with some moving in and others moving out. For example the surnames Upperton and, significantly, Warren appeared during the period, while Lintott and Wheatley disappeared. Fullick was by far the most common name throughout, followed by Shrub(b), Burrow, Marshall and Belton. Together these names accounted for some 16% of the parish population. Today there is hardly a Fullick in the neighbourhood.

There was less variety in Christian names—I noted 102 different ones in

1841, and this rose only slightly to 115 in 1851. In both years the 'top 10' positions were filled by the same names: William, Mary (or Mary Ann), James, John, George, Sarah, Elizabeth, Henry, Ann(e), and Jane, closely followed by Thomas, Charles, and Harriett in its various spellings. Fewer than two dozen names covered 80% of the parish population, and some which are popular today were not used at all—not a single Chris or Pat (of either sex), Den, Don, Geoff, Ken, Paul, Phil, or Ray, nor a Jan, Jean, Jenny, Joan, or Pam—far less a Kylie or an Elvis!

However, this hardly excuses the Powell family of Hollywater, and he an enumerator in 1851 no less, who seem to have been so short of ideas as to call two of their daughters Mary.

All seven censuses 1841–1901 for the parish of Headley have been transcribed in full by members of the Headley Society and are available to researchers. They are also shown sorted by surname on the village website **www.headley-village.com/history**.

All Saints' Headley – view from south-west, 1999

Monumental Inscriptions in All Saints' Churchyard

John Owen Smith

The original churchyard at Headley All Saints' was a small area of ground immediately round the Church and it is there that the earliest graves are to be found. Mr Ballantine Dykes (rector 1848–1872) added half an acre to the west in 1868, and in 1909 Mr Laverty (rector 1872–1928) added a further acre to the west of the old Rectory garden. The third addition, between Mr Laverty's part and Churchfields estate, was brought into use in 1965. To provide for the reverent interment of the ashes of those cremated, a garden of remembrance, surrounded by a hedge and planted with rose bushes, was set apart in 1964 by Canon Tudor Jones (rector 1934–1965) on the south side of Mr Dykes' addition. A further plot for cremations (the 'new garden') was added opposite the south porch in 1989, and a third in 2006.

In 1878, Mr Laverty recorded all the headstones in the churchyard at that time, and had them printed in a pamphlet: *Epitaphs in the Churchyard of All Saints' Church, Headley, Hants.*

In 1980, Mrs J Hobbs and Mr AC Colpus of the Hampshire Genealogical Society (HGS), added to Mr Laverty's list of 200 entries, bringing the total to 1,183 entries. These were published by the HGS and copies lodged in the Hampshire Record Office at Winchester and in the All Saints' Church Office in Headley.

In 1997, The Headley Society decided to update the list again, and the result represented the combined efforts of a number of contributors, mainly from The Headley Society, during the three years 1997/99.

The list is available on the village website,[†] and is updated from time to time with new information—the intention being eventually to add also those burials recorded in the Registers which have no existing monument.

[†] www.headley-village.com/history

Other books from the same Publisher:—

Heatherley *by Flora Thompson*
Her lost sequel to **Lark Rise to Candleford** in which she tells of her time in Hampshire at the beginning of the 19th century after leaving 'Candleford Green.'
ISBN 978-1-873855-29-4   Retail price £7.95

The Peverel Papers *by Flora Thompson*
Nature Notes 1921–27 from the author of **Lark Rise** written while she lived in Liphook. Published here in full and in a single edition for the first time.
ISBN 978-1-873855-57-7   Retail price £19.95

Flora Thompson, the Story of the 'Lark Rise' Writer – *a biography by Gillian Lindsay*
Anyone who has enjoyed Flora Thompson's books will appreciate the opportunity to learn more about this exceptional woman.
ISBN 978-1-873855-53-9   Retail price £9.95

On the Trail of Flora Thompson *by John Owen Smith.* The author of **Lark Rise** lived for nearly 30 years 'beyond Candleford Green' in Hampshire. This book tells of the people and places she met while living locally in Grayshott and Liphook.
ISBN 978-1-873855-24-9   Retail price £7.95

Grayshott *by J.H. Smith*
The history of Grayshott from its earliest beginnings as a minor hamlet of Headley to its status as a fully independent parish flourishing on the borders of Hampshire and Surrey in the 20th century.
ISBN 978-1-873855-38-6   Retail price £7.95

The Hilltop Writers *by W.R. Trotter*
In which we meet Tennyson, Conan Doyle, Bernard Shaw and sixty-three other writers who populated the hilltops around Haslemere and Hindhead at the end of the 1890s.
ISBN 978-1-873855-31-7   Retail price £9.95

John Owen Smith, publisher:—
www.johnowensmith.co.uk/books

Other books from the same Publisher:—

 **Shottermill, its farms, Families and Mills** *by Greta Turner* Two volumes covering the history of this community in the Wey valley from its earliest days up to the start of the 20th century.
ISBN 978-1-873855-39-3   Retail price £9.95
ISBN 978-1-873855-40-9   Retail price £14.95

 **Headley's Past in Pictures** *by John Owen Smith* Three illustrated tours of Headley parish in old photographs: in the village centre and Arford; to Headley Down and beyond; and along the River Wey and its tributaries.
ISBN 978-1-873855-27-0   Retail price £7.95

 **One Monday in November** *by John Owen Smith* The Selborne & Headley 'Swing' riots of 1830, their dramatic events and their after-effects are recounted from the known facts and often contradictory reports and legends which have grown up since.
ISBN 978-1-873855-33-1   Retail price £7.95

 **All Tanked Up** *by John Owen Smith* Tells of the 'invasion' of Headley by Canadian tank regiments during WW2, told from the point of view of both Villagers and Canadians. Including details of the regiments involved.
ISBN 978-1-873855-54-6   Retail price £7.95

 **A Parcel of Gold for Edith** *by Joyce Stevens* The story of Ellen Suter, an Australian Pioneer Woman, who fled the poverty of England and set off alone, aged only 19, to live in the new colony of Victoria on the other side of the world.
ISBN 978-1-873855-36-2   Retail price £4.95

 **Literary Surrey** *by Jacqueline Banerjee* Explores authors from John Evelyn and Fanny Burney to H.G. Wells and E.M. Forster. Contains suggestions for further reading and details about places to visit.
ISBN 978-1-873855-50-8   Retail price £9.95

John Owen Smith, publisher:—
www.johnowensmith.co.uk/books

Other books from the same Publisher:—

A History of the Eade Family in Surrey, Sussex & Hampshire (1250–1990) *by Robyn Lane & Andrew Eade* We follow the fortunes of the Eade family over seven and a half centuries, diversifying into trades such as bricklaying and stonemasonry.
ISBN 978-1-873855-58-4   Retail price £9.95

Churt: a Medieval Landscape *by P.D. Brooks*
How our ancestors lived. Philip Brooks mastered the intricacies of medieval Latin to translate and explain the contents of the Winchester Pipe Rolls.
ISBN 978-1-873855-36-2   Retail price £7.95

An Edwardian Childhood, the making of a naturalist *by Margaret Hutchinson*
The family lived near Haslemere – a life of self-sufficiency where the only machine on the farm was the children's toy steam engine.
ISBN 978-1-873855-47-8   Retail price £8.95

Walks Around Headley *by John Owen Smith*
A dozen circular walks around Headley and over the borders, with maps, illustrations and historical notes.

ISBN 978-1-873855-49-2   Retail price £6.50

Walks Through History *by John Owen Smith*
More circular walks at the West of the Weald, with maps, illustrations and historical notes.

ISBN 978-1-873855-51-5   Retail price £6.50

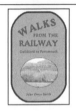

Walks from the Railway *by John Owen Smith*
Circular walks from stations between Guildford and Portsmouth, and linear walks to connect them, with maps, illustrations and historical notes.
ISBN 978-1-873855-55-3   Retail price £6.50

John Owen Smith, publisher:—
www.johnowensmith.co.uk/books